The International Executive Committee, Amsterdam, 1904.

Back Row—Van Kol, Ugarte, Nemec, Vaillant, Soukup, Rosa Luxemburg, Adler, Bracke, Kautsky, Walecki, Vandervelde, Cambier, Longuet, Anseele. Ferri.

Front Row—Cypriani, Troelstra, Hyndman, Bax, Kringen, Katayama, Plechanoff, Knudsen, Hillquit, Navroji.

SOCIALISTS AT WORK

BY

ROBERT HUNTER

AUTHOR OF "POVERTY," ETC.

New York

THE MACMILLAN COMPANY

1908

COPYRIGHT, 1908,

BY THE MACMILLAN COMPANY.

———

Set up and electrotyped. Published April, 1908. Reprinted
October, 1908.

Norwood Press
J. S. Cushing Co. — Berwick & Smith Co.
Norwood, Mass., U.S.A.

PREFACE

"Labor is ever an imprisoned god, writhing unconsciously or consciously to escape out of Mammonism." — CARLYLE.

ALMOST unknown to the world outside of Labor a movement wide as the universe grows and prospers. Its vitality is incredible, and its humanitarian ideals come to those who labor as drink to parched throats. Its creed and program call forth a passionate adherence, its converts serve it with a daily devotion that knows no limit of sacrifice, and in the face of persecution, misrepresentation, and even martyrdom, they remain loyal and true. In Russia its missionaries are exiled, imprisoned, and massacred, but the progress of the movement is only quickened by persecution, proving once again that the blood of the martyrs is the seed of the Church. In Germany and elsewhere it was forced into the night, its leaders were impoverished and hunted through Europe; but underground the movement grew faster than ever. In England it was ignored, defeated it was thought by a conspiracy of silence, when suddenly the nation awoke to the fact that the whole underworld was aflame; and now lords, politicians, and newspapers, consternated and appalled, are rallying for a frontal attack. From Russia, across

Europe and America to Japan, from Canada to Argentina, and from Norway and Finland to South Africa and Australia, it crosses frontiers, breaking through the barriers of language, nationality, and religion, as it spreads from factory to factory, from mill to mill, and from mine to mine, touching as it goes with the religion of life the millions of the underworld.

Its converts work in every city, town, and hamlet in the industrial nations, spreading the new gospel among the poor and lowly, who listen to their words with religious intensity. Tired workmen pore over the literature which these missionaries leave behind them, and fall to sleep over open pages; and the youth, inspired by its lofty ideals and elevated thought, leave the factory with joyous anticipation to read through the night. Its influence reaches throughout all society, and here and there those of the faith are at work in science, literature, and art, in churches and colleges. Millions are already embraced in its organization, and other millions begin to awaken. It has already captured some of the outposts of political power, and it moves on to higher centres of influence, and even now begins to alter the national policy of every European government. Its horizon is boundless, and it quietly works to group its national organizations into an international brotherhood that will abolish war and make as of one blood the nations of the earth.

Strive as I may, I cannot convey to the idle and privileged the full revolutionary portent of this new movement; and strive as I may, I cannot adequately convey to the weary and heavy-laden the grandeur of its thought and the noble promise of its message. I attempt neither. Beyond a brief chapter upon its program, I have not discussed fundamental principles. Others have done that far better than I could hope to do. But I shall have failed in my purpose if I have not brought my reader into intimate contact with the men, the organizations, and the work of this powerful and significant movement. I endeavor to picture a growing organism that already has its ramifications throughout society in every civilized country; and even this is but inadequately done, as the movement has grown with such rapidity, and has developed so differently in the various countries that the task is too great for one wishing to keep to the limits of a sizable volume. One will learn here, nevertheless, something of its leaders, its methods of organization, its congresses and propaganda, and its present influence in the foremost countries of Europe. It should interest those who are curious about current movements; it should prove a warning, if one is needed, to those who live by privilege and by exploiting their fellow-men; and above all, it should help to disillusion those who think that socialism is some supermundane philosophy that has no contact with life, and no especial significance in the world of to-day.

Every new movement has its shibboleths, and the socialist movement is no exception. I have endeavored as far as possible to avoid their use, but the reader will find the terms "class," "working-class," and "class struggle" used very frequently in the following pages. These terms ought perhaps to be defined in this place. The socialists interpret "working-class" very broadly. Karl Marx, in 1850, condemned the extremists in the Communist Alliance for making a fetich of the word "proletariat." And while no socialist would go so far as Frederic Harrison, who says, "The working-class is the only class which is not a class; it is the nation"; Wilhelm Liebknecht declared that, "We include in the working-class all those who live exclusively or principally by means of their own labor, and who do not grow rich through the work of others. . . . It is the party of all the people, with the exception of two hundred thousand great proprietors. . . ."

There is much misunderstanding about the use of the term "class struggle." Socialists do not advocate the class struggle. They recognize that it is inevitable under the present system, and they strive to abolish it. The first International began its preamble by saying, "The struggle for the emancipation of the working-classes means not a struggle for class privileges and monopolies, but for equal rights and duties, and the abolition of all class rule." "The domination of one class," says Jean Jaurès, "is an attempt to degrade humanity. Socialism, which will abolish all primacy of class, and indeed all class, elevates humanity to its highest level." Liebknecht says, "Social democracy, while it fights the class state, will, by abolishing the present form of production, abolish the class war itself."

As nearly as possible in the descriptive portions of the book, I have kept to the limit of my own observations in Germany, Italy, France, England, and Belgium. Realizing, however, that my readers may wish to know something of the movement in other countries, I have asked my friend and secretary, Mr. Charles Lapworth, to prepare a supplementary chapter. I am happy to take this opportunity not only to acknowledge this contribution to the volume, but also to thank Mr. Lapworth for his continuous assistance and helpful criticism during the course of our work. Grateful acknowledgment is also due to Mr. Morris Hillquit, Mr. J. G. Phelps Stokes, and Miss Helen Phelps Stokes, for having read the manuscript and offered many valuable suggestions. Special gratitude is due to my wife, who has worked over the manuscript and proofs with infinite care and devotion.

HIGHLAND FARM,
   NOROTON HEIGHTS,
      CONNECTICUT,
         January 31, 1908.

CONTENTS

LIST OF ILLUSTRATIONS

SOCIALISTS AT WORK

CHAPTER I

THE GERMAN SOCIAL DEMOCRACY

It is rather startling to one whose observation of socialist movements has been confined almost entirely to the United States, to enter one of the largest and most beautiful halls in the world, — a hall seating 10,000 persons — and find it packed to the point of suffocation with delegates, members, and friends of the Social Democratic Party of Germany. I speak of entering; as a matter of fact it took me two hours to enter. Relying upon my experience at home to guide me, I went half an hour late. When I came near the hall, I saw a huge throng of people, surely not less than three or four thousand, standing before the doors. I congratulated myself upon not being later, and hurriedly elbowed my way through the crowd in order to be as near the entrance as possible when the doors should be opened. But before I had gone far I discovered that the hall was already overcrowded, and that we were shut out. None of us were in a mind for that, and in the crush a few window-panes were broken, but it was of no avail; we were informed that the hall would support no more, and the police were unyielding.

It was an impressive sight. They were working men — to a man. And they were of that type of working man one too rarely sees outside of Germany. They

were not pale, anæmic, and undersized, such as one sees
in the East End of London, or in the factory districts of
Lancashire; nor were they the tense, exhausted workmen that issue from the factories of the United States.
It seemed as if they had escaped somehow the perfected
system of labor-exploitation which exists with us. They
looked as if they were getting a loaf or two of bread
the better of the struggle with capitalism. They were
serious-minded, ruddy-faced, muscular; one could see
that they had saved from the exploitation of the factory
enough physical and mental strength to live like men
during their leisure hours; and my belief is that physically and mentally they can hold their own in the essentials with any other class in Germany. These were my
observations shoulder to shoulder with the mass outside.
After a time most of those outside went away, and
when somewhat later a few of those inside came out, I
slipped in.

Inside other things impressed me. I was squeezed
so tight among those immediately about me that I
could not see them, and I contented myself with looking across a sea of faces such as I have rarely seen
massed in one place. Clear and resonant over this sea
came the voice of Bebel. A few months ago I saw in
New York a convention of American citizens standing
on chairs, and for twenty minutes waving their hats and
arms, quite as if they had lost their senses, in order to
show their appreciation of a candidate for office. They
were malcontents, they were in fear lest their liberties
should be lost them, and they wanted a Moses to save
them; this, they thought, was he. Here in Mannheim I
see an old man talking to his sons. He has watched
the movement grow up from its childhood. For nearly

August Bebel.

half a century he has served it with faithfulness and power. He has worked his entire life for this thing; yes, more, he has overworked; and not seldom has he been vexed, wearied, and out of heart. In this service he has grown gray, and furrowed, and great. To-day he is the ablest man in the Reichstag, and one of the most powerful debaters in the world. Every man in this hall knows his worth, knows his greatness, and loves him ; but instead of grovel and hysteria they give him the good round of applause of fellowship and affection. It lasts perhaps fifty seconds, and then they stop *to listen to what he has to say*. If what he says were nonsense, I think they would let him know, for they have not intoxicated themselves with a frenzied and worked-up emotion. It was admirable. Without hysteria, without the worshipping of heroes, or the seeking of a Moses to lead them out of the wilderness, this German proletariat is coming to its own. They know their wilderness, and they are sure of their own capacity to hew paths and bridge streams, making a way out of the miasma of forest and swamp into the warmth and sunshine of the New Time.

Such was the first general gathering, the night before the regular opening of the congress of the Social Democratic Party of Germany. The next morning at eight o'clock sharp the delegates assembled for their regular work. The entire floor of a large theatre was occupied by the delegates from 385 electoral districts of Germany, and by about 80 members of the Reichstag. The representatives of the press to the number of a hundred sat about the tribune, and the galleries were crowded with visitors. Fraternal delegates from other countries occupied seats upon the platform.

It would convey to the reader only a fragmentary idea of the German movement to treat in detail the work of the congress; for unlike our American parties,* the Social Democrats are not mere opportunists. The leading political issue of the moment is not the main topic of comment, nor is the congress merely a nominating body absorbed in selecting winning candidates and devising vote-catching platforms. The conventions are annual assemblies for discussing questions of organization, the reports of the commissions and officers, and for revising, after thorough discussion, the tactics of the party, and perhaps an article of its program. This is all made necessary because the Social Democratic Party, again unlike our parties, has a definite membership, numbering at the present time 530,000 out of the 3,250,000 persons who at the last election voted its ticket. This membership is the sovereign body; it pays dues to support the organization, together with its offices, schools, magazines, and papers. No one can become a member of the party who does not subscribe to its program and obey its rules of political activity. In each locality the members constitute a branch. These branches administer the electoral work, carry on the propaganda, and discuss, weekly or monthly, current political questions. Each year the branches select their delegates to the congress, which is therefore merely the representative body of the whole party.

The German party is the oldest and largest socialist organization in Europe. It represents the thought of a very large proportion of the working men of the entire nation. There are more socialists in Germany than there

---

* Of course in this and similar statements I do not include the Socialist Party of America.

are people in Spain, or Mexico, or in Belgium, Holland, Denmark, and Norway put together. Its present vote would have elected the President of the United States up till the time of Grant's second term. It polls a million more votes than any other party in Germany. By reason of an antiquated distribution of seats the socialists elect to the Reichstag only 43 members instead of 115, which they should have by right of their numbers; and by reason of unequal suffrage, instead of controlling nearly every large city in the German empire, they elect only about a third of the members of the Town Councils.

The party carries on a propaganda of incredible dimensions. Its journals reach no less than 1,049,707 subscribers. There are 65 daily papers, and about 12 weekly and monthly journals. A comic paper, " Der Wahre Jacob," alone has a circulation of 230,000, and " Die Gleichheit," a journal for working women, has over 60,000 regular subscribers. Its organ in Berlin, "Vorwärts," has a circulation of 120,000. The party employs 28 organizing secretaries, who go about the country assisting the branches in the work of organization and propaganda. In September, 1906, the national committee on education opened a school in Berlin for the purpose of training working men as organizers, secretaries, and editors. About 30 students are sent there entirely at the expense of the party.

It will be seen that the German socialist movement is a democratically controlled organization of a character unknown in American politics. Indeed, it is more like one of our scientific or professional societies, drawn together by a definite purpose, and managing its affairs locally and nationally with some definite end in view. As a basis of its organization there has been from its

inception a program including a brief statement of its
final aims and immediate demands. Its socialist principles are clear and precise, involving fundamental economic changes, and its program of social and political
reform includes demands for universal and direct suffrage, direct legislation, the substitution of a militia for
a standing army, international arbitration, free speech
and assembly, compulsory education, free legal and
medical assistance, the abolition of capital punishment,
a graduated income and property tax, the protection of
working men and women, prohibition of child labor,
governmental insurance and the eight-hour day. Supplementary to this general program, the annual national
congress expresses by resolution its opinion upon current political and social problems.

Naturally the most prominent men in the movement
attend these annual gatherings. Now that Wilhelm Liebknecht is dead, the first man is, of course, August Bebel.
He is nearing his seventieth year, and, although gray,
he has in the tribune the appearance of a man of great
physical strength. His rapidity and spontaneity of action seem to denote youthful health and vigor; but
when I spent a Sunday with him afterward, quietly
walking in the woods, I saw that he was small, narrow
of shoulder, and delicate. For nearly fifty years he has
been a leader of German working men's movements,
and for forty years he has had a seat in the Reichstag.
Mrs. Wilhelm Liebknecht once told me of her first
meeting with the two men who built up the socialist
movement in Germany. In the sixties she was taking
English lessons of the sister of the philosopher Büch-
ner, and was invited one afternoon to go for a walk
with a small party of their guests, consisting among

others of "two interesting young men." One of them was sitting in the garden. He was pale and thin, with long hair falling about his shoulders, a serious face, brown eyes, and a languishing, love-sick air. She said she first thought him a sentimental poet. It was August Bebel, then a master turner, in wretched health and threatened with tuberculosis. Despite poverty and illness he was at the time carrying on an extraordinary agitation, and although a youth, was already the leader of one of the largest working men's movements in Germany. When the party reached the top of the hill, Mrs. Liebknecht met her future husband; a tall, interesting-looking man with strongly intellectual tastes. They began to talk of Kant, Hegel, and the other great German philosophers; and directly fell to quarrelling, as he attacked them and their "nonsense" with great vehemence, while she defended them as well as she could. This was about the time that Liebknecht, the disciple and representative of Marx in Germany, was converting young Bebel to socialism. It was fortunate for Bebel that shortly afterward he was imprisoned for disseminating "doctrines dangerous to the state," as in prison rest and food restored him to health.

There is also, at the congress, Paul Singer, that extraordinary organizer, who has done so much to perfect the machinery of the movement. Singer was a rich and successful business man, who after his conversion to socialism devoted all his power and genius for business-like organization to the party's affairs. Liebknecht and Bebel were agitators and politicians; Singer, the quiet and effective administrator building up and strengthening the organized forces behind them. A good part of his large fortune has been devoted to invigorating

the party journals and organs of propaganda. Besides
Singer there are other prominent party leaders, including Auer, another extraordinary organizer; Kautsky,
the scholar of the movement, and Legien, the head of
the trade union forces.

Two days of the congress were given to the debate
upon the general strike, or what the Germans signifi-
cantly call the *Politischen Massenstreik*. Within recent
years the idea of the general strike has gained many
adherents in the European movement. In France and
Italy, where the revolutionary tradition is strong, and
broad generalization seductive, the idea of such an uprising of the workers has taken firm hold on the imagination. In Germany and England it has few advocates.
In Belgium it has been twice employed to force political
reforms, once with signal success. The immense revolutionary power resting in its natural and proper use was
shown once in Russia. In Germany there has recently
arisen a demand on the part of the more extreme sections
of the party, the hotter heads, and especially the anarcho-
socialists, for its adoption as an ordinary weapon of the
working class against the tyrannies of the government.
At the congress of the trade unions at Cologne in 1905,
a resolution advocating the use of the general strike was
rejected. But a few months later the socialist congress
at Jena expressed recognition of its value and advocated
its use. Bebel himself spoke in its favor. Later, however, when the party was considering plans for an immense propaganda to gain universal suffrage in the
elections for the Prussian Landtag, and to retort to the
assaults directed against universal suffrage in certain
other German states, and the general strike was proposed
as a means to that end, Bebel declared that the moment

had not come for such extreme measures and that he would oppose all propaganda looking to immediate action of that character. This series of events created throughout the party a lively discussion, and to clear up the matter the subject of the general strike was put upon the program for discussion at this congress.

Bebel, in summing up its recent history, maintained that the general strike cannot be organized artificially. "It is possible," he said, "only when the masses are in a high ferment. In Russia the use of the general strike has broken down. Such successful strikes as there have been of this character were not artificially organized by the working men's associations. They were provoked by events. In August, 1906, the workers refused to participate in the strike because they considered it inopportune." Bebel's opposition to the use of the general strike, except under extraordinary conditions and with the accompaniment of a revolutionary state of mind on the part of the masses, called forth a heated discussion. Young Liebknecht and Rosa Luxemburg attacked Bebel's position with considerable warmth, but at the close of the debate Bebel was supported by a large vote.

The resolution upon which this debate took place, while reaffirming the declaration of the congress of Jena, recommended with particular insistence consideration of the resolutions which favored the reënforcement and development of the party organization, and the reciprocal affiliation of the members of the trade unions to the political groups. It also declared that as soon as the national committee of the party recognized the necessity for a general strike, it must put itself in relation with the national committee of the trade unions in order to take all the measures necessary to assure to the action a fruitful result.

In one paragraph of the resolution it was declared that trade unions were indispensable to the bettering of the conditions of the workers under the present state of society, but that having a class conscience, the unionists should equally pursue the aims of the Social Democratic Party in seeking to deliver the working-class from the present wage-system. Kautsky created an important discussion by proposing as an amendment that the trade unions should be dominated by the spirit, and *bound by the decisions*, of the party. This brought up one of the most burning questions of socialist politics; namely, whether or not the unions should have an independent existence. In France the trade unionists have assumed an attitude of neutrality ; in America they forbid all politics in the unions; in Belgium they are a part of the political organization; and in England they are a political organization. It is an old and much-debated question of tactics. Kautsky is an uncompromising believer in the unions being dominated by socialist political policies. But he and his supporters were defeated, and the revised amendment which follows was put and carried by a large majority :—

" To assure the unity of thought and of action of the party and of the unions, which is supremely necessary to the victorious march of the proletarian class struggle, it is indispensable that the unions should be permeated by the spirit of social democracy. It is the duty of all members of the party to work toward this end."

The thing that impressed me most at the German congress was its distinct proletarian character, and the extraordinary intelligence and ability of the working

men in attendance. I spoke of this to Ledebour, one
of the most effective and pleasing orators of the party,
and a member of the Reichstag from Liebknecht's old
constituency in Berlin. He remarked that it had become noticeably more so in recent years. The opposition to the party on the part of middle-class parents,
and the prejudice inculcated by instructors in the
schools and universities, had kept the younger men of
better education out of the movement. For this reason
it became necessary for the socialists to have a school of
their own to train the youth of the working-class as
editors and secretaries.

As the proletarian character of the movement struck
me, so did the independent, able, and frank discussion
on all the important matters. The officials, the editors,
and the representatives in the Reichstag were called to
account for every act that could justly be questioned or
was of a controversial nature. The German rank and
file are not being blindly led anywhere; and while
Bebel's power is immense, it results — aside from his
exceptional ability — from the scrupulous care with
which he always presents his side of any case. To
those who hear him there can be no mistaking of his
position. His sincerity, and the way an idea dominates
his mind, so that he can present it to his audience from
every conceivable point of view, enables him to carry
his party with him. Thorough, painstaking thinking,
clear and forceful repetition of his thought with exhaustive care to make his position clear to the most obstinate
opponent or the most stupid auditor, are to my mind
the secret of this extraordinary man's success. It is a
power which Lincoln had, only Lincoln had it in an
even more gifted way. He was usually able to make

his position clear in a few words. Bebel attains the same end, but, at times, only by the most laborious means.

It struck me also that the party was to all outward appearances conservative. It is conscious of its enormous power and feels deeply its responsibility. I do not mean that it is cowardly, that it does not take the most advanced ground in its political program, or that it dilutes in any way the revolutionary aim of the movement. What I mean is that it is not uselessly offending any one. Inside the party the leaders are extremely careful not to offend the more backward and slow-moving elements, which are perhaps as. numerous in the German movement as elsewhere. The more advanced are willing to sacrifice positions which they would otherwise take or hold in order to retain the adhesion of the less revolutionary members. They scrupulously avoid giving offence to the trade unions, and give them all assistance and consideration in their method of advancing the proletarian cause.* I suspect a majority of the congress were in favor of Kautsky's resolution, only they were unwilling to press it against the wishes of the trade unionists.

Outside the party they are quite as careful not to give the reactionary elements in the empire any unnecessary

---

* The party maintains the closest possible relation with the trade union movement, which is now the strongest in the world, numbering in all its branches 2,300,000 members. At the end of 1906 the trade unions connected with the great central organization numbered 1,799,293 members, or an increase of 369,000 over the preceding year. The women in the movement numbered 132,821, as against 89,500 in the previous year. The total receipts amounted to over $10,500,000, and the expenses to $8,000,000. Strikes and lockouts cost about $4,750,000; while sickness and out-of-work pay only absorbed $1,750,000.

excuse for their attacks.   For instance, it is unquestionable that Bebel, aside from what seems to me his sound
theory of the *milieu* which must exist as a soil for the
proper incitement and development of the successful
Massenstreik, is influenced by his fear of the power of
the reaction if it should be too much harassed.   For
instance, in his speech on the general strike, he said :
" My opinion at bottom has never varied.   I have always
said that the general strike cannot be organized in
Prussia as in other countries.   We are in the presence
of a violent reaction, malicious and brutal, against which
we cannot launch an organization such as so important
a struggle demands.   To attempt such an adventure
without being prepared is to furnish to the reactionaries,
to the *agents provocateurs*, the very occasion they
desire to reduce still further that which remains of our
liberties."

That, it seems to me, is a pretty conservative stand
for the leader of the greatest political party in Germany
to take.   But Bebel unquestionably relies upon parliamentary methods and strength for the attainment of
socialist ends.   The working men must still further
unite, must still further become conscious of the historic
rôle they are to play before they will be able, in the
words of Karl Marx, to throw off their chains.   Until
both of these objects of the party are attained it might
lose much that it has already gained if it were to attempt
to move by revolutionary methods.   This attitude is con-
ciliatory and, in a sense, conservative.   Is it not also far-
seeing and wise ?

When we left Mannheim, no one thought that within
a few months the German empire would be in the throes
of an election.   The general opinion was that the gov-

ernment would not soon again give the socialists an
opportunity to prove their strength.   Flushed with success, and enjoying an electoral history of remarkable
achievement, the socialists were perhaps over-confident
of their growing influence and power.   With an organization little short of perfection, with an electoral strength
nearly double that of any other party, with local elections going everywhere in their favor, it were unrea-
sonable to expect a set-back.   To the astonishment,
therefore, of all Europe the German government in
December, 1906, on a ridiculous issue, ordered the
dissolution of parliament, and appealed to the country.
The government had demanded from the Reichstag a
supplementary grant of 29,220,000 marks, a comparatively small sum, for the maintenance of troops in South-
west Africa.   In spite of a pathetic appeal from the
Chancellor, Prince von Buelow, this demand was rejected.   The Conservatives, Antisemites, and National
Liberals were ready to give their 168 votes, but the
Clerical and Social Democratic parties refused their 178
votes.   The latter went so far as to demand a reduction
in the fighting strength in the colony from 8000 to
2500 men.   Military advisers declared that any such reduction would be dangerous to the interest of the German colonial policy.   Buelow, who was anxious to cut
himself loose from the control of the Clericals, insisted
upon the Reichstag voting the required sum, and upon
his defeat, he carried out his threat of dissolution.
There was tremendous excitement throughout the German empire, but the general belief was that the actual
position would not be changed, and that the government
would have to meet the same opposition when the next
parliament assembled.

The Reichstag is elected by universal manhood suffrage by ballot (every man of 25 has a vote), and there
is supposed to be one deputy for every 100,000 inhabitants. But the electoral divisions were settled in 1869
and 1871, and have never since been altered. In 1871
there were 397 deputies, because the population was at
that time about 39,000,000; but since then it has increased
to nearly 60,000,000, and the number of deputies has
remained the same. The rural population of Germany
has during this period decreased, while that of the cities
has increased many-fold. For example, Berlin, in 1869,
had 600,000 inhabitants, and therefore six members. It
now has a population of nearly 2,000,000, and should
have 20 members, but it is still represented by only six.
The Clericals and Conservatives are usually returned
from rural and thinly populated districts, while the
Social Democrats gain their support mainly from the
cities and large industrial centres. For instance, they
elect all but one of the members for Berlin, and have
great strength in Chemnitz, Zwickaw, Stuttgart, Frank-
fort, Karlsruhe, Dortmund, Duisberg, Hannover, Ham-
burg, Munich, Nuremberg, Leipsic, etc. But it is
precisely these places that suffer from inadequate representation, and consequently the Social Democrats,
with over 3,000,000 votes, send only 43 deputies to the
Reichstag, while the Conservative party, with 1,000,000,
returns fifty-nine.

In Germany, as in other continental countries, there
are many parties with different shades of political opinion.
It is difficult to give an American an exact idea of what
they stand for, as they differ so much from our parties.
They represent almost every point of view; sometimes
standing for the interests of one class or another; some-

times for the interests of certain nationalities in the empire; sometimes for specific economic and political principles. It may, however, be said that there are sixteen different parties or fractions, as they are called in Germany, the five most important of which represent as nearly as possible the following definite interests : The Conservatives are a powerful group representing the old aristocracy, and supporting monarchical and autocratic institutions. The National Liberals here, as everywhere, represent the industrial interests, and while politically more advanced than the Conservatives, from the economic point of view their interests are even more opposed to the workers than those of the Conservatives. During the last ten years the Liberals have been forced to support the monarchy. The Freisinnige represent the Free Trade section; their philosophy is mainly that of the Manchester School, and their watchword " Modern Progress and Freedom of Commerce." The two most powerful parties are the Clericals and the Social Democrats ; together they have as many votes as all the others combined ; but the division between them is complete. The Clericals represent the Catholic interests. Their strength is among the most conservative and often the most ignorant classes of the population, and their power is immense. The Social Democrats, on the other hand, represent the wage-earners, and the most intelligent and far-seeing of the small-propertied classes.

With this short statement of the suffrage inequalities and party divisions the electoral campaign will be more intelligible. Having broken with the Clericals, Buelow had now to look elsewhere for the governmental majority. Accordingly, when he gave out the " Wahlparole," he did not publish it in an official paper, but addressed an open letter to the head of the National Party (*Reichspartei*), a section of the Liberals whose chief aim is to combat the socialist movement. The combating of socialism was the bridge which, it was hoped, would join the Conservatives and the Liberals; and it was decided their electoral tactics should be to try to awaken that apathetic part of the propertied class, who seldom trouble to vote, to a sense of the danger of revolutionary socialism. This made it appear that the government was not chiefly combating the Clericals, although, as was subsequently shown, it used underhand methods in its vain attempt to crush their power. Nevertheless, the electoral campaign resolved itself mainly into a struggle of Conservatives and Nationalists against Social Democrats.

At the beginning of the campaign "the honor of the nation" was preached from every reactionary platform, but rather unfortunately for the empire-makers the government itself was obliged, at the end of a week, to admit that the war with the Hereros was at an end. This, however, did not discourage the bourgeois candidates from exploiting the people's patriotism. Votes were obtained by every means possible. The workers were beguiled, by jingoism and imperialism, into forgetting their own troubles; the bourgeois were awakened to the danger in which their privileges stood from socialism. The merchants were terrified into action at the impending danger of a socialist state, and were assured that their only hope lay in joining to form a compact majority. The interested classes were called on to support the institutions which supported them. The disinterested and exploited workers were fed with Chauvinism and fallacies concerning the advantages

c

which would accrue to them from the colonial policy of the government. Glowing pictures of the might of Great Britain, due, it was pointed out, to her comprehensive colonial policy, were played up before them. These chords were harped upon, as we shall see, with considerable success.

Social Democrats make no compromises with the bourgeois. They agree to nothing that will not radically change the present system; and the rulers, knowing that they cannot placate them by passing small reforms, are now awake to the fact that if they are to continue their present power, they must crush socialism. The socialists in parliament had, in some cases, opposed small measures of reform as being inadequate, and their opponents were not slow to misrepresent this action to the workers, telling them that the socialists did not want or intend to pass measures for their benefit. The trade unions look to the socialist members to support reforms in their interest sometimes without regard to Social Democratic principles, and occasionally the socialists in parliament have not done so, preferring to oppose reform measures which only tend to stanch and not to heal injustice caused by the present system. It is easy for the other parties to turn to their own advantage such action on the part of socialists. Besides these "constitutional" methods of attacking socialism, the reactionary parties used others.

It would seem almost unbelievable that in modern Germany methods were used to coerce people to vote against their convictions and interests. Nevertheless, that seems to be the fact, and it has since been proved that the governmental machinery was used to carry out a great scheme of intimidation against the workers. As we know, there is no such thing as free speech in Germany. Every political meeting is under the superintendence of a "gendarme," who may declare a meeting illegal if he considers the speeches dangerous to the powers that be. It is therefore a very simple matter for those in authority to break up and prevent socialist meetings. As this power was used to its greatest extent in the last elections, the socialist campaign was greatly handicapped. Many saloon-keepers were forced by brewers and rich proprietors to refuse to let their rooms to socialists, and meetings were dispersed on the flimsiest pretexts. The socialists in many places took to holding meetings in the open air, but the season was against them. As an instance of really tyrannical intimidation may be cited a case in the industrial town of Saar, where the employers engaged men, armed with cudgels, to attack socialist propagandists.

So much for the battle carried on against the socialists. The figures of the parliamentary strength of the chief parties before and after the election may be given as follows : —

	1903		1907	
	Votes	Deputies	Votes	Deputies
Centre (Catholics)	1,875,292	100	2,183,381	105
Conservatives	948,448	55	1,070,658	59
National Liberals	1,313,051	52	1,654,738	55
Social Democrats	3,010,771	81	3,258,968	43
All other parties	2,348,025	109	2,994,353	135

From these figures it will be seen that the government gained a striking parliamentary victory, but it would be a mistake to think that the socialists suffered defeat.

The strength of socialism in Germany cannot be measured by the number of its parliamentary representatives, because its parliamentary strength depends largely on the electoral law. At present this does not permit the socialists to show their real strength, and the electoral law might be so changed that it would be impossible for them to capture a single seat. These electoral changes have little significance, however. The vote is a better test, as the number of convinced socialists alone is the true measure of the real power of the movement. In the judgment of the leaders the socialists actually gained a great victory. The first reason for this belief is that in the face of a terrific campaign they increased their vote by 250,000. The second is that they have finally forced the more advanced sections of the bourgeois parties into the conservative ranks. In other words they have been fortunate in this campaign in compelling the other parties to form a block to fight unitedly the interests of the working-class. The Liberals, only too glad to throw in their lot with the government, have therefore ceased to be an opposition party; and now that they have sided with the government in favor of reaction, their influence with the people will diminish. This forcing of other parties into the ranks of the reactionaries is a great gain for the socialist cause, for in the next elections hundreds of thousands of voters will see that there is no longer any hope of reform from these other parties.

The loss of socialist seats, then, is not due to a diminution of socialist strength. It is the result of the coöperation of all parties, excepting the Clericals, against socialism, and the bringing to the booths of a great mass of apathetic citizens who seldom vote. Whatever could be done by the government to weaken the suffrage of socialists was done; but these methods have their limit, as "Vorwärts" said immediately after the first election. From 1877 to 1884 the socialist vote only increased from 493,288 to 549,990, but from 1884 to 1903 the party gained an increase in votes of 2,500,000. In the five years 1898–1903 they increased nearly 1,000,000. But these million new voters were not all grounded socialists, while those in the late election, some three and a quarter million, who gave their support to socialist candidates were, it is fair to assume, no raw recruits, but thoroughgoing socialists. All but the very surest were swept away in the tumult of jingoism created by the other parties.

GROWTH OF SOCIAL DEMOCRACY SINCE 1867

	Votes	Deputies
1871	124,655	2
1874	351,952	10
1877	493,288	13
1878	437,158	9
1881	311,961	13
1884	549,990	24
1887	763,128	11
1890	1,427,298	35
1893	1,786,738	44
1898	2,107,076	56
1903	3,010,771	81
1907	3,258,968	43

Figures are sometimes illuminating, and the preceding table will show clearly the growing power of the socialist movement in Germany. No comment is neces-

sary, but it may be of use to the reader if he will
compare for the various years the electoral strength with
the number of representatives sent to the Reichstag.
It will be observed that this is not the first time the
socialists have increased their votes and lost seats.   In
1887 they lost over half their parliamentary representation, and yet they gained an increased vote of nearly
200,000.

These figures show a remarkable and significant
growth, and it is natural to ask what use have the
socialists made of this increasing power ?   It is generally known that within the last thirty years Germany
has developed a daring policy of State Socialism.
Municipal and national ownership of public utilities
and natural resources has proceeded at a pace that
has amazed the rest of Europe.   At the same time
labor legislation for the protection of the working-
class has been developed until it is a model for Europe.
Social and industrial conditions have been revolutionized.   The conditions of the working-class in Germany
have been changed so that what were among the worst
in Europe are now the best.   Some mighty force has
wrought this change.   No one, so far as I know,
believes that it is due to superior benevolence on the
part of the upper classes of Germany, or that they are
more humane than the like classes of other nations.
Indeed, it is sometimes doubted that the German
capitalists are, as a rule, as philanthropically inclined
as, for instance, those of England.   And yet the fact
remains that despite the lack of unusual concern for
the welfare of the masses, Germany has evolved an
exceptional and admirable code of legislation which has
materially improved the condition of the masses.

It is impossible to place this beneficent legislation to the credit of the old Emperor, and no one knowing the history of recent years can feel that the credit belongs to the capitalists. On the contrary, they fought it at every step, and accepted it finally with lamentation. Indeed, it was not a voluntary policy on the part either of the Emperor or of Bismarck or of the capitalists. It was forced upon the nation by the insistent demands and threatening power of a united and uncompromising working-class. It was this force which made a change of policy necessary, and it was Bismarck's shrewd political sagacity that devised a plan to ease the struggle, to soften the lot of the workers, and yet to keep capitalism intact.

The real significance of the matter is that as liberalism in the early part of the century forced its way to freedom through the restrictions and privileges of the land-owning classes, so in these later days socialism is forcing upon capitalism, legislation giving greater freedom to the masses and more generous treatment to the producers. Liberalism gained its object by a series of violent outbreaks and bloody revolutions. The working-class has thus far in Germany pursued its course peacefully, and has gained what has already been accorded to it only by an impressive and insistent solidarity. Just as liberalism revolutionized the economic and political policies of the old feudal powers, socialism begins to revolutionize the economic policy of capitalism.

A bit of history will fully prove this assertion. Social Democracy, naturally enough, made but little progress in Germany before 1871. The agitation of Lassalle, Liebknecht, and Bebel was already putting the working-class into a state of ferment and unrest. Up to that time Social Democracy as a political force was insignificant. But the disintegration of the old political parties, due largely to the financial crisis resulting from the Franco-Prussian war, and Bismarck's adverse laws against the Catholics, gave the socialists their first political opening. Both Liebknecht and Bebel were imprisoned for the publication of treasonable writings; nevertheless, whilst still in prison, both were returned to the Reichstag, and the Social Democratic Party polled a surprisingly large vote. The government became frightened and the police were ordered to carry on a campaign of extermination against the socialists. Instead of this having the desired effect of breaking up and destroying the various groups then existing, it forced them to unite for the common good. In the year 1875 they finally completed their union, and from that time until to-day there has been a united working men's party. In the year 1877 the party polled nearly a half-million votes, elected 12 men to the Reichstag, and many other representatives to state and municipal administrative bodies throughout Germany. The fear of Social Democracy was naturally increased by its continued success. In May, 1878, the Emperor was shot at. In June of the same year he was fired at again and severely wounded. These two attempts upon his life, while in no way connected with the Social Democrats, were nevertheless represented to be the result of their agitation; and they gave Bismarck the opportunity he desired to pass his anti-socialist legislation. Then began a period of governmental repression, carried on by all the powers of the state, against social democracy. Instead, however, of destroying the movement, it merely forced it underground; and through secret organization the party continued to carry on its propaganda, and to gather under its banner new recruits. Herr Richter, the Progressist leader, was quite right when he prophesied, "I fear social democracy more under this law than without it."

Bismarck was too shrewd a politician to use but one weapon in an emergency of this sort. With one hand he made a gigantic effort to annihilate the socialist party; the other he reached out ostentatiously in sympathy to the working-class. By the side of repression he developed his policy of State Socialism. He turned his mind for the time from purely political and diplomatic problems to economic questions, and he frankly stated at various times in the Reichstag that he intended to adopt as a policy every reasonable measure advocated by the socialists, and to carry them out for the benefit of the workers. He went even further and announced that he was himself a socialist, and acknowledged the "right to work," and the responsibility of the state to protect the working-class, and to provide for those broken down in industry. The Emperor also insisted upon the passage of legislation which would positively advance the welfare of the working-classes. "Past institutions," he said in his message to the Reichstag in 1879, "intended to insure working people against the danger of falling into a condition of helplessness owing to the incapacity resulting from accident or age, have proved inadequate, and their insufficiency has to no small extent contributed to cause the working-classes to seek help by participating in Social Democratic movements."

It would be easy to quote from the speeches of Bismarck, Bebel, Liebknecht, and other parliamentary leaders of the time, as well as from the Emperor's messages to the Reichstag, to show that the socialist movement forced upon the government this change of policy.* Other countries have in some rare instances partially abandoned the policy of *laissez faire* on becoming informed of its merciless ruin of the poor; but in Germany social democracy has forced its complete abandonment by the state. Alone in Europe at this time the German working-class was conscious of its power and wise in its solidarity, and alone in Europe the German capitalists were thus early forced to capitulate.

In the midst of these stirring times a plan was put before the Reichstag for the insurance of working men, and in the years that have followed this legislation has been so improved and extended that now every workman's family possessing an income under $500 a year is assured of a pension in case of need due either to sickness, accident, old age, or death. Up to the eighties very little legislation had been passed for the protection of workmen while employed, but an improved code was drawn up, which has become a part of the legislation of the empire. Railroads and other public utilities, mines and other natural resources, have been gradually taken over by the state. Public utilities necessary to the various municipalities have been municipalized, and an improved system of taxation, intended to relieve the pressure upon the poorer classes, has also been drawn up and passed.†

The result of this State Socialism was not felt imme-

* See also pp. 223–224.

† For a fuller treatment of social reform in Germany see Chapter VII.

diately. Indeed, one only begins now to see its effect upon the German nation. When it was introduced, Germany was on the verge of ruin. Trade, industry, and agriculture were depressed, and the laboring-classes were among the most miserable in Europe. The cities were filled with wretchedness and poverty; they were insanitary; the housing of the people was abominable; and everywhere the masses of the poor lived in abject misery. The policy of *laissez faire* had brought Germany to the same bankrupt condition that one still finds in England and that begins to show itself in America. The working-class, hopelessly discouraged, and embittered by poverty, was in a state of dangerous discontent; and Bismarck became convinced that there was no hope of retaining its political allegiance while its misery was unbearable.

It would be folly to maintain that State Socialism has been the sole cause of what is, comparatively speaking, the present remarkable prosperity of the German empire; and yet no one can doubt that no matter what other forces may have been at work, the policy of protecting the working-classes, and of ameliorating their condition of life, has been one powerful cause of the improved conditions. Industry in Germany is enjoying a prosperity equalled perhaps nowhere else. The exports have increased at a rate rarely equalled by any other country. The concentration of wealth has been no less striking than in the United States. Trusts, combinations, and pools have rendered industrial operations more economical, and relieved the nation of some of the ruinous costs of competition. Along with this enrichment of the capitalist has proceeded an amelioration of the living and working con-

ditions of the people. The state insurance system of
Germany distributes over $100,000,000 every year to
the working-class in the form of benefits and indemni-
ties.* The municipalities have so improved the living
conditions in the cities that to-day there are practically no slums in Germany. The aged and sick, the
injured in industry, all have their little patrimony to
keep them from want. There is poverty in Germany,
wages are low, conditions are still intolerable; but the
improvement over the old days and over the conditions still obtaining in neighboring countries gives
one the impression that there is no dire want in the
German empire.

When this enlightened policy was forced upon the
government, and Bismarck pleaded for its acceptance,
the large industrialists prophesied the ruin of German industry. It was repeatedly said that the heavy burdens
placed upon capital by the new legislation could not be
borne, and that German industry would be unable to
continue in competition with the rest of the world.
When liberalism defeated landlordism, it was said, as
we all know, that the ruin of the nations had come. Now
that socialism is defeating liberalism, it is being said
that the ruin of industry is certain. But capitalism forgets one thing; namely, that labor can be exhausted
and made unprofitable. Of course it is not primarily for
the capitalists to remember the interests of labor, and if
the workers did not organize to protect themselves, they
would be exhausted and impoverished. For humanity

* In 1903 the number insured against sickness was nearly eleven million;
the number insured against accident was nearly eighteen million; and
the number insured against old age and invalidity was about thirteen and
a half million.

is a part of nature, and labor, like land, must be enriched in order to make it productive. It is, therefore, a curious fact that a policy which was forced upon capitalists blinded by self-interest, and which it was claimed threatened them with ruin, has in no slight degree actually promoted their present prosperity.

The German movement has much to teach us. To a political reformer it has a lesson; namely, that a " third party " can exercise an influence almost equal to that of a party in power. To the laborer it demonstrates the possibility of improving his own condition even now if he will but unite with his fellows. To the socialist it proves that a party which demands the social revolution has a long struggle ahead of it, but in the meantime it obtains incidentally an increasing and striking amelioration of existing conditions. These are not unimportant by-products of the labor movement in politics, for that is all they can be called, as the social democracy of Germany has never been in power and has never of itself been able to pass a single law. It has rarely collaborated with other parties, and it has been forced during the last forty years to be merely an ominous protest, a source of real apprehension if not of dread to the German government. Without supreme power its final revolutionary program can, of course, never be fully realized. What it has gained is merely the reform of present economic conditions. It has made no serious inroads upon capitalism, but it has forced capitalism to be more just and merciful to the producing masses. In order to win from social democracy its adherents, capitalism has endeavored to render the party powerless, and has given with its own hand, as an indication of what it wishes to appear as its native generosity, the social reforms of the last thirty years. The reason why these same reforms have not been carried out in England and America, or indeed anywhere else, is because the working-class has not expressed its will with the same unity and solidarity.

The working-class in Germany knows how to use its power in its own original way. Its independence of the other political parties, and the fact that the bureaucracy has managed thus far to keep it out of power, has forced upon it the rôle of critic. In this capacity it exercises an incredible influence. Its minorities in the various legislative bodies never allow the parties that rule to ignore social, political, and industrial evils. Under this unfriendly and relentless eye the parties in power do not dare to give franchises, grants, and special privileges to private interests. Graft is almost unknown. No evil escapes the socialists ; no reform satisfies them. Their ideals and aims are beyond any immediate attainment, and national ownership, municipal ownership, labor protection, the demolition of slums, the abolition of child labor — none of these reforms receive from them more than a cold approval. There is always something more that must be done, some other grievance to be removed. The working-class in Germany is like an awful conscience, voicing the evils of society, condemning the acts of the powerful, setting forth the ideal of the future. Autocracy can cripple it, can even render it physically impotent ; but it knows not how to destroy its spirit. For thirty years two great forces, class and mass, have been giving battle, each frankly bent upon the other's destruction. Does any one doubt that that one will conquer whose morality is the truest, whose ideals are the highest, and whose spirit expresses the faith of the time ?

CHAPTER II

THE ITALIAN SOCIALIST PARTY

In the Eternal City, in the new and handsome *Casa del Popolo*, the socialists' own meeting-hall, the congress of the Italian Socialist Party was in session. Every one was alive with excitement, as it had been rumored that the party would be split into a thousand fragments. The Reformists, led by their able and forceful Turati; the Syndicalists, led by their brilliant, emotional, and impractical Labriola; and the Integralists, led by the impressive and not always consistent Ferri, — all were there, and lost no time in giving battle.

It seemed only natural in Rome to be witnessing a battle of giants, a turbulent, hero-worshipping populace broken into factions, and the fate of one of the greatest and noblest nations in the world resting upon the outcome. At any rate, as I sat three days in that hall, this appeared to be not far from the actual situation. With all the lovable qualities; with a fine and sincere admiration for power and greatness; with quick and agile intelligence; with childlike frankness and honesty; with idealism and splendid emotion, quick to resent, quick to forgive; these men sat together for three days backing their leaders like boys with fighting cocks, — apparently deciding nothing of importance except not to split, but discussing almost everything in the wide world of interest. It was a thousand times more engaging than the German congress. It was comic, tragic, lyric, and

absorbing to watch.   At times it was as impressive as
cannonry, and as brilliant as fireworks; but in the end a
thing of wonder and bewilderment.

The middle-class character of the Italian gathering
astonished me most.   In almost every other country the
socialist movement is mainly proletarian.   In Germany
there are few men in the movement not of the working-
class.   In the Italian assembly there were evidently few
who had ever done manual work, and most of the delegates were well, and many even fashionably, dressed.
Not only are the leaders, Ferri, Labriola, and Turati,
what they call on the continent "intellectuals," but so
also were many of the delegates from the unions, co-
operative societies, and other working men's organizations.   This is peculiar to the Italian movement.   In
probably no other country except Russia are there so
many socialists among the scholars, scientists, and eminent writers.   Lombroso, one of the most noted scientists in Europe, and easily the foremost criminologist,
is a member of the party.   As adherents and sympathizers it counts, among others, De Amicis, the most
widely read of the Italian novelists; Ferrero, a social
writer of great influence; Graf, Guerrini, and Pascoli,
among the most talented of the poets; Sanarelli, the
well-known scientist and discoverer of the yellow fever
germ; Chiaruggi, a leading embryologist; and Cat-
telli, the physicist.   Fogazzaro is sympathetic, and Gabriel D'Annunzio stood as a candidate of the party
at a recent election.   To be sure, the other movements
in Europe have some equally well-known sympathizers,
but in other countries they are exceptions.   In Italy
thousands of students, professors, and professional men
openly support the socialist movement.   A careful cen-

sus was made in 1904 to determine the various vocations of the members of the party. The results bear out the statement that the Italian movement is dominated by middle-class elements. It was shown that from 20 to 30 per cent of the members were industrial workers; from 15 to 20 per cent rural workers; and between 50 and 60 per cent professional men, merchants, students, and small proprietors.

The electoral strength of the party is, of course, mainly among the working-classes, but thus far the great mass of Italian working men have been too little educated and too little trained in organization to be capable of assuming official responsibilities. There are, however, exceptions to this general statement. The most powerful labor union in Italy is among the railwaymen. The genius of the organization is Quirino Nofri, formerly an ordinary railway employee, but at present the head of the union as well as member of parliament. A strong organization exists also among the dockers. The leader is Pietro Chiesa, a powerful and influential man who has risen from the docks. He also is now a member of parliament. But men of capacity for leadership and organization are rare among the working-classes in Italy. Most of the organizers and agitators in the unions are men with university training; and Labriola, the leader of the unionists, and the one who most bitterly attacks the middle-class control of the socialist movement, is a university professor and successful advocate.

The middle-class character of Italian socialism was perfectly illustrated by the reports of the congress published in the official organ of the party, "Avanti." After the name of certain speakers was written in

D

parenthesis *operaio*, "workman." This term of explanation was rarely used, as few working men were
heard during the congress. Nearly all the speakers
were middle-class men of exceptional ability and talent.
They were democratic and devoted, but their complete
domination over the congress gave one the feeling
that there is something unsound in the Italian movement, and inclined one to think that there must come
some remarkable and revolutionary changes in the
party itself before it can become a truly socialist organization.

Any one, however, who is inclined to believe that the
Italian movement is badly organized will find himself
mistaken. Although it is one of the youngest movements in Europe, it has during the last fifteen years
made wonderful strides toward a compact and powerful organization both among peasants and working
men. During the first five years of this century the
growth has been striking, and in 1906 it numbered
1250 sections, with over 41,000 members. As in the
German movement, all of the members pay dues and
subscribe to the program and tactics of the party. So
large a number of pledged men makes therefore a credit-
able showing, and indeed, with the exception of Denmark, Belgium, and Germany, the organized movement
is one of the strongest in Europe. It differs from the
German party in one important feature. The unions of
the peasants and industrial workers, the coöperative
societies, and the other purely economic organizations
are affiliated directly with the party. Founded, as they
have been, largely by the party leaders, they have in
almost all cases become branches of the political movement.

The Italian socialist party is one of the few movements in Europe which have made appreciable headway among the peasants. This is a fundamental political necessity in Italy, as it is largely an agricultural country and no party of any consequence can exist without the adherence of the rural workers. The peasant leagues or unions are in some respects peculiar to Italy. They began to take form about twenty years ago under the guidance of the old Garibaldian forces. Even at that time they had a political character, but it was largely limited to republicanism. In the nineties the peasant leagues of Venetia and Emilia developed surprising strength as a result of the fearless and indefatigable propaganda of Professor Enrico Ferri, who about this time threw his entire energies into the socialist movement. In Emilia the peasants are best organized. The unions number at least 70,000 members in this one district, and through their support the party has dominated most of the local governing councils, and has returned several members to parliament. From Emilia the unions spread throughout the north of Italy, until now they number, according to the reports of the Bureau of Labor, not less than 220,000 members.

All of the peasant leagues have a definite political character, and most of them are affiliated directly to the political socialist movement; but their greatest achievement has been on the purely economic field. It would be impossible to estimate in figures the advantages which they have gained for their members. The estimate, made by one Italian writer, that the peasants have benefited to the extent of about $15,000,000 yearly, is doubtless made upon no very reliable data.

These unions have, however, been the backbone of most of the discontent existing throughout this section. And as hundreds of strikes occur yearly, most of which appear to end successfully for the workers, it is not to be doubted that these organizations have wrought a revolution in rural conditions.

The unions of the industrial workers, now coming to be called "syndicats," after the French word, have also a large membership, approximating 400,000. In nearly all the main industries the workers have developed strong and effective unions, and recently they have formed a national body. In about a hundred centres the unions meet in the so-called Labor Chambers, which are workmen's temples, built as a rule by the municipality. In both France and Italy these institutions are under the semi-official patronage of municipal authorities, and in many instances the officials in charge are direct employees of the government. Many of these halls are handsomely built, with every convenience for carrying on the work of the unions; although it must be said that, with the exception of those municipalities under socialist control, neither the Italian nor French cities desire in the least to promote trade unionism. Both governments to a certain extent still look upon working men's organizations as little less than criminal, and it is partly for the purpose of keeping them constantly under police surveillance that they have provided them with these general meeting-places.

Some idea of the popularity of the Italian movement can be gathered from a study of its electoral strength. The suffrage in Italy is restricted by a literacy test, so that only a small proportion of the workers have the right to vote. At the present time the suffrage extends only to 7 per cent of the population, while for instance in Germany it is enjoyed by 20, and in France by 27 per cent. Illiteracy disqualifies a large number of workers in the north, and nearly all in the south. Quite naturally, therefore, the main strength of the party is in the north. In Emilia and Venetia the organization is very strong. Next comes Piedmont, which has returned as many as six socialist deputies to parliament. Lombardy is well to the front, and in Central Italy Tuscany has a strong organization with a large membership. But as one goes further south the movement becomes weaker, and with the exception of times of social unrest and public agitation, it shows but little life. This is due to the fact that the south retains its old feudal characteristics. There are few industries, and the peasantry is among the most abject and illiterate in the world.

The restricted suffrage, excluding from the ballot more than 4,000,000 working men, prevents one from obtaining the true measure of the socialists' strength. But of those who vote, socialism has the support of one out of five; that is to say, that out of the 1,593,000 votes cast at the last election 320,000 persons voted for the candidates of the socialist party. The electoral strength of the party has grown with each election. In 1892 it gained 26,000 votes; in 1895, 76,000; two years later, 135,000; in 1900, 175,000; and in 1904, 320,000 votes. About 100 municipal councils are in the control of the socialists, and the group in parliament numbers 25 out of 508 deputies. The socialists, by right of electoral strength, ought to have not less than 100 deputies, but by corruption and ballot manipulation on the part of the government the number returned was kept down to one-fourth their rightful representation.

Unlike other political movements, the socialist party in each country owns its press. It is supported out of party funds, and its policy is controlled by the party members. The Italians have five daily and over 80 weekly papers. Milan, Genoa, Mantua, and Reggio-Emilia have dailies. The party organ, "Avanti," directed by the central committee, is published at Rome, and edited by Enrico Ferri. Although Rome is not in the strongest centre of the movement, this journal has a daily circulation of over 30,000. Altogether the various party papers reach, it is said, no less than 240,000 readers. The trade union journals issued by the central bodies, and by the stronger professional organizations, all have a socialist bias. One of the most effective papers in Italy is an illustrated comic and satirical weekly called "L'Asino." It has a very large circulation, and is widely read among all classes during times of excitement.

But the propaganda in Italy, like that in France, is not mainly carried on by means of newspapers. As a rule neither the French nor the Italian workmen read a great deal. Few books are sold directly to the workers, and what is called scientific socialism rarely reaches them except through short and simply written leaflets and tracts. The real weight of the propaganda rests upon the speakers. Probably nowhere else can be found so large a proportion of brilliant orators and propagandists as in the Italian and French movements. The political campaigns are stirring, and there are always dramatic features which arouse widespread interest. The population is moved to a pitch of excitement that often ends in violence.

Every occasion is made use of to advance the propaganda, and the most favorable time to reach the working-class is during an industrial conflict. No year passes in Italy without serious strikes, which frequently end in riot and bloodshed. It is no wonder that violence should frequently occur, for in addition to the adverse economic conditions which drive the people to the extreme of hunger and misery, the masses are so ill educated, and so emotional in their temperament, that when aroused, nothing short of a violent outbreak seems to satisfy their spirit of revolt. In all the bread riots, strikes, and demonstrations of recent years the police and army have ruthlessly and brutally put down the people. In one case hundreds of the strikers were court-martialled and condemned to imprisonment. In 1894 Crispi, the Prime Minister, with incredible brutality, kept 2000 Sicilians constantly under police surveillance in the misery of "forced domicile."

Often in Italy the stupidity of the police provokes riots which under a wiser administration would never happen. A writer in " Le Mouvement Socialiste," describing the "Massacres of Class in Italy," gives an illustration of the manner in which these tragedies sometimes occur. It often happens that a labor exchange organizes a fête of agricultural laborers, which may also offer the occasion for a collective protest against those held responsible for an odious and heavy local tax. The crowd peacefully promenade the streets, and then before separating halt at the principal square in order to listen to a few words of encouragement from one of the comrades. The peasant who speaks is ill educated, and, in expressing the sentiments which surge from his heart, may in his ignorance show little regard for the conventions and exigencies of the law. The police officer, considering the public order menaced, commands the crowd to disperse and the peasant to cease his oration. The crowd protests, and, instead of dispersing, gathers round the orator. This forms a pretext for the guardian of the law to order his men to fire. At the first volley the crowd flies, terror-stricken. Some are killed, some are wounded; and as for the "agents of order," not a single one has received a scratch.

It is unquestionable that a large part of the influence of socialists among the working-classes of Italy is due to this sort of stupidity on the part of the government. Perhaps the revolutionary tradition has made the upper classes fear the masses; perhaps it is that they do not understand the workers, and that after brutalizing them by oppression and the refusal of adequate education, the gulf between the classes has been so widened that hatred, suspicion, and fear are the only sentiments that can exist between them. In any case socialism has taken hold of the Italian masses in a way that cannot be paralleled in many other countries. If socialism among the working-classes in Italy does not always represent a conscious, thoughtful, and determined movement for the attainment of a definite end, it at any rate represents a spirit of revolt which is in some respects infinitely more dangerous to the whole capitalist régime.

In considering the Italian movement one must always bear in mind the history and tradition of Italy. It has ever been a land of conspiracy, revolution, and guerilla warfare. "The psychology of Italy," an Italian has said, "permits a vehement tendency to murder. This form of crime is only rarely disclaimed by the national *morale ;* it is often glorified; and many of our moralists admit that the assassination of a compatriot sometimes resolves itself into a duty to the community." The history of all its political struggles, of all its uprisings against oppression, shows a tendency to run to extreme violence, even under the guidance of humanitarians such as Mazzini, Garibaldi, or the present-day socialist leaders. It should also be borne in mind that the Italians were among the first in Europe to accept the anarchist views of Bakounine. His doctrines appealed to the Italian mind as they appealed to the Russian mind, because the hatred of existing institutions was so great that anything short of pan-destruction seemed merely toying with the misery of the people. In the old International, the Italian section represented strongly the anarchist tendency, and until as late as 1882 the anarchists played a more important rôle than the socialists in the working men's movements of Italy.

In the year 1882 a new weapon was put into the hands of the Italian working-class by the extension of the electoral franchise. This act converted many of the leaders, among others Andrea Costa, who presided over the Rome congress, from the anarchist to the parliamentary method. In 1885 another of the many fruitless attempts to organize the Italian workmen took place and a working men's party was founded in Milan with over 40,000 members. The organization had not yet learned the use of the ballot, and it did little more than encourage violence. Anarchist leadership again destroyed the movement, and in 1886 the party was dissolved by prefectoral decree.

Five years later Signor Turati founded a weekly review, called the " Critica Sociale." He was a wealthy lawyer, a thoroughgoing Marxian, a brilliant thinker, with scholarly training. He soon exercised an enormous influence throughout the north of Italy. His review was far over the heads of the working men, but his influence among university men, lawyers, doctors, and the intellectual class generally was so great that within a few years many of the most brilliant of the young men openly supported the socialist cause. In the same year a conference was held at Milan, and a new laborers' party was organized. For the first time in the history of the working-class movement anarchists were excluded. The party adopted a program, and adhered definitely to the political method. This was the beginning of the present-day movement. It is evident that it did not take Italy by storm, as Turati, in his report to the international congress at Zurich in 1893, stated that conditions favorable to socialism had but lately developed in Italy, and although there was hope for its future, at present it was somewhat meagre and wanting in vitality. In fact he thought that for all practical purposes it might be said to be non-existent.

However, from this period on everything favored the rapid growth of socialism. The adoption of a legal and definitely political method put the governing authorities at a disadvantage in dealing with the new movement. Their fear, however, of the labor party was not less great. Under Crispi, the movement felt in all its branches the effect of his policy of repression and reaction. He charged socialism "with raising the right of spoliation to a science," and he accused it of plotting to surrender Sicily to France. His fear of the movement became a mania, and he undid himself in his wild frenzy to destroy it. His brutal oppression, his use of police and soldiery, his imprisoning of the republicans and radicals as well as socialists, brought all the advanced parties together; and, laying aside differences, electoral agreements were finally consummated.

It is not too much to say that all disinterested and patriotic Italians were, in the nineties, ready to welcome a new party. The old political parties were in decay, eaten through with corruption. The idealism which had brought them into existence was dead. The political history of the period shows that instead of moral enthusiasm, there was widespread intrigue. Corruption was on a par with our own. Political jobbery was universal — much as it is in New York or Chicago. The old parties, and nearly all of the old leaders, were involved. There were bank scandals like our insurance scandals; there were franchise thieves and bribers of legislatures. The Mafia and Comorra were political machines similar in some respects to Tammany Hall, in others to Monk Eastman's gang. The police officials were in league with criminals, and all that was vicious in Italian life was dominant. The thieves at the top were prosperous and arrogant — the masses underneath misgoverned, oppressed, and starving. When their misery became unbearable, and they quarrelled with their employers, they were shot down as our workers are in Colorado.

In the midst of such conditions the people looked to the socialists. Their leadership was disinterested and capable, their principles high and aims lofty; and it was not unnatural that they should attract that idealism so characteristic of the Italian people. Bolton King and Thomas Okey say in their interesting volume on "Italy To-day": "Alone among Italian parties the socialist movement stood boldly for purity of public life, and while well-meaning men of Right and Left touched corruption with a trembling hand, the socialists smote and spared not. To the best and most thoughtful of the educated middle classes it appealed through its high idealism, its call to intellect, its protest against the barrenness of public life, its splendid campaign against evil in high places."

From this time on the socialist movement, through its representatives in the chamber, exercised an almost dominant influence in Italian political life. It began with a program of economic and social reforms, and while it has never ceased to draw the attention of all Italy to evil economic conditions, it has been forced to occupy itself mainly with purely political questions. The time was ripe for reform; party machines had to be overturned; corruption both in private business and public life had to be exposed; and it was but natural that the socialist party should throw itself with fervor into the reform movement. In their struggle against corruption, the leaders have come to occupy a position similar to that of a middle-class opposition party; and their alliances with the advanced elements of the bourgeois have served to obliterate the class lines which are really the basis of the party's program and the reason for its existence. In its engaging work of political reform the socialist party has to a certain extent overlooked its fundamental purpose.

During this period economic discontent grew apace. Italy is the land of strikes and the home of misery. Industrial conditions are intolerable, and the people suffer. The masses are in favor of political reform, but hunger is always there; and if the political party and parliamentary method will not bring economic reform, they will abandon it for the old revolutionary methods of the sixties and seventies. In the last few years the new revolutionary weapon, the General Strike, has been resorted to again and again. In 1904 the workers were stirred to intense indignation by the massacre of the striking miners at Buggeru, and at a great and solemn meeting at Milan they declared for the general strike. The central committee, realizing the necessity for preparation, asked for a postponement, and invited the workers to hold themselves ready in case of another massacre. This was not long in coming. At Castelluzzi, in Sicily, a troop of carbineers broke into a meeting of the peasants' league, and tried to seize the papers and arrest the secretary. The members protested energetically, and the soldiers opened fire. On receipt of the news of this outrage the central committee gave the order for the general strike. The solidarity of the working-class was perfect, and in 900 communes, including all the large cities, industry was at a standstill. Although the strike lasted but two or three days, it struck terror to the heart of the bourgeois.

At some demonstrations provoked by the insupportable misery of the people, massacres again took place in the early part of 1906, and the socialist deputies demanded a government inquiry with a view to fixing the responsibility and punishing those responsible. The labor chambers were asked by referendum to proclaim another general strike, but there was only a minority in favor, and the central secretaries resigned. However, several days later a strike at Turin resulting in bloodshed aroused universal indignation. The socialists renewed their demand in parliament, and the government refusing, they resigned and appealed to the country. At the same time at Bologna, Milan, Ferrara, Ancona,

Livorno, and afterward at Rome, the general strike was proclaimed. The bourgeois, less frightened than in 1904, attempted to retaliate with an absurd voluntary police force. The strike, however, was not so effectual, and ceased everywhere in three days, leaving among the bourgeois a profound rancor against the proletariat. Many of the well-to-do left the socialist party, and the leaders, who had for some time been at odds, began to quarrel among themselves more intemperately than ever. Labriola, the leader of the syndicats, accused the party of being dominated by middle-class elements, and voiced his despair of the parliamentary method. Turati condemned the violence of the strikers, and spoke of their leaders as anarchists. Ferri took a middle ground and strove with might and main to re-establish harmony.

It is not for me to take sides in this great battle of tendencies and personalities, and without doing so it is nevertheless fair to say that Labriola's criticisms have some justification; for while it is unquestionably true that men of the exploiting and professional classes can be convinced of the necessity for socialism, they can only most rarely appreciate the proletarian feeling or unreservedly sympathize with its inevitable and irresistible revolt. In other words, they are likely to be unconsciously philosophic about its progress and willing to wait the working out of a long evolutionary process. This at any rate seems to be true of Italy, and their effort to throw on others the entire responsibility for the strikes shows that however good socialists they may be they are extremely sensitive when accused of violence. But whether or not the movement in Italy is to continue indefinitely to be led by professionals and intellectuals, it is certain that for some time the workers have been chafing under the serene parliamentary methods of their middle-class leaders.

In the midst of this general state of unrest, the congress at Rome was held. I was not surprised that it proved a battling of personalities, even more than a battling of ideas. To be sure, each of the three " great men " represented a certain tendency, but hero-worship and personal admiration swayed the judgments of the congressists almost as much as the tendencies to which they adhered. At any rate it seemed to me a fair inference, if not quite just, when an opposition paper designated the tendencies of the party as Turatist, Ferrist, and Labriolist. But this criticism is not the whole truth, as unquestionably Turati and Labriola, in their widely separated doctrines and tactics, and Ferri, in his eclecticism, typify the various tendencies which exist in the Italian movement.

Turati and his followers are reformists. Without agreeing to all their enemies have to say about them, it must be granted that they are frankly and openly pure opportunists, working hand in hand with the advanced Radicals and Republicans. I think they are fearful of the proletarian feeling. Their main effort is directed toward obtaining certain political reforms, and a gradual amelioration in the condition of the masses. Turati honestly and bravely stated the difference between his faction and that of the Syndicalists. " The conflict is not only a question of etiquette, it is at the same time in ideas, in sentiments, in action. Between the bourgeois parties there is not a hostility so great or so violent as that which separates us from the Syndicalists, in spite of the soft lie of sweet fraternity in our party." This is certainly meant to be unequivocal, and it is. Turati thinks the Syndicalists are anarchists, at least in tendency, and he expresses himself with his admirable and characteristic frankness. He is absolutely honest and sincere, so that even those who differ from him strongly in opinion are forced to admire him. He is the ablest man among the members of the party because he has the clearest and most logical mind. He is a keen and powerful debater, never leaving the field of pure and careful reasoning. He apparently has no desire to sway the emotions, and his ability in critical and logical debate is, although used for a different tactic, similar in quality to that of Bebel in Germany, or Jules Guesde in France. Turati is an incorrigible reformist — in other words, a logical reformist, and arguing from that basis he is clear, consistent, and courageous. His opponents think he should leave the party or be expelled, as his views are those of John Burns and of Millerand. At least from the socialist point of view, one must so consider them ; and if the socialist party were as uncompromising and the working-class as self-reliant in Italy as it is in France, or even in England, Turati would be faced with the same situation that confronts, in these countries, men of similar views.

Ferri is almost an exact counterpart of Turati. He is an emotional and powerful orator of the ordinary type. He is a man of good phrases, of epigrams, and generalities. He is eclectical, and a harmonizer, often regardless of violent contradictions. He considers that socialist parties must everywhere have their advanced revolutionary tendencies, as expressed by the Syndicalists, and their slow-moving, timid, and compromising tendencies, as expressed by the Reformists. In other words, the party must always have, in parliamentary phraseology, a left wing and a right. It is the rôle of the Integralists to sit in the centre, and to harmonize the two extremes. Any one can see what a difficult position this is to fill, and Ferri is attacked by both extremes for holding this middle ground, and for his unwillingness to support either the logic of the Syndicalists, or that of the Reformists. Labriola thinks integralism only a veil for those who are secretly Reformists, while Turati is impatient with it for not supporting the reformist position, and thus enabling his section to adopt a consistent reform program upon which to stand before the country, and upon which the party could fight unitedly in parliament.

Opposed to both the Reformists and the Integralists are the Syndicalists. What their exact opinions are, it was impossible to gather from the congressional proceedings. They had few representatives, and I must think that the views Labriola gave as those of his faction were only his own served up as syndicalism. With a brilliancy not exceeded, with a handling of facts and theories that was truly remarkable, and with fearlessness and power, this very extraordinary young man presented his case. It created a tremendous sensation, and as it was he who forced the fighting during the entire congress, it is only just that I should speak at greater length of his personality and views; although I am bound to think that the enthusiasm which he invoked was not so much because of his thought as because of the revolutionary spirit, and the superb feeling that characterized his address.

It may be that Arturo Labriola, if he did not express the workmen's thought, fairly well expressed their revo-

E

lutionary feeling, in that he seems to be going through a crisis of thought which may lead him, as it may lead them, to anarchism. But whether considered as a socialist or as an anarchist, Labriola cannot be explained. At present he is illogical and contradictory both in his thought and in his activity. But with all that to be said against him, he has rare personal magnetism. I sat for three hours listening to him, and I may say that, with few if any of the ordinary gifts of the orator, he is the most thrilling speaker I have ever heard. At times his discourse was like organ music, rising and falling with a peculiar harmony. His climax was not a usual one; it was climax upon climax until at last one seemed to burst in profusion, like a giant sky-rocket. And then at times his oratory was disjointed and discordant. It made one think of Browning's line, "Why rushed the discords in but that harmony should be prized?" It was a most remarkable speech — apparently the sincere and frank expression of his own soul. He kept nothing back. He was illogical but conscientious, and he seemed not to realize that his own individual crisis in thought was hardly to be presented as syndicalism.

The battle between the tendencies was not to Labriola, but he won a personal triumph that was immense. The various factions had again and again interrupted him during his address. At times it looked as if there might be a riot, and several times during his discourse, the chairman could not maintain order for many minutes together; but at the end of his address, and after a superb peroration, the entire audience rose to its feet and applauded with all its power, while those near the platform ran forward to embrace and kiss him.

I can only briefly sum up his views. He spoke in

favor of a vigorous campaign of propaganda against clericalism, against the monarchy, and against the military. He spoke disparagingly of parliamentary methods, and confessed his reliance upon the economic organization of the workers for the important changes that were to come. He criticised the leadership of the party as being middle class, and as forgetting its reason for being, and its direct responsibility to the working-class. He said *Intellectualism* ought not to be parasitic. It ought to be put at the service of socialism. It ought to illuminate the way in advance of the socialist cause. He thought it unimportant whether or not the laborer were forced to work an hour or so more in the day. " Let him work," he shouted ; " society will enrich itself thereby, and we will find a far greater harvest when the day of our victory and ascension shall come." He said it was folly to hope for the transformation of society by parliamentary action alone, and that " the emancipation of the workers can only be accomplished by the workers themselves, and not by their proxies, by some persons interposed." The nationalization of public utilities was to him unimportant because the state exploited the workers quite as mercilessly as private capitalists. Socialism of the state was only another word for capitalism of the state.

After disposing of the various methods advocated by socialists of whatever view to improve the condition of the proletariat, he asked: "What then remains, what is there essential and truly revolutionary in socialism, if it is not the free effort of the working-class, the economic organization of the proletariat upon the field of the class struggle, the grouping of the workers in their trades, federated among themselves for their common interests and preparing themselves to take one day into their own hands the direction of social work. . . . In order to arrive at this result political action can only play a secondary rôle; it is the general strike which is the decisive weapon, the supreme means of emancipating the working-class."

This is the view of a new school rising in Europe. Sorel and Lagardelle in France, and Leone and Labriola in Italy, are doing a very useful work in forcing the purely parliamentary socialists to recognize more than they otherwise would the value and indeed the necessity of strong organization among the working-classes on the economic field; but the socialists of the United States, and England especially, know how absurd it is to consider this the sole means necessary by which to combat capitalism. It is common knowledge with us that the union movement is revolutionary and often violent in the early stages of its development. Wherever the organizations are weak, they are the most combative. As they grow more experienced and develop strength, they become more careful about risking defeat by hastily considered or ill-advised action. The trade union movement in Italy is still in its early stages, and while the members are mostly socialists, the leaders may become, as many of our trade union socialists of the seventies and eighties became, extremely careful not to endanger the funds and standing of their economic organizations. The English and American unionists, after a long period of syndicalism, are now beginning to realize that they have left undeveloped and unused one of their most effective weapons of defence and of aggression; namely, their political power. It will therefore be a cause for profound regret if the Italians discard this method of emancipating the working-class upon the assumption that they can gain more by the development and use of their economic organizations. Neither the one nor the other method alone suffices for this tremendous task. What is needed is a more comprehensive organization of the workers, both in the trade unions and in the branches of the party. To change from the parliamentary to the syndicalist method, or *vice versa*, can have but little effect, except to cripple the working-class in the midst of a difficult war.

The whole congress was occupied in this struggle between the three factions. In the voting Labriola was badly defeated by a union of the Reformists and the Integralists. The movement goes on united, if unity is possible where there is so much ill-feeling between the factions. How much it is a mere unity of form, without a unity of spirit, one cannot say. Certainly the divisions between the factions seem very deep and forbidding. They make one feel grateful that one is not an Italian socialist. One would not know what to do or whom to support. This must be a very common feeling among the Italians, with the effect that their work must be, to a certain extent, weak, uncertain, and halting, all of which is especially deplorable for Italy. The working-classes there, perhaps more than anywhere else in Europe, need the training and development that come from participation in organizations of their own. They need its steadying influence, and the education it gives in self-reliance. They need both their economic organizations and their political organizations, and anything which retards the growing and strengthening of these resources of the working-class of Italy does it a very bad turn.

To one sitting in that hall, not in the heat of a faction or under the spell of a personality, the spectacle was of a kind to make one despair. At the end all was tumult. There were shouts, congratulations, exultations — there were the victors and the vanquished. The congress of the Italian Socialist Party was another thing of the past in the city of things of the past. It was not without a feeling of relief that one left the new temple to walk through the wastes and ruins of the old. From the terrace of the senatorial palace one sees the white, deserted temples of a thousand gods, vast wastes of the precious, unrewarded, and gigantic labor of the poor. By the love and labor and hope of the disinherited the temple of Saturn was built, and that of Castor, and that of Vesta, and that of Futura, and that of Concord. The arch of Septimius was their labor, and so too were the towering arches of the basilica of Constantine. And to-day it is but a step, as it was three thousand years ago, from this spacious, but now *dead* city into the narrow alleys of the *living* poor. It was the work of the poor. It was they who had built it all. They had cut its marble from the hills, dug the trenches, laid the foundations. Every wall, column, arch, they had put in place. The city of palaces, of baths, of circuses, of arches, of temples, they had built again and again. They had laid its pavements and adorned its streets with exquisite beauty. They had built palaces for their tyrants, for their kings, emperors, and senators, for their priests, for their demagogues, and for the mistresses of their tyrants, and emperors, and priests, and demagogues. But for themselves they had in B.C., and they have in A.D., hovels and alleys.

Is this new movement going to repeat the old, old story? That is hardly conceivable; but in Italy, instead of union, education, and organization, the party brings to the proletariat the quarrels, tendencies, hair-split-

tings, and personalities of a few middle-class intellectuals.   It is, I fear, a party of Roman patricians, with
the votes of a restive, revolutionary proletariat.   Is this
too harsh ?   Perhaps it is.   It may be that these impres-
sions of the Italian socialist movement are all wrong,
and no one more than I can hope that they are; for
Italy needs socialism as much as any land under the
sun.   It is her only hope; and I should think that any
man with heart would be a socialist in Italy.   The misery is so great there that even the hardest must be
touched.   I think of one valley, so smiling, so beautiful,
with a thousand terraced gardens on its exquisite slopes,
under skies that enrapture the soul; and with men,
women, and children whose forms and faces lacerate
the heart.   After one sight of that humanity, there are
no more skies, no gardens, no valleys, no hills.   I would
rather live forever in Dante's hell than there among my
wretched human brothers.   Great God, is not the Valley of Tirano all the school Italy needs for socialism ?
Are not the streets and alleys about the temple, living,
and about the Coliseum, dead, all that is needed for propaganda ?   The faces one sees there are the faces with
big eyes and sunken cheeks.   They are faces that, once
seen, can never be forgotten.   They are with you when
you eat, and your food sickens you.   They are with
you when you dress, and your clothes become hateful to
you.   They are with you when you try to sleep, and the
night haunts you.

It may be that some men in Italy can close their
hearts to these faces and eyes.   It may be that some
men must do what St. Francis did — give all, absolutely
all.   But is it possible that any one with compassion
can know and see and feel, and not be a revolutionist ?

CHAPTER III

THE German congress was an impressive gathering of intelligent and wide-awake men. The Italian congress was full of excitement and pyrotechnics. The French congress, held at Limoges, in the heart of the great potteries, was impressive, interesting, and also not without its fireworks. The delegates thought with a thoroughness not inferior to that of the Germans, and debated with a vivacity and charm not exceeded by the Italians. They were men from the workshops, men from the study, men from the "sanctums" of the great journals; and there were there men of international reputation in science, economics, and politics. The congress was therefore not so exclusively working-class as the German, nor so middle-class as the Italian. Those who were Intellectuals took their inspiration from the people, and those who had come from the workshops were as capable as the Intellectuals of thought and of leadership.

The movement in France is superb. It has all the necessary qualities and elements of a great party. If it has its opportunists, it has also its impossibilists. If it has its cautious ones, it has also its impetuous ones. If it has its pure theorists, it has also its thorough practicians. And the balance is admirable. But it is not the balance which comes from the dominance of one powerful mind. Criticism runs high; each tendency is represented by some mind and voice of a high order. And a tactic or a policy which runs the gantlet of the keen intelligence of men with such different points of view is pretty certain to be sound.

For the first time I have seen some good resulting from divisions among socialists. The French socialists are to-day united, but for thirty or more years they have been separated into various groups, sometimes attacking each other, often competing with each other, and at times maligning each other. Again and again they have achieved a sort of unity, only to break again into bitterly antagonistic groups. Schism after schism occurred, and the weary years of propaganda dragged on, without that unity of the proletariat which was the watchword and fundamental doctrine of all their teaching. There was a bad side to these divisions which no one could wish to minimize, but at least they had one good result. Great men were produced, — skilful debaters, indefatigable propagandists, powerful polemical writers. And now that unity has come, and all the men of the old groups are fighting together for the common end, the French party has in its fold a remarkable number of brilliant and capable men. Each of the four or five old factions has contributed its quota of extraordinary men. Some of the groups had drawn to themselves the ablest minds from among the workers; others had drawn from the intellectual proletariat men of exceptional ability; and all together contribute now to the united party the valuable results of their labors.

But what a history the French movement has for discord and division! France is the birthplace of nearly all the idealism that gave rise to the modern

movement. Ever since the great revolution, the philosophy of socialism has fascinated some of the most
brilliant minds in France; but the fulness of their inspiration and the variation in their tendencies have
prevented them from establishing one school. It is not
strange, therefore, that among a people so enamoured
of ideas and ideals, in a country where men register
their convictions in blood, in a nation that has a revolutionary tradition of which every child is proud, it
has been only through infinite toil and anguish that
coherence in organization and doctrine has been brought
into being.

In France socialism often means revolution, and
the most widely varying doctrines, from extreme anarchism to extreme statism, are frequently embraced
within its scope. Before the insurrection of 1871 the
old International exercised a powerful influence in
France, and included within its organization nearly
every phase of socialist thought and revolutionary
action. The Proudhonian anarchists, with their program
of decentralization, anti-parliamentary action, and the
abolition of all forms of government, together with a
belief in the efficacy of coöperation and mutual aid among
the workers to achieve the complete emancipation of
the proletariat; the Blanquists, with their conspiratory
methods of taking the state by surprise and wresting
it from the hands of the capitalists; and a small group
of Marxists, who believed in definitely organized political action by the working-class; were all carrying
on a feverish agitation, which consisted almost as much
of internal warfare as it did of active efforts against
capitalism. For a period of over ten years these various factions carried on their strife. They had only

one thing in common, and in that they were also in agreement with the republicans of that period — they were all against the empire. As the social unrest developed, and the masses became more and more agitated and revolutionary, one of those periods of explosive energy and violence arrived to give an outlet to the growing class antagonism, and in 1871 a terrible struggle between the capitalists and the workers broke forth in all its fury. For a moment the workers were victorious; then came defeat, followed by wholesale massacres.

At almost the same time the International, torn by dissensions after a vain attempt to harbor all revolutionary elements, was abolished by Marx. Its warring factions were broken and dispersed and their revolutionary force spent in the upheavals of Paris and Spain. With the crushing of the Commune nearly all the leaders were forced to leave France, and every vestige of their organizations was shattered. Blanqui, that inveterate revolutionist, was again in prison, Vaillant and many of his friends were in exile in London, and the anarchist leaders in Switzerland. The workers were left without leadership, and the brutal methods by which the government had put down their uprising left them broken and cowed.

But the irresistible impulse of working men to organize did not long remain quiescent. As early as 1872, a few workers came together for concerted action. They disclaimed all revolutionary views; nevertheless, the government dispersed them. Again, three years later, in Paris, the representatives of various groups came together to establish a working men's movement. They all agreed that it should be exclusively working-

class, and that politicians, theoreticians, and revolutionists should not be admitted. They expressed
themselves in favor of trade union action, and the
development of coöperatives. They wished solely,
they declared, to modify the present state of society
in a way more equitable for the workers; and they
avoided with care all revolutionary and socialist utterances. The revolutionists in exile read with amazement
the declaration of the congress, and issued manifestoes
condemning the conservatism of the workers. To all
appearances the proletariat had abandoned all radical
views, and the moderates and the republicans, who
were leading the movement, intended to prevent the
revolutionists from gaining control of it again.

At this time there appeared in France, Jules Guesde,
one of the most remarkable personalities in the socialist
movement. He had returned from exile in Switzerland and Italy. Before the Commune he had collaborated actively with some other revolutionary journalists
in attacking the empire, and under the patronage of
several men who later were the leaders in that insurrection, he founded a paper called " The Rights of
Man." When Guesde was twenty years old, he so
outraged the imperial régime that he was condemned
to six months in prison. On the famous fourth of
September, without knowing what had happened in
Paris, he marched with a small group of republicans
upon the prefecture of Montpellier and captured it,
and then after the insurrection he was condemned to
five years. Instead of going to prison he left France,
and during his exile at Geneva he became an active
socialist, and assisted there in creating a section of the
International and in founding a daily paper. He then

Jules Guesde.

became a wandering agitator, passing through all the industrial centres of Italy, carrying on a ceaseless propaganda. By word and pen he attacked the present order with bitterness and fearlessness. Often hungry, in rags, and homeless, he suffered privations which would have killed any man without his indomitable will-power. Threatened for a time with tuberculosis, he had to go to southern Italy, but as soon as his five years' exile was over he returned to France.

But while abroad Guesde had been schooled in the thought, tactics, and language of Marxian socialism, and when he returned, he had a far different conception of revolutionary methods than he had had when he left. The brilliant example of the German organization was before him, and he set out to capture the French working-class movement and organize it into a definite political party. In 1877 he established "L'Égalité" to sustain his views, and in addition to his own editorial work he wrote for two journals with a similar tendency. Along with some other Marxists he gave battle to the anarchists and the insurrectionists. He became the very genius of agitation, rushing from one end of France to another to carry on his propaganda among the masses, and to convert the leaders of the trade union movement to political action. Guesde's belief as to the necessity of a violent revolution did not change, but he began to realize more and more the futility of insurrection and street-rioting. From this time on he appears as the most striking figure in French socialism, and while perhaps Marxian views have never appealed so completely to the French as to some of the other nationalities, it is almost entirely due to Guesde that the working-class movement has abandoned the old methods and settled down to organized political action founded upon a coherent and logical doctrine.

At the trade union congress held at Lyons early in 1878, it was decided to organize an international working men's congress to be held in Paris the same year upon the occasion of *l'Exposition Universelle.* All plans were made for it, but the police informed the unions that it would not be tolerated, and they abandoned their project. The socialists, under the leadership of Guesde, decided to ignore the authorities, and to proceed with the congress; and the unions promised their support. By this audacious move Guesde and his friends appeared before the foreign delegates as if they were the leaders of the entire French movement. When the congressists came to assemble, they found the hall surrounded by police, and the organizers of the illegal assembly were arrested. Guesde presented a collective defence before the court, but nevertheless he and his associates were condemned to six months in prison. However, the defence, which was in the nature of a manifesto, was circulated throughout France, and created a profound sensation. Guesde was soon to be in reality the head of the working men's movement.

During the next few months the agitation was at fever heat. The Marxists were fast making converts of the leaders, and already several important unions had declared for socialism. In October, 1879, a congress, "ever memorable," as Guesde afterward said, was held at Marseilles. Over the door of the hall was hung an inscription which foretold the outcome of that historic meeting, "The land for the peasant; the tool for the laborer; and work for all." The events of the past few months had had their effect, and the delegates, caught in the storm of enthusiasm, were ready for revolutionary action. Even the moderates seemed to have given themselves over to the common impulse. The note of the gathering was sounded by Jean Lombard, the organizing secretary of the congress, who urged that the new program ought to show a sensible progress over the previous ones; and he proposed to change the name of the gathering to "The Socialist Labor Congress." The proposition was accepted with unanimity. A delegate arose to declare that unions have a rôle to play; that is, to be a nursery of revolutionary ideas. Another delegate announced the failure of the co-operative idea. Fournière, in a passionate address, said that as things were going there would be in ten years neither small employers nor proprietors. Two classes only would be face to face, the idle rich and the poverty-stricken workers. In the midst of the general tumult in the congress almost every revolutionary tendency found expression. One of the delegates went so far as to exclaim that the only propaganda worth while was to declare to the people that " in place of capturing the central government it is necessary to bombard and destroy it," which showed that if there were socialists in the assembly, there were also anarchists.

But despite the strong revolutionary feeling, no one seemed to have a program. It was a golden opportunity for the Marxists, for their thought was clear and their program definite. It is useless to analyze the addresses relative to the constitution of a political party. The delegates found themselves in accord, and Guesde and Paul Lafargue, the son-in-law of Karl Marx, together wrote the program which was adopted.

After the confusion of years, from amidst the many
revolutionary tendencies bequeathed to the French
working men by the great thinkers of the past, Marxian
doctrine and tactics had captured the French movement, and placed it in accord with the other political
socialist movements then arising in all the neighboring
countries.

The following year the congress was held at Havre.
The republicans, who had launched the movement in
Paris, in 1875, a few old and rich unions which had joined
it, and some coöperative societies which had supported
it, had been surprised at Marseilles, when the socialists
had taken the congress by storm; and they decided to
attend the next gathering solidly organized.   The socialists exerted themselves to the utmost to return to the
congress as many delegates as possible, but when they
presented themselves, they were refused admission by
the moderates; and they retired in a body to assemble
in an adjoining hall.   There were only 57 delegates,
representing a variety of tendencies, and it seemed as
if they had been defeated.   The moderates appeared to
be victorious, but they had no faith, no doctrine, no
ideals, and despite their strength they ceased to exist
after a subsequent congress a year later.   The socialists
on the other hand stood for what appealed to the French
working men, and after the Havre congress their influence became dominant.

Socialism began to take hold in France, and there
collected around the movement Guesde had started
many brilliant and capable men.   The party was united.
It had a clear and definite program, and in all parts of
France agitation and organization were making headway.   A number of journals were launched, and among

others "L'Émancipation," edited jointly by Guesde, Paul Brousse, and Benoît Malon, the latter a most admirable and capable man. The same year parliament voted complete amnesty to the militants of the Commune, and returning from exile they threw themselves into various radical movements. A number of them followed Clémenceau, who at that time was directing the extreme Left, while others founded a new socialist organization. J. B. Clément, Jules Joffrin, Jean Allemane, and others, affiliated themselves with Guesde and Malon. Vaillant, Granger, and others reconstituted a Blanquist group. All things seemed to point to the rapid success of the socialist movement.

The elections of 1881 were, however, an immense disappointment, and unfortunately served to arouse new dissensions. Certain factions of the party attributed the failure to the Marxian program of Guesde and his friends. They said it was not adapted to the French spirit, and was written in a vocabulary little known. Besides failing to take account of the traditional forms of French thought, it introduced new ideas which, it was said, did not appeal to the French working men. One of the candidates of the party, Jules Joffrin, altered the program to suit himself, and this lack of discipline infuriated Guesde. The journal, "L'Émancipation," was abandoned, after it had issued twenty-four numbers, because of differences between Guesde and Malon. Paul Brousse, who was ambitious to lead, and his friends undertook to drive Guesde from the movement. Brousse in his youth had inclined toward anarchism, and had been associated with Bakounine in the work of the International. Later he adopted the collectivist position, but he remained a bitter opponent of Marxian

F

tactics, and especially of what seemed to him, as it had to Bakounine, the dictatorial attitude of some of the Marxian leaders. The general dissatisfaction with Guesde's leadership gave Brousse an opportunity to attack him, and he undertook the battle with almost sinister delight. During the next year or so Brousse and Guesde spent the force which ought to have been given to organization and propaganda in bitter personal attacks; and when the next congress of the socialist party assembled at St. Etienne in 1882, every one foresaw that it would end in a rupture. Brousse and his friends succeeded in their campaign, and Guesde and his sympathizers retired from the congress amidst lively scenes. At this time the Broussists, or, as they were called from this time onward, the possibilists, were numerous; but their party was loosely organized, and with the exception of a few victories in Paris they made little impression. Guesde and Lafargue dominated the industrial regions of the north, where their adherents were active and serious, and it was inevitable that Guesde and his followers should, despite their apparent defeat, exercise the more powerful influence in the rising tide of revolt.

During the eighties and early nineties various attempts were made by the Guesdists to recapture the trade union movement. At times they appeared near to success, but again and again they were vanquished; and at last the trade unions and labor exchanges definitely adopted an anti-parliamentary attitude. When later " The General Federation of Labor " was formed, it decided that the sole revolutionary means to employ for the emancipation of labor was the general strike. Guesde has never known compromise, and despite the inevitable tendency of the French masses to violent action, he has never wavered in his opposition to the general strike. With all the power of his keen and logical mind he condemned and demonstrated the futility of the purely economic strife, but without avail ; and finally the main body of the union movement passed from under his influence.

It would seem, among such personal and doctrinal divisions, that socialism would have had but little chance of developing strength ; but what would have made a movement impossible in other countries helped the movement of France. Nothing interests and attracts a Frenchman more than a good fight, whether it be in the streets, in the journals, or in the assembly. A century's struggle for liberty has not been without its effect, and it is, therefore, a part of the French nature to admire individuality. An Englishman or an American likes to be in accord with others, and to conform to the views of others. A Frenchman prefers to differ, and he detests conformity. As a result the various groups, with their differences in doctrine, their sectarian schisms, and even their violence, drew to themselves adherents, all of whom seemed proud to have views that differed from those of the other groups ; and no less proud that the views of the various socialist groups differed fundamentally from those of the bourgeois parties. In addition to this individualism, there is among Frenchmen little respect for the definite and detailed organization that exists among the Germans. In the old International the Frenchmen were anarchists and supported the principles of decentralization and federalization. While the Germans, even as outlaws, were secretly building up their political organization, the Frenchmen were discussing great ideas, and by the force of thought arrived at a solidarity of action that has at times made the French movement much more formidable even than the German. The German working-classes have few dissensions, and for thirty years have worked mostly in concert. The French movement is most of the time torn by conflicting views, but at rare moments it demonstrates a solidarity of action that seems instinctive.

Despite differences, therefore, French socialism began, in the early nineties, to impress itself upon the national life. There were no less than five well-organized groups. The possibilists were led in two sections, one by Brousse and the other by Allemane. The collectivists, supporting the Marxian position, were led by Guesde, Lafargue, and other doctrinaires. The Blanquists maintained the traditions of the old conspirator, and announced themselves ready for revolution. There was still another group, the independents, led at that time by Millerand, Jaurès, and Fournière. It was composed largely of radicals, who were beginning timidly to support the socialist position. The leaders were of the middle class, and they brought into the movement a brilliant coterie of university men, journalists, and students.

The elections of 1893 proved a striking victory for the socialists. Forty deputies were elected to parliament upon a collectivist program, and the vote was four times larger than that of 1889, amounting in actual numbers to nearly half a million. The Guesdists and all the other groups had elected their strongest men. This unexpected victory led to a kindly feeling that had not before existed between the various sections, and in order to make their influence as powerful as possible, they organized a united socialist group in the chamber.

Jean Jaurès.

The work done during the session of 1893–1898 was most effective. The principles and program of socialism were for the first time placed before the entire country with clearness and power. Guesde took every opportune moment to explain the fundamental doctrines of socialism. He developed Marx's view concerning the evolution of modern capitalism, and showed how inevitable it was that socialism should follow. He also forced upon the chamber a consideration of the eight-hour day, and, in connection with a municipal pharmacy which the socialists were endeavoring to establish at Roubaix, he expounded the whole socialist program for municipal reform. Jaurès, Vaillant, and the other members of the group developed other phases of the socialist position. For the first time a just conception of socialism penetrated into every corner of France. Printed in the official journal, these socialist addresses were reprinted in the columns of all newspapers and journals. Collectivism was decidedly to the front, and every editor in France began to discuss the growing power and influence of the new movement.

During this session Jaurès was the leader of the parliamentary group. As everything in the early years of the movement centred around the personality of Guesde, so everything during the last fourteen years in France has centred around the personality of Jaurès. He is without question one of the most powerful personalities in the International movement, and one of the most popular in France. He is still in the prime of life, barely forty-eight years old, although he began his parliamentary career over twenty years ago. He is of middle-class parents and was graduated with honors from the École Normale Supérieure. Immediately after graduation he was made professor of philosophy, and his studies led him into the field of socialist thought. The surging life about him, and his natural sympathy with the masses, contributed to a growing discontent with the quiet of the university, so remote from the field of action. In 1885 Jaurès stood as candidate for parliament, and was elected. He immediately became one of the leaders of the radical group, and although he did not announce himself as a socialist, he was at that time entirely sympathetic. Upon his defeat in the elections of 1889 he returned to the university again as professor of philosophy. While there, he prepared two studies for his doctor's degree, one of which was upon Origins of German Socialism. In 1893 he announced himself as a socialist candidate, and was elected by an enormous majority. He, Millerand, Viviani, and others then formed the independent socialist party.

Jaurès is a man of extraordinary capacity for work. He has a powerful physique that knows no fatigue. It is doubtful if he has an equal as an orator, and his abilities as a debater are hardly less remarkable. It is intolerable to him to follow, and while he is modest and reasonable, his exceptional mental and physical power enables, indeed forces him, to occupy a leading part in parliamentary battles. The number of debates in which Jaurès is engaged is incredible, and alone they would occupy the entire time of most men. But he is also a student, and his researches into the history of the French revolution are said to be exhaustive, especially in their examination of original documents. At the same time he is the editor of a daily paper, " L'Humanité," and there is hardly an issue that does not contain a leading article by him. But even these various occupations do not seem to exhaust the energies of Jaurès, and few men in the socialist movement carry on throughout the country a campaign of propaganda equal to his. During elections and in other times of excitement he seems able to preach to the whole of France the philosophy of socialism. He conducts what we should call a whirlwind campaign in parliament, in the journals, in drawing-rooms, in the streets, and among strikers. In the strike that broke out in Carmaux, he led the splendid campaign of the strikers, and moved the sympathies of all France by his vivid portrayal of their conditions.

Poor old Guesde was jubilant. Sick and exhausted after the weary years of persecution and strife, he turned to Jaurès as the one who should continue his work. I am told that one evening, after they had dined together, Guesde said: "Jaurès, I am tired. I have fought as best I could. My strength is gone. I have looked for some one else to carry on the battle, and now I know you are the one to do it." Guesde is not often sentimental, and is rarely carried away by enthusiasm, but he thought at that time that the socialists would in a few years control the government of France. He could not have foreseen the days of trial that were coming to test the movement to its foundations. Above all he could hardly have realized that Jaurès and he were to be opponents in one of the greatest internal battles the socialist movement has known.

Up to this time Jaurès had refused to recognize the divisions in the party, and he always spoke for any of the groups that desired his services. It is unquestionable that he wished unity, and used his utmost power

to achieve it. In 1898 the Dreyfus case came to occupy the thought of France, and in a flash the nation
was thrown into tumults of passion. Aside from the
rights or wrongs of this case at the beginning, when
it became *l'Affaire* its political importance could
hardly be ignored by any parliamentary party. The
Guesdists and a few other socialists looked with alarm
upon its intrusion into parliamentary life, for to them
it meant that social reform and socialism were to be put
in the background, and a purely personal and political
question forced to the front. They decided, therefore,
to have nothing whatever to do with the matter. But
Jaurès followed his conviction, and, as we know, led
one of the most brilliant battles in the history of the
French chamber. For the moment he seemed to forget
he was a socialist, and all his energies were diverted
from the movement and devoted to *l'Affaire*. This
naturally led to difficulties between him and Guesde,
who is ever jealous for socialism and knows no diver-
sion.

Another event transpired at about the same time that
led to an open rupture between Guesde and Jaurès.
When Waldeck-Rousseau formed his radical ministry
in June, 1899, he found the active support of the socialists a political necessity. In order to win it he decided
to invite one of their most capable members, Millerand,
to come into the cabinet. Jaurès supported the idea,
and openly urged Millerand to accept the position. At
the same time General de Gallifet, who had crushed the
Commune with terrible brutality, was also invited to be
a member. It was serious enough for a socialist to take
a position in a non-socialist cabinet, but for one to enter
along with General de Gallifet stirred the party to its

depths. The Guesdists and the followers of Vaillant, an old Communard, issued a scathing manifesto, excluding Millerand and his defenders from the party. The only union then existing between the various socialist organizations was in their parliamentary work, and the followers of both Guesde and Vaillant retired from the parliamentary group. It is possible that Jaurès had not fully realized the seriousness of Millerand's action, and to mend matters he urged the immediate necessity of complete union; and against the will of his opponents forced a general congress of all socialist bodies. As a result a central body was formed for the purpose of carrying out the details of unification; but the diverse elements were too deeply hostile to one another, and too much absorbed in the Millerand-Waldeck-Rousseau ministry, to consider calmly proposals for unity. The International Socialist Congress, which was held in Paris in 1900, was forced by the situation in France to give almost its entire time to the "cas Millerand." The French socialists held themselves in check as best they could during the international gathering, but a short time later at a national congress, which it was hoped would establish unity, the Guesdists and the followers of Vaillant left the assembly in a body.

Indeed, there was no possibility at that time of union between the various socialist groups, and during the next four or five years the differences between them were accentuated. Various efforts were made toward conciliation, but without result. Guesde was uncompromising, and Jaurès was passing through a crisis of thought that appeared to lead him farther and farther from the accepted political tactics of modern socialism. To read the masterly defence of his

policy which he delivered at the Bordeaux congress
of 1903 leads one to the realization that a crisis faced
not only the French, but the whole international,
movement. "Guesde is wrong," Jaurès said, "in thinking . . . that the state is exclusively a class-state, upon
which the too feeble hand of the proletariat cannot yet
inscribe the smallest portion of its will. In a democracy, in a republic where there is universal suffrage,
the state is not for the proletarians a refractory, hard,
absolutely impermeable and impenetrable block. Penetration has begun already. In the municipalities, in parliament, in the central government, there has begun the
penetration of socialistic and proletarian influence. . . .
If it is in part penetrated by this democratic, popular,
socialist force, and if we can reasonably hope that by organization, education, and propaganda this penetration
will become so full, deep, and decisive, that in time by
accumulated efforts we shall find the proletarian and
socialistic state to have replaced the oligarchic and
bourgeois state, then perhaps we shall be aware of having entered the zone of socialism, as navigators are
aware of having crossed the line of a hemisphere —
not that they have been able to see as they crossed it
a cord stretched over the ocean warning them of their
passage, but that little by little they have been led into
a new hemisphere by the progress of their ship. . . .
I acknowledge that this complicated policy which I am
trying to formulate before the party, a policy which
consists in at once collaborating with all democrats, yet
vigorously distinguishing one's self from them ; pene-
trating partially into the state of to-day, yet dominating
the state of to-day from the heights of our ideal — I
acknowledge that this policy is complicated, that it is

awkward, that it will create serious difficulties for us at every turn."

It is difficult indeed to overestimate the dangers of this policy. It opens the way to compromise and corruption. It destroys the independence of the movement, and in the end confuses it with the purely political manœuvring of the other classes. It endangers the socialist ideal, and leaves to the movement only a policy of petty reform. Although Jaurès saw reefs ahead and warned Millerand that his policy would allow them to abandon all "but what can be easily assimilated by the governmental action of to-day," the difficulties and dangers did not deter him. These questions, so vital to the party, which were only superficially considered at the international congress of 1900, were the subject of a historic debate at the international meeting of 1904 at Amsterdam.

The year before, at the Dresden congress of the German party, a great struggle had taken place between Bebel and his followers and those who have come to be called revisionists. The latter had for several years been criticising the uncompromising tactics and political methods of the party. They were of the opinion that infinitely more could be accomplished by so powerful a movement if it compromised with the other political parties and participated in governmental power. The methods advocated by the revisionists were those used by Jaurès in France, and their contention seemed to be making headway. At Dresden the entire subject was examined from both a theoretical and practical standpoint. The revisionists were defeated, and what has since been known as the Dresden resolution was almost unanimously passed. It condemned in the most ener-

getic fashion the revisionist tendencies. It declared
that the socialists should pursue a policy strictly independent of all other political parties, and should in no
wise consent to participate in a capitalist government;
and it expressed its entire belief in the wisdom and
utility of the old political tactics which had enabled
the party to reach its present strength and to accomplish
so much for the welfare of the working-class.

Guesde and his followers considered the decision of
the Germans of supreme importance, and they decided
to bring the matter before the International for the purpose of defining the political method of the international movement. Nearly all the great speakers —
Bebel, Vandervelde, Ferri, Adler, Anseele, Guesde, and
Jaurès — participated in the debate, and what has been
described as "a titanic international duel" took place
between Bebel and Jaurès. The latter, in a series of
masterly addresses, defended his position in France.
He endeavored to prove that it was impossible to have
the same political tactics in all countries. There was,
he maintained, an essential difference between the political methods to be adopted in a republic and those
necessary in an autocracy. He claimed that the very
helplessness of the German party was adequate reason
for their adoption of an uncompromising and hostile attitude toward the governing and all other parties. On
the contrary the power exercised by the proletariat in a
republic forced it to accept a responsible part in government. Pleading for Millerand and the political policy
of his section, he claimed they had aided in saving the
republic to France, they had defeated the reactionary
bloc, and crushed the conspiracy between cæsarism
and clericalism. He portrayed the advance made in

recent years in France toward a system of social legislation, measures for the protection of labor, and the
nationalization of public utilities. When he finished, he
was given an ovation, and shouts of approval came from
all parts of the hall.

When Bebel arose, it seemed impossible that he should
overcome the powerful arguments and torrential eloquence of Jaurès. His reply was quiet, logical, and in-
cisive. He condemned the policy of compromise, and
showed that the hostile method of his own party had
gained for the German working men a far greater range
of social reforms than those existing in France. He
showed how in France, under the ministry of which
Millerand was a part, the workmen were intimidated
and the army used against the strikers in a way never
done in Germany. While declaring himself a republican, he demonstrated that whatever political form of
government existed, the capitalists gained control of it,
and used it against the interest of the workers. He did
not deny that Jaurès and the French socialists should
exert themselves to save the republic, or to fight with
the bourgeois to separate the Church from the State, but
a collaboration with other parties should be temporary,
and as soon as the particular battle was over the old
uncompromising attitude should be resumed.

It is impossible in a few words to sum up a debate
which was on both sides succinct and yet comprehensive.
Hardly a phrase could be eliminated from either address
without injury to the subject-matter. But the victory
was to Bebel, and a revised resolution based upon that
of Dresden was passed almost unanimously. Jaurès
fought brilliantly, and defeated, he was loyal. He accepted the decision of the congress, and submitted

himself to that discipline which is so striking a characteristic of the socialist movement. Upon his return to
France union was established, and since that time it
has not been seriously in danger. Jules Guesde had
in 1879 forced German political tactics upon the French
movement. Twenty-five years later, he repeated his
extraordinary achievement.

With this rapid historical survey, let us go back to
the Potteries, where the united party assembled in congress. It was held in a big, barnlike structure, which
belonged to the Coöperative Union of Limoges, and
which under ordinary circumstances served as a great
storehouse for their supplies. Two splendid banners
were displayed above the platform. One bore the
motto of socialism, and its rallying cry throughout the
world, which carries in its five words both the philosophy and the program of the contemporary struggle
for freedom: "Working Men of all Countries, Unite!"
The other, a banner with letters of gold, breathed forth
the spirit of internationalism with which the French
movement is specially permeated and glorified: "*Parti
Socialiste: Section Française de l'Internationale Ouvrière.*" This, then, is a congress of a great national
section of the International Socialist Party!

At ten o'clock in the morning 220 delegates, representing 67 sections of the French party, took their
seats. They were a strong-looking lot of men, and
while, as I have said, the middle-class element was
large, the delegates were mainly working men. I
almost instantly picked out Jules Guesde. One would
remark him anywhere. The pallor of his dark skin
gives one the first impression of physical weakness.
He has great masses of long black hair which he

tosses back over his head and ears. He is upward of sixty, but his eyes still burn and his thought comes in flashes. Every expression, word, and act tell of what Guesde is and of what he has always been. He is a zealot. His whole being loathes the system under which we live, and he fights it, not calmly, but at fever heat. His voice is piercing, almost painful at times, but his thought is as clear as a mountain stream, and it tears its way through all obstacles at a rate which is almost unbelievable. He knows no compromise and gives no quarter. He is fearless and imperious. His words come like rapier thrusts, and he often uses them as unmercifully. By the side of Guesde sits Gustave Delory, who was breaking stones on the streets of Lille two years before he was elected mayor of that great city, and who is now a deputy in parliament. In both places he has astonished friend and foe alike by his extraordinary ability.

The fine, jovial face with merry twinkling eyes and white hair in abundance is that of Paul Lafargue. One could see that it must be he who had written the fantastic socialist tracts one reads with such pleasure, and who, as Émile Vandervelde has said, loves nothing so much as to shock the timid by his extreme paradoxes. The strongly built, gray-bearded man, with blue glasses and a small cap, is Edouard Vaillant, the veteran revolutionist, and a leader of that terrible insurrection of '71. He once made the remark that he had never known any kind of revolution that he was not in favor of. He is still fighting at the head of the movement, and perhaps no other man in France is more long-headed in times of stress than Vaillant.

Jaurès sits far away to the back of the room. He

is a short, thickset man, powerfully built, with leonine head. He shows in every movement quickness of action, tireless energy, and the enormous quantity of physical and mental power which he possesses. One can feel the sentiment of the South in him. He is a man of emotion whose whole being revolts at the cruelties, the miseries, the brutalities, of the present system. One can see that he likes to be in the thick of the fight. He bears a striking resemblance to Senator La Follette. Physically and mentally as well as in their power of debate and oration they are as alike as brothers. Besides the men I have mentioned there were many others of international renown, such as, for instance, Gustave Hervé, the great apostle of anti-militarism, who has only recently come out of prison, where he had been sent for his propaganda among the conscripts. But I should take too much space if I were to attempt to describe all the noted men who were present. There were others almost as well known as those named, and many younger men of brilliant ability who are fully prepared to take the places of the older men when they are gone. My purpose must be now to tell a little of the work of the congress.

The reports of the administration showed a remarkable progress in the growth of the movement. When the various parties were united, there were only 27,000 persons definitely affiliated and paying dues. Now there are more than 52,000. The party is organized in over 70 different federations, with affiliated groups in 80 out of the 97 departments of France. There are 2160 municipal councillors, 149 mayors, and 219 vice-mayors in the various cities, towns, and villages of France. In parliament the socialist group numbers 52

members, and at the last elections the total vote given
to 346 candidates put forward by the party was approx-
imately 900,000, an augmentation of 12 per cent over
the vote obtained in 1902. The press of the party includes three daily papers: " L'Humanité," in Paris, " Le
Populaire du Centre," at Limoges, and " Le Droit du
Peuple," at Grenoble ; and in addition there are two
biweeklies, 37 weeklies, and two monthlies.

These interesting reports as to the progress of the
movement were followed by several debates, the most
important of which was perhaps that concerning the
relation between the trade unions and the socialist
party. It was the old controversy that has agitated the
movement for thirty years, during all of which time
Guesde has made repeated efforts to capture the unions
and to persuade them to adopt a parliamentary attitude.
Indeed, it is the most vital question before the socialists
in all countries, except in England and in Belgium, where
the workers, politically and industrially, are closely and
firmly united. It was the real problem back of the discussion of the general strike in Germany, and it was also
at the bottom of all the discussions of the Italian congress.
And with us in America, it is one which must be solved,
or the socialist movement may long continue in its present ineffective condition.

The question was brought before the congress in a
motion made by the Guesdists, which was aimed against
what is called the neutrality of the unions ; that is to
say, their non-political attitude. In France, as in Italy,
the trade unions are extremely revolutionary, and the
advanced wing and some of the most ardent fighters are
bitterly opposed to parliamentary methods. Some of
them are, of course, anarchists; others are " syndi-

G

calists " ; that is to say, believers in direct action by the
workers themselves by means of the general strike.   The
Guesdists wished to begin a war upon these elements
and by resolution to condemn the independent action of
the unions.   They also asked for the constitution of a
permanent committee to consolidate the unions and the
socialist party.   The resolution called forth an immense
and heated debate.   Two days and all of one night were
consumed in discussion.   About forty delegates inscribed
their names as wishing to take part, but after several had
spoken it was seen that this question alone would occupy
the entire time of the congress unless some limit was
put either as to time or as to the number of speakers.   As
the French have a prejudice against a time limit, it was
decided to ask all those desiring to speak to retire and
select from among themselves those who were best fitted
to place the various points of view before the congress.
Eleven out of the thirty who still desired to speak were
then selected, and among others Jaurès, Hervé, Allemane,
and Guesde.

The debate was both brilliant and instructive.   While
it comprehended questions which we do not have in
America, much of the discussion was upon the relative
power of the two organizations, — the unions upon the
economic, the socialists upon the political field, — to
achieve the emancipation of the working-class.   The
only view that was not represented was that of "the
pure and simple" trade unionist, for there is no one of
importance in the labor movement in France who would
consider that the working-class should concern itself
merely with a struggle for shorter hours and better
wages.   Nor, on the other hand, would any one suggest
that the labor movement should ally itself with one of

the old parties. The movement is too far advanced for that. The fundamental question is whether the unions shall take industry into their own hands, by means of the general strike and any other direct revolutionary method available, or whether they shall pursue the parliamentary method, and in this way gradually capture the state, and through it socialize industry.

So much for the ground of the debate. The Guesdists are revolutionary parliamentarians, who are convinced that the workers can do nothing without having the state in their hands, and they are apt to underestimate the importance of trade union action. The opposing elements in the party, like Vaillant and Jaurès, desire to leave the unions independent, and to neutralize by their own propaganda that of the anarchists. Vaillant feared the resolution of the Guesdists would only serve to aggravate the conflict between the party and the unions. The congress, he said, ought to affirm the necessity for the economic movement, and it ought not to wish to subordinate the unions to the party. It ought to recognize the Federation of Labor as the economic unit of the proletariat, and to say that the socialist party will give it every aid in its economic struggle. This was very much the trend of the debate against the motion. Jaurès made a very long, but, it seemed to me, not very effective address, although it was delivered with all the power and magnetism of his personality and impressive oratory.

There was an effort made by both sides to arrive at an amicable settlement of the difference of opinion, but neither could conscientiously yield upon the vital issue. After two days of discussion, representatives of the varying views were sent into a special committee to arrive, if possible, at a compromise. Having sat most of the night without reaching a settlement, the two following resolutions were submitted to the vote. That supported by the Guesdists declared: "It is the same class, the same proletariat, which organizes and acts, both on the economic field through its unions, and on the political field through its socialist party; and if these two methods of action and organization cannot be blended, they cannot ignore one another, without mortally dividing the proletariat against itself and rendering it incapable of emancipating itself; it is necessary, therefore, according to circumstances, that the trade union and political actions of the workers should be in concert and unison."

That supported by Jaurès, Vaillant, and others was to the effect that: "The congress, convinced that the working-class will only be able to fully free itself by the combined force of trade union and political action, by the unions going as far as the general strike, and by the conquest of all the political power, in view of the general expropriation of capitalism; that this double action will be much the more efficacious as the political organizations and the economic organizations shall have their complete autonomy; and taking official notice of the resolution of the trade union congress at Amiens, which affirms the independence of the trade union movement of all political parties; invites all militants to do their best to dissipate all misunderstanding between the Federation of Labor and the Socialist Party."

These two resolutions were put to vote, and the latter was carried by 148 mandates against 130, with nine abstentions. The closeness of the vote shows that the policy of the party in this matter is not finally settled. And it is needless to say that had the vote gone the other way it would have offered no solution to the vexing problem of harmonizing the tendencies of these two great movements of the working-class. The solution lies not so much in resolutions as in convincing the proletariat that there is danger in the present friction between those who would take the view that parliamentary action is alone necessary to emancipate the working-class, and those unionists who are constantly proclaiming that the economic movement with revolution as the end is the sole method worthy of engaging the energies of the proletariat.

Upon the report of the socialist group in parliament another interesting discussion took place. This time it was as to the attitude that the party should take in its relation to the Clémenceau ministry which had been formed on the eve of the congress.* Two of the ablest socialists, Briand and Viviani, had taken posts in the new cabinet, and Millerand had been offered a portfolio, but had refused it. The entire cabinet was made up of men of radical opinion, and the parliamentary session at hand promised to be most interesting. There were many questions upon which the opinion of the socialist party could not easily be distinguished from that of the ministry. It was decided, therefore, that there should be a resolution formulated expressing the views of the congress as to the relation which should exist. After some discussion, in which Jaurès and Guesde took part, the following resolution was passed : —

" The congress, considering that any change in the personnel of a capitalist government could not in any way modify the fundamental policy of the party, puts the proletariat on its guard against the insufficiency of

* See also p. 250.

a program, even the most advanced, of the 'democratic bourgeoisie'; it reminds the workers that their liberation will only be possible through the social ownership of capital, that there is no socialism except in the socialist party, organized and unified, and that its representation in parliament, while striving to realize the reforms which will augment the force of action and the demands of the proletariat, shall at the same time oppose unceasingly, to all restricted and too often illusory programs, the reality and integrity of the socialist ideal."

Every one rejoiced that there was no serious difference of opinion in this matter, for many had feared that Jaurès would be inclined to view favorably the new ministry. The passing of the above resolution without a dissenting voice proved beyond question that the party was firmly cemented in its bonds of union, and needless to say, it was a cause for supreme happiness to the entire congress. In conversation Jaurès was overheard to say to a few comrades who were speaking to him of this resolution and the "socialists" Briand and Viviani: "Outside of the united party, there are no socialists."

Unity, submission to the will of the majority of the party, friendly words between those of different views on tactics, the absence of ill feeling of any kind, all of these things impressed one with the new life of the French movement. The desire for accord was so great that Hervé remarked on one occasion that the congress was afflicted with a strange malady, that of unanimity. Nevertheless, one could still see signs of the old divisions, and occasionally the factions seemed on the point of breaking forth in their old lines of battle; but the desire for unity was too strong, and I am sure that Guesde expressed the view of every one who attended the congress when he said afterward : " Unity has come to stay, and no man in the party is strong enough to destroy it." This is the word of courage that, after thirty years or more of quarrels and schisms, the French socialist movement now sends forth to the world.

CHAPTER IV

THE BRITISH LABOR PARTY

No other socialist body in Europe was founded under what seemed to be such favorable auspices as the Social Democratic Federation of Great Britain. The time was ripe for socialist agitation and organization. The reaction against the barren and treacherous policy of the liberal party, which had been returned to power in 1880 under Gladstone, was in full swing, and gave birth to a political revolt led by some eminent democrats and reformers. In 1881 they held a meeting in the Westminster Palace Hotel to discuss plans for united action. It was a notable gathering. There was Joseph Cowen, the intimate friend of Mazzini and Garibaldi, an ardent republican and radical, who with Sir Charles Dilke, Bradlaugh, Auberon Herbert, and others, had in the seventies carried on a courageous campaign against monarchy. Professor Edward S. Beesley, who had in 1864 presided over the inauguration of the International Working Men's Association, was also there. He was an eminent positivist, a brave and fearless thinker, and had been a warm friend of the trade union movement in the day when to be its friend meant persecution and social ostracism. At a second meeting, H. M. Hyndman occupied the chair. He was a Trinity College, Cambridge, man, a brilliant journalist who had specialized in Indian affairs, and had aroused immense interest in that colony by his remarkable portrayal of the evils prevalent under British rule. After his defeat as an independent candidate for parliament in 1880, he had thrown himself into a campaign of protest against the coercion policy of Gladstone in Ireland. Helen Taylor, the niece of John Stuart Mill, Herbert Burrows, and Belfort Bax were also among the early members. As a result of these conferences the Democratic Federation was formed, and a definitely socialist program was adopted. Directly afterward, William Morris, Edward Carpenter, and Walter Crane came into the Federation ; and John Burns, Jack Williams, and Tom Mann, three of the most effective labor agitators in England, joined a year or so later.

About the same time another socialist organization, the Fabian Society, was formed. Professor Thomas Davidson had gathered about him a group of young men to whom he presented with lofty sentiment and fine humanism his philosophy for perfecting individual character. He held their attention for some time, but at last, Bernard Shaw says, "Certain members of that circle, modestly feeling that the revolution would have to wait an unreasonably long time if postponed until they personally had attained perfection, set up the banner of socialism militant; seceded from the regenerators ; and established themselves independently as the Fabian Society." Bernard Shaw, Sidney Webb, Sydney Olivier, now Governor of Jamaica, Hubert Bland, and Graham Wallas were among the secessionists.

To any one who knows anything of English affairs, the names of the founders of these two socialist organizations are ones to conjure with. All men of brilliant ability, they threw themselves into the rising movement with boundless energy. A socialist paper, "Justice,"

was started with Edward Carpenter's money, and was
kept going by William Morris, until a few years later he
launched "The Commonweal," where he printed some of
his noble contributions to socialist literature. All of
these men carried on, up and down the country, a campaign of meetings that seemed to promise for the English
movement a series of brilliant successes.

In 1886 socialist agitation began in earnest, as a
result of a depression which had paralyzed industry,
and had rendered the condition of the unemployed
desperate. Huge meetings were held by the socialists to bring to the attention of the government
the misery of the people. After one of the gatherings in February, 1886, the famished workers rushed
through Pall Mall and other streets of the West End,
and inflamed by the jeers of some young men sitting in
the windows of one of the fashionable clubs, they broke
into a riot. The meeting had been organized by the
Social Democratic Federation, and had been addressed
by Hyndman, Burns, Champion, and Williams, all of
whom were indicted for having incited the mob to insurrection. The upper classes were thrown into a panic ;
all sorts of vague rumors were rife as to a violent uprising of the people, and the trial of the leaders attracted
the attention of the whole country to the views of the
socialists.

During all that year and the next, the agitation
was kept up with unabated vigor, and on the 13th of
November, 1887, another uprising occurred which is still
remembered in England as " Bloody Sunday." A meeting in Trafalgar Square had been advertised to protest
against the policy of the government in Ireland. It was
a huge gathering of discontented, impoverished peo-

Jean Jaurès.

ple, led mainly by the socialists. Burns, Cunninghame Graham, and others were leading groups toward the Square, and William Morris, at the head of a long procession, was making his way toward the same centre. Mackail, in his "Life of Morris," says that: "No one who saw it will ever forget the strange and indeed terrible sight of that gray winter day, the vast sombre-colored crowd, the brief but fierce struggle at the corner of the Strand, and the river of steel and scarlet that moved slowly through the dusky swaying masses when two squadrons of the Life Guards were summoned up from Whitehall. Morris himself did not see it till all was nearly over. He had marched with one of the columns which were to converge on Trafalgar Square from all quarters. It started in good order to the number of five or six thousand from Clerkenwell Green, but at the crossing of Shaftesbury Avenue was attacked in front and on both flanks by a strong force of police. They charged into it with great violence, striking right and left indiscriminately. In a few minutes it was helplessly broken up. Only disorganized fragments straggled into the Square, to find that the other columns had also been headed off or crushed, and that the day was practically over. Preparations had been made to repel something little short of a popular insurrection. An immense police force had been concentrated, and in the afternoon the Square was lined by a battalion of Foot Guards, with fixed bayonets and twenty rounds of ball cartridge. For an hour or two the danger was imminent of street fighting such as had not been known in London for more than a century." This shows the character of the agitation carried on by the socialists during the eighties. All of them, together with many of the old radicals,

were involved again and again in street riots and collisions with the police for asserting the right of free
speech.

A general awakening of the working-class seemed to
be taking place as a result of socialist activity, and 1889
marks the beginning of a new epoch in English trade
unionism. The unions had lost nearly all of their old
idealism and humanitarian sentiment. They had become
little more than societies for mutual aid, content to protect themselves in their own trades, leaving the rest of the
working-class to struggle without organization for the
barest necessaries of life. John Burns and Tom Mann,
imbued with socialist idealism, began a bitter campaign
against the narrow exclusive policy of this aristocracy of
labor. "How long, how long," Tom Mann demands of the
trade unionists, " will you be content with the present
half-hearted policy of your unions ?   I readily grant that
good work has been done in the past, but, in Heaven's
name, what good purpose are they serving now ?   All
of them have large numbers out of employment even
when their particular trade is busy. None of the important societies have any policy other than that of endeavoring to keep wages from falling. The true unionist
policy of aggression seems entirely lost sight of. In
fact, the average unionist of to-day is a man with a fos-
silized intellect, either hopelessly apathetic, or supporting a policy that plays directly into the hands of the
capitalist exploiter."

John Burns was no less vehement in his attacks.
"Constituted as it is," he writes, in September, 1887,
"unionism carries within itself the source of its own
dissolution. . . . Their reckless assumption of the duties
and responsibilities that only the state or whole com-

munity can discharge, in the nature of sick and super-
annuation benefits, is crushing out the larger unions by
taxing their members to an unbearable extent. This so
cripples them that the fear of not being able to discharge
their friendly society liabilities often makes them submit to encroachments by the masters without protest.
The result of this is that all of them have ceased to be
unions for maintaining the rights of labor, and have
degenerated into mere middle and upper class rate-re-
ducing institutions."

But the attitude of the socialists was not solely a negative one. In July, 1888, the misery and suffering of the
girls employed in making lucifer matches aroused the
indignation of Mrs. Annie Besant, one of the most brilliant women in England, who had for some time been
working with the Fabians. Finally her agitation caused
these unfortunate women to revolt, but without funds or
organization their struggle seemed utterly hopeless.
As a result, however, of the efforts of Mrs. Besant and
Mr. Herbert Burrows, the appalling conditions existing
in this trade were brought to the attention of the public,
and several hundred pounds were subscribed to support
the strike, until finally the employers were forced to
make some concessions. Burns was then leading the
gasworkers, who up to that time had been unorganized,
in a successful battle against their employers, and as a
result they obtained an eight-hour day and an increase
in wages.

The success of these two strikes of the most miserable
workers in London gave a tremendous impetus to the
struggle for a wider and more inclusive unionism; and
they were followed by an even more notable victory.
For two years prominent London socialists had been

agitating among the dockers, whose condition was perhaps the most hopeless of English workmen. The trade was so badly organized that none of the laborers received more than a few hours work each day, and the wages were so low that only casual workmen, semivagrants, and single men could remain at such employment. Ben Tillett, a laborer in one of the warehouses, was attempting the apparently hopeless task of organizing these workers. The new union made little progress, but despite that fact the conditions became so unbearable that in August, 1889, a strike was declared. Tom Mann, at the very height of his power, and John Burns went to the assistance of Tillett. They worked night and day, and by assembling every morning near the old London Tower a hundred thousand starving strikers, they managed to dissuade them from abandoning what seemed to be a hopeless conflict. For four weeks the greatest port in the world was completely paralyzed. The big, enthusiastic Tom Mann, with his gifted eloquence and religious faith in the cause of the workers, awakened in all classes a sympathetic interest in the dockers. For perhaps the first time in England there was general disapproval when the companies attempted to obtain scabs to replace the strikers, and nearly a quarter of a million dollars was subscribed by the public to support the strike. With this large fund at their disposal, the leaders established an elaborate system of strike pay, and finally the united pressure from editors, clergymen, shareholders, shipowners, and merchants enabled Cardinal Manning and other prominent Englishmen to effect a conciliation, the men being conceded most of their demands.

In the same decade the Fabians were developing

their own method of forwarding socialism. They were meeting in some of the most aristocratic rooms in London. "Our favorite sport," Bernard Shaw says, "was inviting politicians and economists to lecture to us, and then falling upon them with all our erudition and debating skill, and making them wish they had never been born." A well-known member of parliament, who was lured into their web on one of those occasions, afterward wrote a furious article, entitled "Butchered to make a Fabian holiday." In 1888 twenty-eight Fabians sent postcards to convince the newly born "Star" newspaper that London was aflame with socialism. The ruse worked successfully, and as a result the "Star" became a Fabian organ, with one of the ablest editors in England writing socialist leaders. However, the capitalist proprietors soon discovered that the interest in socialism was still limited to a small group, and the Fabians were cleared out.

Nevertheless the society was making a profound impression upon the old parties.* Instead of limiting their activity to socialist circles the members joined as many liberal and radical associations as possible. By constantly moving resolutions they did excellent work in education, and created a general impression of a widespread socialist sentiment. Graham Wallas formed in London the Metropolitan Radical Federation, representing working men's clubs, having a total membership of 25,000, and under his direction they adopted a program which embodied nearly all the Fabian proposals. By persistently attending all political meetings and besieging with questions nearly every liberal candidate, they finally developed a group of progressives in the liberal

* See also p. 204.

party who were willing to accept most of the immediate
program of the socialists.

British socialism at this time was making splendid
progress among the middle class. A great number of
groups were organized, drawing-room meetings were
held, and even at the universities circles were formed to
study socialism. A number of propagandists were at
work in the churches, and as a result "The Christian
Socialist Society" and "St. Matthew's Guild" were
formed, both of which adopted a Christian-Socialist
program. In the provinces the movement was making
headway among the Dissenters, while in London at one
time there was a group of over forty clergymen, nearly
all of whom were socialists, working to bring to the
attention of the upper classes the miserable condition
of the people. In fact, strange as it may seem, socialism was winning its most enthusiastic adherents among
the educated classes, and in addition to the prominent
men already mentioned as the founders of socialist
organizations, Grant Allen, the scientist, and Professor
Alfred Russel Wallace announced themselves as converts.

The times were stirring, and seemed to be of good
promise for the rapid rise of British socialism. Unfortunately this was a forlorn hope. The working-class for
the most part remained inert, and the middle-class
leaders were quarrelling among themselves. Morris
and his followers broke away from the Federation early
in the eighties and formed the Socialist League. The
Fabian Society, which from the beginning had opposed
the policy of the social democrats, doubted the wisdom
or necessity of an independent political party. Annie
Besant, who had done such splendid work among the

women, withdrew from the Fabians, and Burns and Mann, who had almost accomplished the difficult task of uniting the middle-class socialists with the new unionism, resigned from the Social Democratic Federation. By the unfortunate loss of these two men the Federation suffered seriously as a revolutionary influence among the workers.

There were at this period two fundamental weaknesses in British socialism: lack of unity, and the incapacity of the leaders to bring the workers into a socialist organization. In nearly every other country some one has arisen who has been able to unite the various factions upon a common program and method of action. Unfortunately in England there was at this time no such leader, and the groups became more and more widely divided. The leaders were all middle-class men of great ability, of unquestionable sincerity, making every sacrifice to promote socialism; but their views and tactics differed so profoundly that harmony was out of the question.

It is not to be doubted that despite these divisions important work was done in spreading socialist ideas, which unfortunately, however, seemed to make no considerable impression upon the working-class. Morris early recognized this weakness, and when he left the Federation, he said, "I cannot forego the hope of our forming a socialist party which shall begin to act in our own time instead of a mere theoretical association in a private room, with no hope but that of *gradually permeating cultivated people with our own aspirations.*" In this utterance he struck upon the fundamental defect in British socialism during the eighties. Jaurès, in the great debate at Amsterdam, expressed a similar view

H

when he said that in his belief socialism had not made headway in England because from the beginning it had not been sufficiently in contact with the actual life or with the needs of the working-class. Not only Morris, but many other English socialists realized this weakness of the movement, and efforts were made to penetrate into the unions; but this is almost impossible in England for middle-class men.

As a result of the gulf between the socialists and the workers, socialist ideas underwent a peculiar development in London. The Fabians evolved an original philosophy that the middle and upper classes are the revolutionary element in society, and the proletariat the conservative element; and therefore, as Bernard Shaw says, they went to work "to place socialism upon a respectable bourgeois footing." The social democrats, on the other hand, became more and more revolutionary in their phrases, and more and more narrow in their sectarianism. Failing to effect a great political organization, they became almost anarchistic in tactics. "It will only need a compact minority," their organ declared, "to take advantage of some opportune accident, that will assuredly occur, to overthrow the present system, and once for all lift the toilers from their present social degradation." During this period the social democrats seemed to be expecting at any moment to see capitalism disintegrate of itself, and they cherished the fond hope that after the catastrophe the workers would take industrial operations into their own hands and administer them for the welfare of all. By becoming more and more absorbed in this philosophy of economic fatalism the Federation grew intolerant of the activities of the trade unionists on the one hand, and the Fabians on the other.

It is, of course, evident that middle-class leaders alone cannot make a sound socialist movement. Nevertheless the propaganda during the eighties and nineties was extraordinarily effective. There was little work done in organizing the movement on broader lines, but it is unquestionable that socialist ideas were making great headway. In this phase of socialist activity the Social Democratic Federation played a leading part. It was not able to move the working-class as a body, but it schooled some of the most capable men in the labor movement; and by constantly lecturing and campaigning it acquainted a vast number of earnest young men and women with the economic doctrines of socialism. Fabian groups, branches of the political bodies, and labor churches were organized through the country. The Land Nationalization Society was carrying on a vigorous campaign of education, and the lecturing vans of the Land Restoration League were sent throughout the rural districts, carrying speakers and literature.

About the same time the "Clarion," the best edited journal and perhaps the most effective organ of socialist propaganda, was started by Robert Blatchford and a group of his friends, all of whom were able journalists. For a time each of them wrote under a *nom de plume*: Robert Blatchford as "Nunquam," E. F. Fay as "The Bounder," Alex. Thompson as "Dangle," and Montague Blatchford as "Mont Blong." The journal met with a warm reception throughout all England, and Clarion Cycle Clubs and other organizations were started for propaganda purposes. It would be almost impossible to estimate the value of the "Clarion" in these early days of the movement. It created an enthusiasm of an entirely new order, not only among the working men, but among journalists and others fond of good literature. Its readers were entranced by the "Unsentimental Journeys" of the jovial, big-hearted Bounder; the lilting, satirical lyrics of Mont Blong; and they found a new interest in comedy and drama under the tutelage of Dangle, recently in New York in the interests of his two plays "Tom Jones" and "The Dairymaids." Above all their hearts were touched and their enthusiasm was fired by the wonderfully simple, charmingly written articles of Nunquam. His writings are perhaps more eagerly read than those of any other English author. His "Merrie England," giving the economics of socialism, sold upward of a million, and "Britain for the British," a similar book, has been read by hundreds of thousands.

When I was in London in 1899, I found many circles of influential people discussing socialism. The Fabians were absorbed in municipal affairs and in their efforts to permeate the Liberal Party with socialist ideas, but missing no opportunity to lecture and laugh at each other and everybody else. There was also a small group of the Independent Labor Party, an organization founded by Keir Hardie in the early nineties, with its strength mostly in the provinces. It was serious, hard at work, and, apparently without reason, hopeful for the future. I saw a good deal of John Burns. He had broken away from all socialist bodies, and was busy in parliament and in the London County Council; but he was making no effort to form a movement among the workers, and indeed quite frankly without hope that one could be formed. I saw a few members of the Social Democratic Federation. Their movement, then nearly twenty years old, was standing still, and nearly all the London members were bitter and disheartened. So far as I could see there was no movement of consequence. The various sections did not like each other, the propertied interests looked upon socialism without alarm, and evidently the working-class was fighting shy of it. Later in the summer I attended the conference of the Social Democratic Federation at Manchester, but I was not led to change my conclusion.

In fact, it was not until I spent a few days with Keir Hardie at his home in Scotland that I began to think my estimate of the socialist movement was wrong. Late one afternoon I arrived at Old Cumnock, and was met at the station by Mr. and Mrs. Hardie. As night came on, with a fine, full harvest moon, they took me for a walk; and after listening to my rather despondent remarks concerning the failure of British socialism, Hardie said: "But you have only seen London, and every one who breathes the air of London loses hope. If you want to see the socialist movement, spend some time in the provinces, and you will see that everywhere socialism is making headway."

As a matter of fact, Hardie had made socialism a thing of consequence among the workers outside of London. He early saw the necessity for uniting into one political organization the trade unions with their million and a half adherents, the coöperatives with their million members, and the various municipal organizations working on a program of vital interest to the workers. Hardie and his friends of the provinces were convinced that by working persistently among these organizations they could bring them all together into a political party. In this work he was joined by Tom Mann, who with John Burns had been gradually breaking down the conservatism of the British

trade unions, and had at their Liverpool congress in
1890 scored a great victory for the newer ideas.

Hardie had for years been quietly at work among
the unions of the north. He was born almost in the
mines, having gone to work underground at seven
years of age. He never had a day's schooling, but his
mother taught him to read when he was so young
that he cannot remember when he could not read.
When quite a youth, he began reforming as a
temperance advocate, and although without interest
in the union movement he was induced to become the
secretary of a miners' organization, because he was the
only one who could write the minutes and properly prepare the papers. As soon as the employers discovered
that this youth was the secretary of the union he was
discharged, and he came, in a very practical way, face
to face with economic problems. This act of the employers made Hardie a labor agitator, and gave to the
workers of England the most powerful, consistent, patient, and painstaking leader the movement has known.

But this Scotch miner " could not long be the voice of
the wronged and bruised labor of the mines alone," as
John Spargo has so eloquently said. "Whoso would
cry for one single toiler's weal must cry equally for all.
There is no weal for any while there is woe for any.
Keir had not come to that, but when the docker appealed to him, he became the docker's voice. And
when the seeker for work, tired of seeking in vain, beck-
oned with wasted finger, Keir answered and straight-
way became the voice of the workless one's woe. Then
Keir realized that the wrong of the miner and the
wrong of the docker and the wrong of the workless
one were the same wrong. So Keir became a socialist.

He was the voice of toil in the street, by the dockyard gate, in the market-place, — he became the voice of toil in the parliament of the exploiters of toil. It needed Courage, and it needed Faith, and Keir lacked neither the Faith nor the Courage. Sometimes Labor was afraid of its own voice — afraid of Keir; and when he cried aloud for Peace, and shouted defiance to the red dragon of war, miner and docker and workless one cried out against Keir with a voice not their own and would have stoned him — would have stilled their own voice. But Keir's Strength and Courage and Faith increased; he voiced wronged and bruised and blinded Labor's woes in spite of its own unfaith and ignorance and fear."

At the Trade Union Congress held in Bradford in 1892, Hardie gathered about him a small group of working men for the purpose of forming a labor party. His idea was at that time, as it has been ever since, to unite all the workers into an independent political movement. He found it increasingly difficult to believe in the value of socialism without any labor party to accept it. He was entirely of the view of Wilhelm Liebknecht, who once declared that "it is crazy tactics for a working men's party to seclude itself away up above the workers in a theoretic aircastle, for without working men there can be no working men's party, and the laborers we must take as we find them." Many of the socialists opposed Hardie in this work, and he once said rather bitterly, " It is remarkable that the only serious opposition we have had to encounter has come from the men who ought to have occupied an inner place in our councils. It has been said that the words of the apostate are ever the harshest; and we are experiencing the truth of that."

Nevertheless the I. L. P., as it is now called, was organized, and began almost immediately to make headway in the provinces. Upon the birth of the new party, Tom Maguire, a working man, a poet, and one of the most lovable spirits in the British movement, wrote to Edward Carpenter: "As you may not have heard, be it mine to mention that now the mountain, so long in labor, has been delivered of its mouse — a bright, active, cheery little mouse, with just a touch of venom in its sharp little teeth. . . . To come to the point, an Independent Labor Party is born unto us — long may it wave. You will find in your travels that this new party lifts its head all over the north. It has caught the people as I imagine the Chartist movement did. And it is of the people; such will be the secret of its success. Everywhere its bent is socialist, because socialists are the only people who have a message for it." Many of its members at the succeeding elections were carried to local governing bodies, and the party won to its cause not only the strongest of the younger men in the labor movement, but a large number of disinterested and loyal friends outside the working-class.

The new movement early demonstrated, what had been doubted before in many quarters, that a third party could become an effective power in British politics. The doubt that a labor party could get a footing was due in part to the failure of the Social Democratic Federation in its electoral struggles. In 1885 it had run two candidates in London. Mr. Williams in Hampstead got 27 votes, and Mr. Fielding in Kensington 32 votes. This wretched showing proved a disaster to the socialist movement. The Federation lost many of its members, and some extremists repudiated political action altogether. The English feeling at that time was similar to that which still exists among a great many radicals in the United States. It was recently expressed rather bitterly in an editorial in the single-tax weekly of Chicago, "The Public." "Under the present electoral machinery," runs the editorial, "the socialist party can no more become a dominant or even a second party than a cabbage can become a cow. They cannot continue to draw their own vote. Machine politicians understand this, and are accordingly indifferent to side-party voting." This is a vigorous expression of what seemed to be the view of many English socialists in the eighties and early nineties.

Among others the Fabians had condemned the third-party idea. It was, therefore, of immense importance to socialism when the victories of the I. L. P. proved that a third party could become a political force. Almost immediately after its formation one of its candidates ran in opposition to both Liberal and Tory candidates, and after a short and brilliant campaign succeeded in polling over 1400 votes. Scarcely a by-election took place in an industrial constituency in which the I. L. P. did not carry on an active campaign. At the General Election of 1895 all of its parliamentary candidates, including Hardie, were defeated, but the total vote ran up to nearly 50,000, which meant that the I. L. P was proving to be, even at this early date, a disturbing political factor. In municipal elections it made distinct gains. In Glasgow, Bradford, and other places, it elected representatives to the municipal councils, to the School Boards, the County Councils, Parish Councils, and Vestries. From that time on independent political action was recognized as one of the most effective ways of demonstrating socialist strength.

The I. L. P. was unquestionably the strongest socialist organization in Great Britain at the time I was visiting Hardie. But he was dissatisfied. He said the unions had not come into the movement as he had hoped, and the coöperatives were entirely out of it; above all, the various socialist organizations were not united. It was not his purpose merely to start a new political association to compete with the other socialist bodies. He considered the first and most important work to be done was to take all unions, coöperatives, and other labor organizations out of the Liberal and Tory parties, and to have them form an independent political body. He realized that in the beginning this organization could hardly be socialist, but he was confident that inasmuch as socialism expressed the hopes and aspirations of the working-class, an independent political movement undertaken by the workers themselves must, in the end, become socialist. Hardie was at the time at work on this larger and more inclusive organization, but it had hardly assumed form when I bade him good-by in 1899.

Returning to England in 1903, I went to see Hardie at his rooms in London. He lives in an old court reminiscent of bygone centuries, in the very garret of a fourteenth-century house. In this quaint old place he spoke with enthusiasm of the rising labor movement, and indeed, a new stage was developing in British socialism. The trade unions had decided at their congress in 1899 to call a conference on labor representation in parliament. In February, 1900, a large meeting was held of the representatives of nearly all of the most important labor organizations in the country, and of the three socialist organizations. As a result it was decided that labor candidates should be run for parliament on a footing independent of the two old political parties. Unfortunately the committee had to face a general election when only a few months old, and as nearly all of the candidates had opposed the Boer War, and as jingoism still ran high, they were only successful in electing two candidates, Richard Bell and Keir Hardie. However, several by-elections were won, which made a profound impression upon the country. The movement was taking definite form, and Hardie prophesied that at the next general election at least twenty-seven labor men, the majority of them socialists, would be returned to parliament.

But it was not the propaganda of the socialists alone that forced the inert unions into politics. It was to no small degree the result of an attack upon the very existence of the trade union movement. A decision of the courts, now known to history as the Taff Vale decision, threw the entire trade union movement into a state of excitement and dismay. The Taff Vale Railway Company had sued the Amalgamated Society of Railway Servants for having conspired to induce the workmen to break their contracts, and also with having conspired to interfere with the traffic of the company by picketing and other alleged unlawful means. A prominent justice granted an injunction against the society, and while this was later reversed by the Court of Appeal, the House of Lords finally sanctioned the decision as at first rendered. It decided that a trade union might be sued, and as a result of the suit the railway union was forced to pay damages to the amount of over $100,000. This verdict was staggering, and the unions saw very clearly that unless something was done to alter the situation their movement would be destroyed. According to the English law, the decision practically amounted to new legislation against the unions, and a nullification of the old rights which had been won in 1871. There was a tremendous agitation among the unions, and they immediately set to work to find ways and means of exerting their political power upon parliament, from which they demanded a new law which would give them again the rights they had enjoyed previous to the Taff Vale decision. This attack upon the unions, coming as it did at the very climax of the socialist agitation for a working men's political movement, gave an immense impulse to the organization then taking form.

The new party first came into existence under the form of the Labor Representation Committee of the Trade Union Congress, but as the movement developed, it took the name of The Labor Party of Great Britain. It is a federation of trade unions, trades councils, socialist societies, coöperative societies, and local labor associations. All members elected under its auspices are paid an equal sum not to exceed $1000 per annum, but this payment is made only to those members whose candidatures have been promoted by societies which have contributed to the funds. Absolute independence of both the old parties is enforced upon those elected, and absolute loyalty to the constitution and rules of the party is insisted upon. In the short time of its existence, it has grown to a membership of over one million. In other words, this enormous number of voters severed their connection finally with the two old parties, and the only candidates who could hope to obtain their support in the parliamentary election were those pledged to the principles and objects of the Labor Party. The object, as defined in the constitution, is to organize and maintain a parliamentary group with its own whips and policy, and to secure the election of candidates for whose candidatures affiliated societies have made themselves responsible financially, and who have been selected by regularly convened conferences in their respective constituencies. Candidates must accept the constitution; agree to abide by the decisions of the parliamentary party in carrying out the aims of this constitution; appear before their constituencies under the title of Labor Candidates only; abstain strictly from identifying themselves with or promoting the interests of any party not eligible for affiliation; and they must not oppose any candidate recognized by the executive committee of the party. Candidates must also join the parliamentary labor group if elected.

The independence of the party should not be confused with what is known on the Continent as neutrality. It is definitely a class party working to improve the conditions of life among the workers of Great Britain, and while sections of the Tory and Liberal parties are not permitted to join, all the socialist bodies of Great Britain are welcomed. Both the I. L. P. and the Fabian Society are at present affiliated, and their members are put up as candidates of the party. In other words, it is independent politically of all except the socialist parties. Indeed, although every effort has been made by the capitalist papers and politicians to create a division between what they call the socialist section of the party and the trade union section, there is no real distinction, for most of the 20,000 affiliated socialists belong to trade unions and many of the 975,000 affiliated trade unionists are also socialists. The strength of the socialists cannot, therefore, be measured by the number of the adherents coming direct from the socialist groups. For instance, out of seven candidates successfully promoted and financed by the I. L. P., three of them were trade union officials whose societies comprised about 50,000 members, and of the 23 successful candidates put up by the trade unions themselves, 10 were leading members of the I. L. P. Altogether 13 members of parliament are both trade unionists and members of the I. L. P., and they represent trade societies with a total of 330,000 members. Another indication of the unity between the two sections is the fact that nearly all of the ablest militants are socialists. The chairman of the Parliamentary Committee, the chairman of the Executive Committee, and the chairman of the Congress are all socialists, and of the members of the new Executive Committee only three are not socialists. In addition to these evidences of socialist strength, a large majority of the candidates selected at present to contest new seats in the next general election are well-known socialists. It is with complete unity between the sections that the Labor Party has carried on its electoral campaigns. The brilliant results are known, and, at the last general election, 29 working men were returned to parliament, a majority of them socialists.

It was a great achievement, and when the news was cabled round the world, it was received with amazement. The old political parties, the metropolitan newspapers, the leaders of thought, and the grave and wise governors of the destinies of the British people could not understand. It seemed incomprehensible that such a movement could have arisen, could have attained such proportions, without their knowing of its existence. British labor in politics! Fifteen or twenty socialists returned to the House of Commons! It seemed incredible. Of all the workers in the world none appeared less class-conscious, less imbued with socialist sentiment or revolutionary ideals, than the British working man. He had patiently suffered every injustice. He lived in frightful conditions of squalor and poverty, and when old age, unemployment, or serious illness deprived him of a livelihood, he and his family went to the workhouse or subsisted on the meagre rations of outdoor relief. His submissiveness had been so complete, and his complaints so rare and mild, that a political revolt seemed unbelievable. It was the general belief that the grossly immoral thing called socialism would never appeal to the Briton, and the governing classes, sure that it never would, were almost paralyzed. The working man had severed his connection with the capitalist parties, and what they had failed to give him as a matter of common human justice he demanded now in no uncertain way by sending his own representatives into parliament.

With these things in mind, I went to the Labor Party congress which convened at Belfast on the 24th of January, 1907. There I found 350 delegates, all but half-a-dozen of whom were working men, who had come as representatives from the most important trade unions in Great Britain. It was a most significant gathering, — significant because it represented a mass movement of the manual workers to express politically their discontent with the present order. In combining with almost perfect solidarity all the varied working-class organizations of Great Britain, the party had accomplished a remarkable work, the importance of which, from the point of view of the advance of socialism, could not be exaggerated. There were representatives from practically every trade — miners, iron founders, steel smelters, engineers, firemen, gas workers, railway men, dockers, printers, postmen, textile workers, carpenters, bricklayers, and general laborers, and as a whole they represented a million workers, who during the last seven years had been assembled together in the independent political movement.

Practically every one in the assembly had come from the workshop. Most of them were self-educated men, who, despite the hard conditions surrounding their early life, had fought their way into responsible executive positions in their powerful organizations. Nearly all of them knew the evils of capitalism at first hand. They had suffered from poverty, unemployment, insanitary homes, insanitary workshops, and many of them had begun as children their lives of labor in mills, mines, and factories. And yet most of them were men of capacity and ability. Their work as organizers had schooled them, and nearly all were capable debaters and impressive speakers. Probably in no other class of society could one find men more familiar with economic and political questions, or better trained in the businesslike methods of parliamentary procedure. Some of them administered the affairs of trade organizations with over a hundred thousand members, and handled year in and year out hundreds of thousands of pounds. The striking growth of the movement since its inception in 1900 is illustrated by the following figures: —

YEAR	TRADE UNIONS		SOCIALIST SOCIETIES		TOTAL
	No.	Membership	No.	Membership	
1900–1	41	353,070	3	22,861	375,931
1901–2	65	455,450	2	13,861	469,311
1902–3	127	847,315	2	13,835	861,150
1903–4	165	956,025	2	13,775	969,800
1904–5	158	885,270	2	14,730	900,000
1905–6	158	904,496	2	16,784	921,280
1906–7	176	975,182	2	20,885	998,338*
1907–8	181	1,049,673	2	22,267	1,071,940

* This total includes 2271 coöperators.

It will be seen that the party has trebled in size since its beginning, and the number of unions affiliated has increased over fourfold. The miners' unions, which have fifteen members in parliament under the auspices of the Liberal Party, have not yet decided to join the independent movement, although the balloting on the question last year was very close, and indicated a growing sentiment in favor of affiliation. The only defection from the ranks of the Labor Party since its foundation has been that of the Social Democratic Federation, which withdrew in 1901 when the party declined to adopt a socialist program.

Impressive as the gathering was, there was one significant contrast between it and the other congresses abroad. With the exception of Hardie, Pete Curran, Bruce Glasier, and one or two others, none of the most prominent militants of the socialist movement were

I

in attendance. The withdrawal of the Social Democratic Federation prevented, of course, the attendance of
Hyndman, Burrows, Irving, and others of that body,
and the organization, composed as it is almost solely
of manual workers, has not thus far made adequate
provision for obtaining the active and enthusiastic participation in its affairs of such eminent socialists as
Bernard Shaw, H. G. Wells, Sidney Webb, Robert
Blatchford, and a host of writers, professors, economists, and clergymen who have become ardent sympathizers. In fact, the only middle-class socialists who
were there were MacDonald, Bruce Glasier, and S. G.
Hobson, from the I. L. P., and Edward Pease, the able
secretary of the Fabian Society. Thus in the absence
of some of the foremost British socialists one could
hardly think of the Labor Party as occupying the same
position in Great Britain that the socialist parties occupy
in other countries ; and there is no question but that
the movement must make some provision for unifying
the intellectual with the manual workers if it wishes
to exercise an influence equally powerful with that of
the continental parties over the thought and life as well
as over the institutions of the community.

The first day's session of the congress was exces-
sively dull. Only details of organization were considered, and the discussion was brief and uninteresting.
It also was a decided contrast to the continental assemblies, as indeed all British meetings are. Britishers
abhor general discussion, and their meetings are organized to keep the assemblies strictly in hand and to
limit rigidly the speaking to the point at issue. On
the continent provision is made for thorough general
discussion before the details of a question are consid-

H. M. Hyndman.

ered. In Germany it is usually thorough, scientific, and doctrinaire; in France and Italy it is the opportunity for a really brilliant play of wit, humor, and intellect. To one of the Latin temperament every question makes an appeal both to his reason and conscience. Necessarily it takes time to obtain an agreement under such conditions, but it is a great incentive to intellectual life. Over a matter that is settled in Great Britain after a few five or ten minute speeches, the Frenchmen spend hours and even days in debate. The question is examined from every possible point of view, and in its relation to every other conceivable question. And when one has been living for some time in the midst of men keenly enjoying this play of intellect and emotion, the British assembly seems to have organized out of existence nearly everything that is worth while in a conference. A long speech is not tolerated, and unless the orator is exceptionally clever he dare not give expression to his emotion. As a result of such parliamentary traditions the congress of the Labor Party seemed all machinery and organization, — like a Lancashire cotton mill.

There was little of importance in the first session, beyond the discussion which was brought up by a resolution of the executive committee to increase the administrative and electoral forces now employed by the committee, so as to enable the party to take an active part in municipal elections, and the report of Keir Hardie as chairman of the parliamentary group. Hardie showed that labor is becoming a powerful force in British politics. In one session they had forced through parliament three important measures, and for perhaps the first time in the history of labor they had obtained serious consideration for all their proposals. The greatest victory was, of course, in passing the Trades Disputes Bill, which defined anew the legal position of the trade unions, and reversed entirely the Taff Vale decision.   A bill for compensating workmen injured in industry was also passed, which realized a great gain in principle as well as in the provision made for those rendered incapable of further labor.   These two bills were directly in the interests of the trade unions, and another bill was passed of a still wider social bearing.   For years there had been agitation to provide meals for necessitous school children, and at last under pressure from the Labor Party a bill was passed which enables the local authorities to make such provision.   Hardie was justified in saying that no party in British politics ever came out of a single session with a better record of good work accomplished.

The second day of the congress was largely devoted to a discussion upon general principles. There was an effort on the part of several members of the Social Democratic Federation, who had come to the congress as trade unionists, to force a constitutional amendment, defining the object of the party to be the overthrow of the present capitalist system. The amendment was so framed that if carried, it would doubtless have split the party, and have forced those who were not out and out socialists to withdraw from the organization. This naturally called forth the opposition of nearly all the socialists who had been working for years to build up the independent political movement. The executive of the party asked Pete Curran, an old militant, to oppose the motion. He said that the resolution, if carried, would destroy the movement, and he insisted that it was neither in the interest of solidarity nor in the interest of socialism throughout the trade unions that the motion had been proposed. This was very much the line of discussion taken by the ablest socialists at the congress, although Hardie regretted that the motion had come up in the form that it had, as it prevented socialism being discussed on its merits. Many good socialists present who would have voted for a socialist statement, would, he said, be compelled to vote against the proposed amendment to the constitution. As the socialists voted with the other organizations, the resolution was hopelessly defeated.

The last day of the congress was interesting only because of one incident. In the few minutes immediately before the close of the session, after a number of questions had been hurriedly voted upon, and other matters decided, a resolution came up dealing with Women's Suffrage, a question which has recently been brought to the front by a campaign of sensational agitation led by some able women. Ever since the movement assumed definite form, Hardie has manifested great sympathy for it. During the last session the party in the House pledged itself to the effect that women's suffrage would be one of the first measures it would advance the following year. A resolution was, therefore, brought before the conference which read as follows: " That this conference declares in favor of adult suffrage and the equality of the sexes, and urges an immediate extension of the rights of suffrage, and of election, to women, on the same conditions as to men." This left to the parliamentary group freedom to support any measure in the direction of complete adult suffrage. Mr. Harry Quelch, the editor of " Justice," who was there as a trade union representative, but who was really the spokesman of the

Social Democratic Federation, moved an amendment.
He expressed himself in favor of equal voting rights being extended to all men and women, but he demanded
that the party oppose any restricted measure. The
amendment was, of course, intended to prevent the Labor
Party from supporting in any way the limited suffrage
bill then before parliament. For reasons unnecessary
for me to dwell upon, a majority of the delegates were in
favor of passing the amendment, and all over the hall
there arose cries of " Vote." Nevertheless, when Hardie
rose to speak, the conference listened to him. It had
been said that the bill would only permit women with
property to vote, and Hardie was accused of having
dropped the unemployed agitation to support this limited
form of women's suffrage. In answer to these and other
objections Hardie said briefly that if the bill contained
a property qualification, he would not support it; neither
would he support it if it were an attempt to put women's
suffrage before a remedy for unemployment. What was
the fact? Women to-day were classed with criminals
and lunatics as being unfit to exercise the vote. There
were no men so classed! (Voices: There are.) " No;
a man does not require to have property to have a vote,
he has a householding qualification. The bill does not
propose to establish any new qualification at all. Under
it two millions of women would be enfranchised, and of
these one and three-quarter millions would be working
women. The difficulty about the bill is that people will
not take the trouble to understand it."

A vote was taken, and it was found that the amendment was carried by a large majority. A loud cheer
from the victors, almost the only demonstration of the
kind that had followed any vote of the conference,

greeted the result.   No one thought that the amendment would carry with it any serious consequences, but to the astonishment and dismay of every one, Hardie, after expressing the thanks of the congressists for the hospitality of the Belfast workers, made the following important statement: —

"Twenty-five years ago this year I cut myself adrift from every relationship, political or otherwise, in order to assist in building up a working-class party.   I had thought the days of my pioneering were over.   Of late I have felt with increasing intensity the injustice which is inflicted upon women by the present political laws. The intimation I wish to make to the conference and friends is that, if the motion they carried this morning was intended to limit the action of the party in the House of Commons, I shall have seriously to consider whether I can remain a member of the parliamentary party.   I say this with great respect and feeling.   The party is largely my own child, and I would not sever myself lightly from what has been my life's work.   But I cannot be untrue to my principles, and I would have to be so were I not to do my utmost to remove the stigma resting upon our wives, mothers, and sisters of being accounted unfit for political citizenship."

These words fell upon the conference like a bomb. The congress of the Labor Party was over, but for a long time the men stood about the hall not knowing what to do.   Hardie's action was a surprise to every one, and no one, not even his most intimate friends, had felt that he would treat his defeat so seriously. But Hardie believes that suffrage is a fundamental right of democracy, and he afterward wrote, in answer to a friend who had written him urging him not to resign, and that socialism must be first: "What my friend overlooks is the fact that with us it *is* socialism first *because we already have the vote*. With our voteless fathers it was votes first. In Russia just now it is votes first; in Belgium the same; and so it would be here if men were outside the franchise as women are. Our fathers fought against class disability just as the women are now fighting against sex disability. If only that fact could be grasped, all the trouble would disappear." Later, in the same statement, Hardie says: "The spectacle of women being treated as though they were dogs or pariahs revolts and humiliates me; their admission to citizenship on terms of political equality with me is with me a sacred principle; and I would not wish to be in association with any movement or party which could be guilty of the unfairness and the injustice of denying to women those rights which men claim for themselves."

It was not an uplifting conference. The first day bored every one, and in the end, as the reader must well see, we went away sad and depressed. In contrast to the continental congresses, the men of the Labor Party lack the passion and warmth which come only with the possession of a great ideal. Nearly everywhere else in Europe the masses are fired with a new religion, and the cold, machine-like methods of the Labor Party chilled one's enthusiasm. There are perhaps many explanations that might be given for this lack of idealism. Perhaps it is because the movement is still in its earlier stages, and the details of organization press themselves forward, leaving little time for developing the fundamental ideas which the movement must have as a basis if it is to rank with similar movements the world over. Perhaps this coldness is inherent in the British temperament. But whatever the cause, the lack of far vision in the labor movement irritates and saddens a great many socialists.

But the average Britisher has no theories. He is quiet, thoughtful, but stolid. Above all he is practical, and the thing he is doing is an end in itself. And the British workman is no exception. If he is interested in coöperation, trade unionism, or a labor party, he is interested in it for the practical good that can be obtained by the use of that thing itself. The Frenchman has his unions and coöperatives, but not at all because he cares about the immediate ends of these institutions. To him they are merely weapons, ammunition in the social revolution. But to the British working man these things are too often an end. If he wishes to exercise his power in coöperation with others in buying, selling, or producing; if he wishes to exercise his economic power by coöperating with his fellow-workmen in trade unions, or if he desires to exercise his political power by uniting politically with his fellow-workmen, he does these things because he feels that there is some concrete immediate end of distinct advantage to himself to be obtained by these means. Formulas, fundamental principles, and eternal verities irritate him. Yet it is perhaps because of these traits of his character that he has formed one of the most distinctly class movements to be found in the world; but he refuses to call himself class-conscious or at present to discuss very seriously or exhaustively the advantages of the socialist state. One cannot help admiring the quick intelligence, the enthusiasm, and the high ideals of the Latin peoples, and the thorough thinking and fatal logic of the

Germans, but there is much also in the British temperament that appeals to one. Simply because the movement in Great Britain refuses to accept phrases which it
does not fully understand is not a good reason for thinking that it is not equally advanced with the movement elsewhere. So long as it moves definitely on
the lines of the class struggle, that is the most important matter; and if the working-classes can be
united politically and economically against the exploiter
of labor, the rest will come of itself.

However, many prominent English socialists do not
agree with this view, and they refuse to identify themselves with the new movement because they fear it
is not, and never will be, a socialist organization. But
even if this were granted, it would only prove that
the British working men are inaccessible to socialist
ideals ; and if that is true, there cannot be a conscious
socialist movement in Great Britain. The Labor Party
represents the working-class. It carries the class struggle into politics. It is an organization of working
men, maintaining absolute independence of the capitalist parties, while at the same time extending an open
hand of welcome to every socialist, whether of the
working-class or not, who belongs to an affiliated organization. No better opportunity has been offered
the socialists of any country to carry on their propaganda, and even to lead the workers into the lines of
socialist development. If the socialists cannot impress
their ideas upon the Labor Party, they will fail to impress them upon the workers outside of the Labor Party.
The worker of the Labor Party is the typical Britisher.
He is suspicious of theoretical considerations and broad
generalizations. For this reason he may resist to the

18.8.'99 faithfully yours
J. Keir Hardie

J. Keir Hardie, M.P.

end the thoroughgoing comprehensive programs upon which the movements of other countries have been built. But because of that, shall we say the Labor Party is not socialist?

Socialism is surely less a matter of program than it is a movement of the disinherited. Hardie very well said at the conference that formed the I. L. P., "The labor movement is neither a program nor a constitution, but the expression of a great principle, *the determination of the workers to be the arbiters of their own destiny*." * Marx himself said that "a movement was worth ten programs." Liebknecht, de Paepe, and nearly all the ablest socialist leaders have considered working-class organization and unity more important than the program. Engels indicated that he was of the same view when in 1892 he wrote of the British movement, "It moves now and then with an over-cautious mistrust of the name of socialism, *while it gradually absorbs the substance*." * The fact is the British worker is building up a powerful working-men's movement. It will represent, it must represent, the aspirations of the working-class, and every day it must come into conflict with the selfish and narrow policy of the present order. Whether it works consciously or unconsciously, its end must be socialist, and curiously enough by the very nature of its political revolt it follows the lines of the Marxian philosophy.

When socialism in England was largely a matter of programs, broad generalizations, and critical analysis, it made little impression. It was a thing by itself, not yet embodied into the constitution and action of working-class life. Socialist thought had not yet been brought into proletarian life, and proletarian life had not

* The italics are mine.

yet been brought into socialist thought, as Jaurès so
well puts it; but the socialists to-day who are in the
Labor Party are in contact with proletarian life, and are
gradually infusing their spirit into the mass of British
workers.   In the old days when the socialists limited
their activities to permeating cultivated people with
their aspirations, to use Morris's phrase, they were
scoffed at or ignored.   To-day everybody in England
is discussing socialism, and every capitalist influence is
being exerted to the utmost to split the Labor Party by
separating the trade unionists from the socialist members.*   The "Daily Express" during the whole summer of 1906 ran a column entitled "The Fraud of
Socialism."   Always bitterly antagonistic to every
aspiration of the working-class, it has consistently
fought every measure for the benefit of the workers;
but in this campaign it posed as the friend of working men.   With a sensational appeal to the mass of
trade unionists it endeavored to rouse them to what
it called the raid the socialists were making upon
their funds.   According to the "Express" the socialists
were endeavoring to capture the trade unions by
stealth, and to use them for furthering their own
nefarious and anti-social purposes.   Other papers came
into the battle.   All Great Britain was discussing socialism and the Labor Party.   Everybody wrote letters
to the papers, as every one does in England, expressing their views upon the matter; and bishops, ministers, politicians, and even the nobility began to take
sides.   Nothing has ever happened that has done more
to advance socialism, and the socialists came out of the
fight stronger than ever.

* See also p. 231.

The real test of the strength and conscience of the workers is at hand. The socialists are being held up as atheists, as believers in the confiscation of all private property, and as advocates of free love.* The labor men with conservative views are being patted upon the back and flattered. Their vanity is worked upon, their jealousies and ambitions fed, and so the campaign progresses, publicly and privately, openly and underhandedly, to disrupt the party and disorganize the working-classes.

The most subtle, and not the least important of the efforts being made to destroy the Labor Party, is the shrewd politics of the Liberals. They have given labor all and more than it has asked. The measures already obtained by labor are not of fundamental importance; and yet even these petty measures in the interests of the working-class could not have been obtained except by bringing to bear on the old parties powerful political pressure, and that pressure is exercised best by an independent party. The old parties see very plainly that if they do not endeavor to placate labor, it may return a hundred or more members to the next parliament, and may even within a few years become the second party. They begin, therefore, to realize that they are in an awkward situation, and they now lavish upon labor evidences of good-will. They do not do so because they love labor any more than they have loved it in the past; it is because their political life has been threatened, and the wise British masters have their own way of acting under such circumstances. They give nothing until they have to, but when no alternative is open to them, they give gracefully. This is a very

* See also pp. 232–233.

skilful method of retaining power, and even some of the labor members are puzzled, and perhaps a little inclined to think they have too harshly judged their masters.

There are reefs ahead, and trying times. No other workers in Europe have such an astute class to battle with. To divide and thus to conquer is the present policy of the old parties, of the press, and of nearly all the most prominent leaders of British opinion. Bismarck, endeavoring to destroy socialism, persecuted the leaders, threw them into prison, drove them into exile, and for several years forced the whole movement underground. He meant to destroy it, but instead he gave it an enormous incentive. As we have seen, his action consolidated the warring factions. In France the upper class use a somewhat similar method, and in Italy they shoot down discontented, starving workmen; but the English statesmen divide, disrupt, create suspicion, flatter, and corrupt, and if necessary, grant, apparently with real sympathy, some of the claims of an advanced movement. These subtle methods are far more effective than those known to continental politicians, and despite all the reform movements that have risen and political revolutions that have occurred in England, the rule of the upper classes has never once been in danger. Taine has well said, " Such a country as this is, based on the whole national history and on the whole national instincts, it is more capable than any other people in Europe of transforming itself without recasting, and of devoting itself to its future without renouncing its past."

In the face of such traditions and inherited instincts, in the face of the native dislike of general principles and abstractions, it is a stupendous task to impress upon British labor the comprehensive revolutionary ideals of socialism. Whether it can be done or not remains to be seen, and in the meantime there is no question but that a real danger confronts a party without well-defined principles and high ideals. No one realizes that fact more than Hardie, and it seemed to me that when he spoke at Belfast the following words, it was with a note of wistfulness, and a sentiment of sorrow : " A labor party without an ideal cannot last. There must be some Holy Grail which they are ever in search of, which they are making sacrifices to reach, and which will inspire and enable the men and women comprising the party to do mighty deeds for the advancement of their cause. Many of the Labor Party — most of them — find that ideal in socialism. They are not content to be merely a Red Cross Brigade to stanch the wounds caused by the system under which they live. They stand for reform, for progress, and finally for freedom of the class to which they belong."

NOTE. — As the manuscript goes to the printer the following report (from "The Labour Leader ") of the Hull Congress of the Labor Party reaches me : —

"At last the Engineers' resolution was reached. In animated sentences J. J. Stevenson, of the Engineers, moved : —

" ' That in the opinion of this Conference the time has arrived when the Labor Party should have as a definite object the socialization of the means of production, distribution, and exchange, to be controlled by a democratic State in the interest of the entire community ; and the complete emancipation of Labor from the domination of capitalism and landlordism with the establishment of social and economic equality between the sexes.'

" When the result was read out, it was found that the resolution was carried by 514,000 against 469,000 votes. This is the first time the extent of socialist conviction has been seriously tested in the Conference."

CHAPTER V

THE BELGIAN LABOR PARTY

I HAVE come from the " Classic Land of Capitalism " to what Karl Marx has called "The Paradise of the Capitalists." One would need to be an adept in fine distinctions to make clear the difference. If the working-classes of England are poverty-stricken, and live in overcrowded and squalid quarters, so do the workers of Belgium. There is one distinction, however. There are certain classes of workmen in England who have, by organization and united action, established for themselves a tolerable existence. In Belgium there is practically no such class. The entire mass of workers, when not actually beneath the poverty line, live but slightly above it. In both the classic land and the paradise an immense body of citizens live in abominable conditions, and toil their lives away without enjoying the benefits of modern civilized life.

Belgium is not a comfortable, joyous place where the people lead happy lives and the souls of children are full of gladness. It is true that in many parts of this tiny country, the smallest in Europe, there are spacious and beautiful estates and handsome châteaux, enjoyed by capitalists who control the powers of government and the institutions of the land. But beneath them is a nation in poverty. The capitalists have created for themselves a paradise; and in order to support it, they have made for the people an inferno. Outside their magnificent estates there is the never ceasing hum of industry; the great factories, the mines, the quarries, the vast docks and wharves, the canals stretching throughout the country, and the minutely and intensively cultivated fields, where multitudes of men, women, and children labor unceasingly. Travelling in Belgium, one passes through such a conglomeration of industrial centres as to make one feel that Packingtown, the great steel mills of Pittsburg, the mining districts of Pennsylvania, the textile mills of the South, and the docks of the Great Lakes had all been crowded together in this little handful of country.

Since 1830, when the capitalists began their rule in Belgium, the population has steadily increased until now it is the densest in Europe. The increase in wealth has been prodigious, and the factories, mines, commerce, and cultivation of the soil have developed to such an intensity that perhaps no similar bit of space in the universe is so adequately and variously industrialized. The figures of the increase in the wealth of Belgium show that during these years of capitalist domination, there have been amassed 35 milliards of francs, with an annual revenue of $3\frac{1}{2}$ milliards. Louis Bertrand shows that if this wealth were equally distributed among all the people, each family would possess a capital of 25,000 francs, or an annual revenue of 2500 francs. This would mean in Belgium that every man, woman, and child would be assured a comfortable and in a small way even a luxurious existence.

But there is no such distribution of wealth. Instead of comfort in the year 1896, 170,000 workmen, or about 25 per cent of all laborers investigated, gained less than 40 cents per day, and 172,000 workers, or 25 per cent

K

again, earned between 40 and 60 cents per day. This, of course, means that these workers were under the poverty line, and therefore unable to supply themselves and their families with the necessaries of life. Perhaps as striking as any of the figures illustrating the poverty in Belgium are those concerning the dwellings of the workers. In Brussels the conditions are by no means the worst, and yet 17,597 of the families investigated, or 34 per cent, are forced to live in one room, the sole space they have for sleeping, eating, and living. But it is not only in wages or in housing that such appalling conditions exist. Even the capitalists under the present system cannot easily remedy these things. The injustice and wickedness of their rule are even more clearly shown by the woman and child labor, and by their resistance to the demands of the people for the education of their children. In 1902 the proportion of militiamen in various European countries who were entirely illiterate was as follows : —

	Per 1000
In the German Empire in 1900	0.7
In Sweden	0.8
In Denmark	0.2
In Switzerland	20 *
In Holland	23
In England (marriage statistics)	37
In France	46
In Belgium	101

* Read only imperfectly.

From these figures it will be seen that the Belgians are by far the most illiterate and poorly educated of all the peoples of industrial Europe. Children have been needed for the mills and mines, and protest on the part of the people has not availed to prevent the capitalists from exploiting them. Capitalist rule in Belgium has been perfect, for, as with us, there were until 1886 but two parties; when the one was defeated, the other was in power, and both parties represented the elements that are enriched by cheap labor.

It would seem impossible to expect from the workers of Belgium an intelligent and consistent revolt, as they are the most oppressed and badly educated workers of the industrial countries of Europe, and accustomed to work the longest hours at the lowest pay. Indeed, it is the opinion of many Belgians that they are weak and submissive. A well-known socialist, Louis de Brouckère, writes: "Belgium, the battlefield of Europe, has known for centuries nothing but uninterrupted oppression. Spain, Austria, and France fought for our provinces which had already suffered from the brutal treatment of the Dukes of Burgundy. The rival powers took possession of them, lost them, and took them again at various intervals. At every new conquest our country had to be forced to surrender and to obey. . . . We have been assailed by all the reactions since the Inquisition, and they have raged in our country more furiously than in any other except Spain, until the Restoration. We have had to submit to the despotism of every power from Philip the Second down to Napoleon, a cruel and long tyranny which ended by forcing us into servitude. During the time of our misery we learned habits of submission, from which these twenty years of socialist organization have not been able to entirely free us."

This is a strong statement, and in the face of such

odds it is little wonder that the workers have submitted. But where any other course has been possible, they have availed themselves of it. In the old days in Ghent the mediæval guilds used to flock into the public square to raise their standard of revolt. There also Gerard Denys used to lead the weavers against their oppressors. And there to-day stands the *Maison du Peuple*, representing the modern revolt of the workers. The Walloons of Liège, known always for their industry and hard labor, used to take the weapons which they manufactured so skilfully to use against their oppressors. A writer of the old day says : "The history of Liège records a series of sanguinary insurrections of the turbulent and unbridled populace against their oppressive and arrogant rulers."

And so it has always been. The strongest section of the International was among the Belgians, and their leaders were among the most capable and uncompromising. Indefatigable in their labor to keep alive the spirit of revolt, they fought with incredible energy and devotion. César de Paepe, Jean Pellering, Désiré Brismée, Eugène Steens, and Laurent Verrycken were men of whom any country might well be proud. Unfortunately the International, as a whole, was a body dominated by intellectuals, and although exhorting the workers to union and persistently urging that " The emancipation of the workers must be the work of the workers themselves," it was filled with the poison of sectarian strife. It was, despite all, ideological, and above all a continuous battle between two great intellects.*

Especially in Belgium they were dreary years of quarrels, creating antagonisms that made unity of action impossible. The death of the International in 1872 was

* See also p. 305.

followed by blank despair. Some of the leaders came to believe with the Russians that the only hope left to the workers was pan-destruction. Others retired to their workshops, hopelessly discouraged. Still others went into bourgeois politics, having lost all hope of working-class organization. Two "brilliant" members of the International planned to interview Napoleon the Third, who was then in England, and to endeavor to persuade him to become the emperor of the workers and peasants! One of them was so infatuated with the idea that he soon imagined himself vice-emperor, and to expound his views he printed a little tract on " The Empire and the New France." Pessimism was general, the labor movement was dormant, and capitalism in Belgium as elsewhere grew more arrogant and oppressive.

It was some time before new blood began to make itself felt. Two of the most remarkable of the younger men came from among that wonderful people, the weavers of Ghent. They were Van Beveren and Anseele. Other youths began to work in other parts of Belgium, and pretty soon throughout the country, workmen's leagues, democratic federations, rational and republican organizations began to spring up. Some of the old sections of the International were revived and a Chamber of Labor at Brussels was founded, while in Ghent and elsewhere the coöperative and socialist organizations took on a new development. Everywhere with the reviving movement there came to birth again the old longing of the oppressed for unity and concerted action. With this spirit there arose leaders to give it voice: Jean Volders, Van Beveren, Anseele, and Bertrand, while old César de Paepe and Verrycken began to work again with renewed enthusiasm.

In 1885 a hundred working men, representing 59 groups, came together in Brussels to discuss what they should do.   It was a remarkable gathering, which ended in the formation of the Belgian Labor Party.   To the thought of every one the condition of the workers had become unbearable, and the longing for unity among the working-classes was profound.   They were weary of dogma and intellect, and came very near excluding that grand old man, César de Paepe.   They gave no thought to program, and the socialists themselves, with the exception of two or three, agreed that it was better to leave the word " socialist" out of the title of the party.

They had reached a stage more fundamentally revolutionary and more dangerous to capitalism than ever rested in any thought, dogma, or statement of what the future society should be.   They intended to unite the working-class, no matter what the individuals believed. They wanted the stupid and backward elements as much as the advanced and more intelligent.   In this memorable year something more profound than doctrine agitated the souls of the workers, and unionists, mutualists, socialists, democrats, republicans, rationalists, catholics, protestants, revolutionists, and positivists came together and formed a class party.   It was a union of oppressed against oppressors, a union of workers against capitalists, a union of exploited against exploiters.   They did then precisely what they are now doing in England.

It was the birth of a party, determined to free itself from political connections of any sort with capitalist parties.   The members did not say they were socialists ; they simply said, " The working-class of Belgium is organizing itself politically against its exploiters," and that means that they intend some day to take Belgium into their own hands and administer it in their own interest. Some of the socialists were not satisfied, but they all freely and generously assented to the decision of the congress. Whatever their opinion was at that time, it certainly came later in accord with that of César de Paepe, who wrote not long afterward : " What more immense and at the same time more simple and precise ! Why add the words socialist, collectivist, communist, rationalist, democrat, republican, and other limiting epithets ? He who says *Parti Ouvrier* says Party of Class, and since the working-class constitutes itself into a party, how could you believe that it may be anything else in its tendencies and principles than socialist and republican ? "

After the Belgian party was constituted it became the most strikingly solidified and integral party in Europe, and it was not long before it adopted a complete social-ist program. Vandervelde has well said : " Belgian socialism, at the conflux of three great European civili-zations, partakes of the character of each of them. From the English it adopted self-help and free association, principally under the coöperative form; from the Ger-mans political tactics and fundamental doctrines, which were for the first time expounded in the Communist Manifesto ; and from the French it took its idealist ten-dencies, its integral conception of socialism, considered as the continuation of the revolutionary philosophy, and as a new religion continuing and fulfilling Christianity."

In accord with this eclectic spirit, the Belgian Labor Party includes in itself every organization that expresses working-class aspirations. The trade unions ; the co-operatives with their " Houses of the People," their great stores, and their public meeting-halls ; and the friendly societies with their insurance schemes, are all closely and definitely associated in one political party, which carries on a gigantic propaganda, and has its press and its fighting force in parliament and upon municipal bodies. It is not surprising, therefore, that this complete organization and almost perfect solidarity brought the workers hope for the future and for the present great confidence in themselves.

During the year 1886 riots broke out in various industrial sections. The working-class had long stood oppression, and now at last it seemed the time had come to remedy the misery of their condition. During all the years of capitalist domination the two old parties had ignored the necessities of the poor. There was no legislation of importance to benefit or protect the working-class. The total disregard of the capitalists for the misery of the workers is shown by their treatment of a bill introduced as early as 1872 to regulate child labor. It was an effort to prevent boys under thirteen years of age and girls under fourteen years of age from working underground in the coal mines. The bill was ignored for six years, and only in 1878 did the parties take time to consider it. And then, even after the horrible conditions of child slavery had been stated, out of 155 representatives in parliament 150 voted against the bill. But things began to change immediately after the formation of the Labor Party. The capitalists were then forced to consider seriously the condition of the people. A commission of inquiry was established, and in the years following 1886, law after law was voted for the benefit of the working-class. They were not important laws perhaps, but as I have shown in the chapter on the British movement, even such miserable concessions are

Maison du Peuple, Brussels.

wrung from the ruling powers only after a complete
political revolt of the wage-workers.

Early on Easter Sunday, 1907, I went to the "House
of the People" to attend the annual congress of the
Belgian Labor Party. In one of the busiest and most
important sections of the beautiful capital of Belgium
the socialists have built their temple at a cost of over
1,200,000 francs. It is a veritable palace, containing
the offices of the International Socialist Bureau, the
Belgian party, and the trade unions. There are also
several large meeting and committee rooms, and of
course, the stores, tailor shops, etc., of the coöperative.
On the ground floor there is a large and handsome café,
which is filled to overcrowding every evening with
working people and their families. Besides this House
of the People there are five branch establishments, all
of them handsome buildings, and one of them with
large grounds in addition.

On this Easter morning the building was gorgeous
in the sunlight; red flags were flying, and a great
banner with "Welcome to All" was flung over the
broad entrance. From the top of the building were
hung four tablets bearing the names of Marx, Proudhon,
Volders, and de Paepe. How significant are these
names! Marx and Proudhon bequeathed to the Belgian movement, as to all other working men's movements in the world, intellectual lines of guidance.
Volders represents the genius of agitation, one who
literally destroyed himself by days and nights of
feverish propaganda. At the time of his death, he
was the master of Brussels. César de Paepe was a
friend of Proudhon, of Bakounine, and of Marx; a
great scientist, and an indefatigable propagandist. It

was his spirit and counsel more than any one else's that made possible the unity and impressive harmony which rules the Belgian movement. His was the genius of working-class solidarity.

At the top of this House of the People is a superb hall, ordinarily used for dramatic purposes, with seats for perhaps 2000 people. The night before I had seen it crowded with the poorest working men, women, and children of Brussels, who had come to see the popular cinematograph. This morning working men from every part of Belgium, from the mines, quarries, docks, glass-works, mills, and all the great industrial enterprises, were gathered together to deliberate upon their common affairs. There were about 400 delegates, representing coöperatives, mutual societies, trade unions, socialist circles, and "locals." They were almost all working men, for the movement in Belgium is predominantly proletarian, and in this respect it resembles markedly the British Labor Party. The mass of the delegates are builders and organizers of working-class movements. Many of them are masterly in debate and powerful propagandists, but few outside of Belgium know their names, or can appreciate the immense rôle they play in party affairs.

There were, however, a few men of note. There was Louis Bertrand, who in the early days of the movement carried on an effective propaganda, and was also president of the conference at which the Labor Party was founded. Professor Émile Vinck, who has specialized for many years upon municipal questions, delivered an important report. Senator Lafontaine, an extraordinarily brilliant man, Jules Destrée, and Louis de Brouckère were also in attendance. Camille Huysmans, the secretary of the International Socialist Bureau, was as efficient in the Belgian congress as he is in all congresses and committee meetings, whether national or international. Vandervelde, perhaps the most able parliamentary leader, and a scholarly and conscientious writer on economic subjects, was unable to be there because of illness; but he sent a report which was read and discussed.

The youthful-looking person in the chair was Edouard Anseele. I had always wanted to see this militant ever since I learned that socialism was not a dream or a utopia, but a present-day movement full of purpose and vitality. I had imagined that Anseele was now old and fatherly-looking, with white hair, benevolent face, and kind eyes. Instead, I saw a short, powerful, well-muscled, youthful-looking man with a small head and a strong neck. His jaws are those of a fighter, and in action they open and shut like a steel trap. He is the soul of conviction, and to express this soul he has a body of iron that knows no ache or pain. Overcoming obstacles is to him a joy. He loves to meet them, to battle with them, and to conquer them. He is strenuous as even Roosevelt knows not how to be. He never rests; he cannot walk, he runs. In fact, Anseele does the work of half-a-dozen men, and his accomplishments are prodigious. Besides managing one of the largest coöperative undertakings in Belgium, which does an annual business of over 5,000,000 francs, he is an aggressive deputy, and no discussion takes place but finds him on the fighting line. He is the *bête noir* of the capitalists in the chamber. He annoys them, routs them out of their lethargy, prods them into activity, and goads them into

fury. He is also an indefatigable propagandist, flying
to all parts of Belgium to carry the message of socialism. The son of a workman, Anseele is the very in-
carnation of the working-class revolt.

It is recorded that once, when about eighteen years
of age, he heard by chance some socialists speak. One
of them described the misery and wretchedness of the
weavers of Ghent. Anseele wept. That meant something for that lad, and since that hour he has been a
revolutionist. In his youth he sold papers on the
streets, he wrote socialist novels, and in the evening
hours he carried on a ceaseless propaganda. As he
was extremely poor, he often sold shirts and other articles to his audiences to pay his travelling expenses
and to assist the propaganda. Later he became the
editor of the local socialist paper, and was sent to
prison for some months because after the soldiers had
shot down some workers on strike, he called King Leo-
pold, Assassin I, and issued a passionate appeal to the
mothers, sisters, and sweethearts of the soldiers, beg-
ging them to write to their dear ones in the army, demanding that they refuse to fire upon their brothers, the
working men. It would be impossible to recount what
this man has accomplished by his superhuman activity
during the last thirty years.

The congress reminded me very much of the English
one. It was cool, even-tempered, and efficient. There
were no great orations delivered, and the questions discussed had to do with definite and practical party work.
For an outsider there was not a great deal of interest.
After considering reports from the parliamentary group,
the trade union group, the coöperative group, and the
federated municipal councillors, the congress gave con-

sideration to certain detailed questions of administration, and to other matters largely of local interest. Louis Bertrand read an important report upon the eight-hour day, and the old fight for universal suffrage came up under the form of a proposed electoral affiliation with the Liberal Party. Vandervelde in his report traced the history of the struggle for universal suffrage, and advocated affiliating with the Liberal Party for the purpose of combating the Clericals. The latter have always been the most obstinate opponents of universal suffrage. It was, therefore, the opinion of Vandervelde that a general and concerted electoral affiliation should be worked out between the Liberals and the Labor Party which would enable them together to control practically all the municipal bodies of Belgium.

The struggle for universal suffrage in Belgium has been a long, bitter, and insistent fight, extending over a half century. There have been two general strikes, countless riots, imprisoned and martyred workers. At all the congresses since the formation of the party, there has been a discussion of this question. One cannot over-estimate what the working-class of Belgium has suffered in the long struggle to obtain a more equitable electoral system. After the general strike of 1895 the old law was repealed; but the new law, while marking an advance, well deserves the name that Anseele gave it, " The law of the four infamies." This legislation still irritates the workers, and the suggestion of Vandervelde was considered as perhaps the only means now available of forcing the government to grant a further extension of the suffrage. It should be said incidentally that electoral affiliations among the opposition parties are customary in Belgium; but although the wisdom of such action is doubted by some members of the Labor Party, each section or federation has been left to do as it pleased in such cases, and the party statutes provide only that the principles of the party program shall not be sacrificed. The proposal of Vandervelde was, therefore, not so unusual as at first appears. It proposed that instead of isolated instances of affiliation, the Labor Party should work out a consistent plan for affiliation with the Liberals in all parts of Belgium. After an interesting debate it was decided not to agree to a general plan, but to leave to the local federations freedom to do as they desired.

This is perhaps the chief matter of interest to the outsider that came up for discussion. It was not what transpired at the congress that impressed one with the vital power of the Belgian movement. It was what was back of the congress. It was the thousands of working men, women, and children bound together in a multitude of circles, coöperatives, mutualities, and unions that form the basis of working-class action. The Belgian movement is not dominated by politicians, nor held together by oratory. It is the expression of a class impulse. It is the precious result of the work of the men and women of the mines, mills, and factories, who after the hard toil of the day, give their love and labor to the upbuilding of their emancipatory institutions. Determined to free themselves from the unbearable conditions of capitalism, they have created for themselves numberless organizations to support them in their conflict.

To begin with, there are the *syndicats*, or trade unions. Although they have existed in Belgium from early times, and while almost every type can be found there,

including "The Knights of Labor," copied from the
American organization, the trade union movement as a
whole is weak. The reasons for this are various. In
the first place the law has been most unfriendly to its
development, its members have not seen the necessity
for large dues and efficient, well-paid secretaries, and at
present they have practically no paid organizers. At
the time of a strike they often depend more upon assistance from the coöperatives than from their own
treasuries. The trade unions also usually have a political or religious bias. There are, for instance, four
types of unions: (1) those connected with the Liberal
party; (2) those connected with the Clerical party; (3)
those connected with the socialist party; and (4) the
Independents who refuse to affiliate themselves definitely with any party. There are now about 148,483
trade unionists in Belgium. Only 17,000 are Catholics,
2000 are Liberals, about 31,000 are Independents, while
94,000 are affiliated with the socialist party. It is
obvious, therefore, that outside of the socialist and
independent unions the movement is of little consequence.

The Labor Party, realizing the weakness of the
unions and their importance in working-class action,
is now using all its power to build up a strong and
virile trade union movement. Several of the ablest
leaders are devoting their entire time trying to infuse
a more militant spirit into the workers. Propagandists
are at work in all parts of Belgium, agitating for paid
officials who can give all their time to the affairs of the
unions. New organizations are being formed, and the
old ones that have fallen into decay are being revived.
As a result of these energetic efforts, one begins to see

a great increase in membership that promises well for the future.

Not all the unions, however, are badly organized, and those of Ghent have been of enormous service to the workers. The coöperatives, the mutualities, and the party work in perfect harmony, and together they have realized an immense progress. Through their political influence the unions have obtained from the city of Ghent an insurance scheme for assisting the unemployed members. Since 1901 the municipal council has given to unemployed union men one dollar for every dollar expended from the trade union treasury. This is a significant and important development, for it means that the unions no longer have to bear the entire responsibility for the unemployed. The scheme has spread from Ghent to other cities in Belgium, which now undertake a part of this heavy burden and coöperate with the unions to the extent, at least, of sharing the load.

The next group of organizations connected with the Belgian movement are *les Mutualités*. They are mutual insurance societies such as we have in America. They existed in Belgium long before the formation of the Labor Party, when a number became affiliated to the political movement. Some, however, were unable to do so at that time, as they included in their organization both employers and employees. In 1905, according to the Bureau of Labor, there were about 7000 such societies, organized to insure the workers and their families against sickness, old age, death, and similar misfortunes. Although this seems a large number for so small a country, there are still many others which do not report their affairs to the Bureau of Labor, and are, therefore, not included in the official reports. One of the most interesting of the latter is the *Bond Moyson* at Ghent, named in memory of one of the pioneer socialists of Flanders. In 1890, after a long discussion and a rather heated battle, all of the insurance societies in Ghent, excepting one, affiliated themselves to the group of socialist organizations centring about the *Maison du Peuple*. This consolidation was followed by an era of prosperity, and the members of the insurance organizations increased from 4600 in 1897 to 10,323 in 1904, or including families to nearly 30,000 persons. Soon after the reorganization several new insurance measures were adopted. A new fund was established to provide against invalidity, and another for ordinary life insurance. The members of the *Bond Moyson* now obtain three classes of benefits: pensions, the care of a physician and medicines, and bread supplies from the coöperative stores. In case of the death of the insured one, a pension is also given to the family. Special assistance is provided at the time of childbirth. As a new development a pension is now given to all those who have bought regularly at the coöperative stores for twenty years. And when they are 60 years old, they are given practically all their necessary supplies. Not only in Ghent has the system developed, but organizations similarly constituted and managed are a part of the movement in all the industrial districts of Belgium.

The third group of organizations — the coöperatives — is perhaps the most important. They comprise almost every type of associated effort. One sees now in all the industrial towns of Belgium handsome stores, large assembly rooms, cafés, and restaurants, owned and administered by the working people themselves. In ad-

L

dition to the stores, where the activity is largely commercial, there are also several productive enterprises of note,
and almost every town has at least one model bakery.
In these bakeries the workmen have an eight-hour day
with the maximum trade union wage. There are also
breweries and cigar-making establishments, boot and
shoe factories, printing shops, cotton mills, and dairies,
— all conducted on the coöperative plan.

It is again at Ghent that the organization is the best
developed. To begin with there is the beautiful house
of the *Vooruit*, which is called "Our House." In addition to being a large department store, where almost
everything that is required by the working people can
be bought, it is a working men's club. There are rooms
for meetings and for recreation, which in many ways resemble those of the University Settlements in America.
On the first floor of Our House is a large café, where
about 1000 people can sit comfortably at the tables.
No strongly alcoholic drinks are sold, although one can
always obtain light beers and wines, tea, coffee, milk,
and similar non-intoxicating drinks. In the evening the
café is invariably filled with men, women, and children,—
the weavers of Ghent. Above this room is a large and
beautiful library, which is also used at times for lectures
and meetings. On the same floor there are several
committee rooms, while on the top floor there is a large
assembly room, occasionally used as a theatre. All the
rooms are handsomely decorated with mural paintings,
illustrating in heroic forms the subject of Labor.
Throughout the town there are many branch stores,
and on the outskirts of the town there is a new model
bakery with the most improved machinery, which pro-
duces about 200,000 pounds of bread each week. In ad-

First Oven of the Coöperative Bakery, Brussels.

Present Ovens of the Coöperative Bakery, Brussels.

dition, there are several branch libraries, a large cotton mill, and a well-equipped printing establishment, where two daily papers and most of the books, pamphlets, tracts, and other publications of the party are printed. For twenty cents a year every member of the coöperative, including altogether about 155,000 persons, receives regularly all publications of this print shop.

Perhaps no more significant move has been made by the ever enterprising Anseele and the working men of Ghent than the buying of a fine old house in one of the most aristocratic quarters. It was formerly occupied by an exclusive club, but it was found too expensive to keep up! Suddenly and quite secretly this house was bought by the weavers of Ghent, and it is now their club. It has a café, a library, a handsome theatre, and meeting-rooms, in addition to a large garden, which is used on Sundays and other fête days, for the games and assemblies of the socialists. In the midst of this old aristocratic quarter Vooruit has placed its standard, and the neighbors now see the working people at games and dances, and hear at close hand the singing of the "Internationale," and other revolutionary songs.

It is, of course, impossible to give in a short chapter an adequate conception of the development of the coöperatives, but the following figures may convey some idea of their extent. The annual sales of the distributive stores in Belgium during 1906 amounted to about 32,000,000 francs, and out of the profits benefits were allotted to the members amounting to over 3,000,000. This latter sum was distributed to about 120,000 persons who were affiliated with the coöperatives. The total sales from the various productive enterprises, which include breweries, bakeries, dairies, and so forth, during

the same year amounted to about 1,500,000 francs. The
value of these organizations, however, does not lie only
in the amount of money which they distribute to their
members; they also furnish supplies in immense quan-
tities to the strikers when there is any great battle on
between employers and employees. In addition they
supply funds to carry on many other working-class activities. The *Maison du Peuple* of Brussels, to mention
but one instance, during the six years, from 1897–1903,
gave to the socialist propaganda half a million francs.
Another useful service rendered by the coöperatives is
the aid they give to those agitators and propagandists
of the labor movement who have been blacklisted by
their employers. These men can always find work to
do in the coöperative establishments, and still have time
free to carry on their propaganda.

The fourth development of the working-class spirit is
the Labor Party itself. It is the bond which unites all
the various activities. It is meant to express the
views and aspirations of the working people politically.
The party has now in parliament 30 deputies and seven
senators. In the municipal councils of Belgium it has
500 representatives, and its total socialist vote is about
half a million. While the unions fight the battles
of the workers on the economic field, and endeavor to
force the employers to accord them better conditions
and higher wages, the coöperatives strive to displace
the middle man in commerce, and to gain for the
workers immense advantages in buying the necessaries
of life. But the workers of Belgium realize that neither
of these efforts alone can accomplish their complete
emancipation. They do not undervalue the economic
movements. On the contrary, they promote and

strengthen them in every possible way ; but they fully realize that so long as the capitalists control the machinery of government, the workers must remain a subject class. They, therefore, seek to conquer the government, and toward this end the party carries on a ceaseless propaganda with its six daily papers, reaching over 106,000 persons daily, 22 weeklies, and 14 monthlies.

The printing establishment of the Brussels " daily " is in a handsome building, with spacious quarters and everything required for publishing a first-class daily paper. There are large editorial offices, light and airy workrooms for the compositors, and ample quarters for the five large presses. The biggest press was at the time of my visit printing the daily papers for two other towns about two hours from Brussels. On another machine an illustrated weekly was being printed. The Brussels daily, " Le Peuple," sells for one cent, while the papers for the smaller towns sell for two centimes, or less than a half cent. The committee in charge of the press has decided recently to issue a new daily for one centime, or one-fifth of a cent. This gives some idea of the enterprise and business methods of the Belgian socialists.

Of course there are efforts made in other directions as well to promote the propaganda. A large number of party members are speaking and agitating all the time. At the coöperative theatres socialist plays are given. A clever method of spreading the party views among the poorest workers is through the medium of cinematographs. Between scenes there are shown mottoes, and short phrases expressing socialist opinions. Political criticisms, words of enthusiasm and revolt are

thrown on the canvas, and in this way the poorest and
most ill-educated workers gain some idea of the aims
of socialism. There is also a university in Brussels
under the control of the socialists.

The efficiency of the Belgian socialists is impressive.
For poor working men to have built up these great
properties, and now to carry them on with such ability,
is nothing short of miraculous. They are proving in
the face of a hostile class their own capacity, and learning day by day their own worth. Collective enterprise
has its difficulties, associated effort its trials. They
are learning what these difficulties and trials are; and
they are also learning something more profound — how
to suppress brutal egoism, and how to serve the commonweal. It is that which glorifies the Belgian movement, and gives even to the observer a profound and
comforting spiritual uplift. But the workers have a hard
fight against a reactionary government, which never
ceases to combat their coöperatives, unions, and political
party.

To the workers of Belgium nothing has been given;
not a step has been taken without suffering. Indeed,
it was misery that drove them together. Their own
suffering and the memory of martyred brothers have so
united their life and spirit, that not a single important
division has occurred in the movement during the last
twenty years. They are not moved by doctrines, and
they give free play to any one who has a plan for re-
lieving distress. They would never think of neglecting
any opportunity open to them to fight the battle of the
disinherited. They scorn no method; they eagerly
use and develop all. They believe in coöperation, in
trade unions, in municipal ownership, and in national

ownership; they believe in economic action and in political action; indeed, when any one of these is but weakly developed, the whole party with hearty good-will devotes all the energy at its command to the task of strengthening it. While others have been discussing theories and quarrelling over differences in method, the working-class movement in this little paradise of the capitalists has been born and has grown to full maturity.

It is not hard to explain why it is the Belgian working-class is so fortunate, or why, in the face of so many difficulties, it is able to accomplish such a magnificent work. It has learned the value of unity and the power of concerted action. The advice and example of old César de Paepe was ever before them. He coun-selled solidarity the day the party was born, and he never ceased urging its supreme importance. It is, therefore, significant that in 1890, as he was carried away from Brussels to die in Southern France, he should have written these words to the then assembled congress of the party: "I beg of you one permission, one only. Permit an old socialist, who has been in the breach for more than thirty-three years, and who has already seen so many ups and downs, so many periods of progress and of reaction in the revolutionary Belgian parties, to give you counsel. That is: be careful above all, in all your deliberations and resolutions, *to maintain among the different factions of the party and among the more or less extreme or moderate tendencies the closest possible union, and to prevent all that can con-stitute even a suspicion of division.* Naturally this implies that it is necessary to commence by forgetting the divisions that have existed in the past. To divide

you in order the better to oppress you, such is the tactic
of your enemies.   Flee from divisions; avoid them;
crush them in the egg; such ought to be *your* tactic,
and to that end may your program remain the broad-
est possible, and your title remain general enough to
shelter all who, in the Belgian proletariat, wish to
work for the emancipation, intellectual and material,
political and economic, of the mass of the disinherited."

CHAPTER VI

THE PROGRAM OF SOCIALISM

It is but natural that the reader should begin to ask, What is all this movement about? What is wanted? Why this extraordinary organization of working men in every country, and what do they seek to accomplish? It is not my purpose in this book to attempt to answer adequately these questions, but rather to describe the movement, and to convey a precise impression of its present influence; I must, therefore, refer inquiring readers to other books which treat particularly of the aims and principles of socialism.* Nevertheless, I realize the necessity for a brief outline here of the historic basis of modern socialism, and of its fundamental doctrines.

Many people appear to be more interested in the methods by which socialists endeavor to obtain their ends than in the ends themselves. To such persons the word "revolution" is apt to signify merely a question of method, confused, therefore, with violence and insurrection. When socialists use the term, as they do frequently, it is almost invariably without any implication of violence. There are unquestionably a few semi-anarchists who from time to time associate themselves with the movement, and by inflammatory addresses convey the impression that the socialists expect to

* See p. 364.

attain their ends by resort to open warfare. Liebknecht once said, " The frothy and theatrical phrases
of the fanatic supporters of the 'class struggle' dogma
are at bottom a cover for the Machiavellian schemes
of the reactionaries." In nearly every country such
irresponsible agitators have been excluded from the
movement. But while modern socialism condemns
violence, it is everywhere frankly revolutionary.

It is perhaps too much to expect that the present
struggle between labor and capital should proceed at
all times peacefully. History has known many revolutions, nearly all of which have been the culmination of
class struggles, wherein the force of the people has
been spent without their knowing precisely what they
sought to attain. Nearly all the early struggles, as for
instance the struggle of the serfs against their masters,
or that of the present dominant class against the old
feudal landowning aristocracy, ended in violence and
bloodshed. In the face of history, therefore, it would
seem absurd for one to prophesy concerning the outcome of the present struggle between the workers and
the capitalists, for certainly none of the previous uprisings were as truly revolutionary as the present. And
if one considers that when the contemplated revolution
is accomplished it means the rise to power of the working-class, and the abolition of private property in the
means of production, it would seem almost incredible
that it should take place in all countries without violence.
Nevertheless everywhere, and at all times, the responsible leaders urge the masses to pursue a peaceful
political course. Marx and Engels spent a good part
of their lives trying to convert the working-class from
the methods of violence, conspiracy, and insurrection

advocated by the anarchists. In 1850 Marx resigned from the central committee of the famous Communist Alliance because they sought to substitute "revolutionary phrases for revolutionary evolution"; and he told them with biting sarcasm that they would very likely have to go through a half-century of preparation before they could change themselves and make themselves worthy of political power.

Both Liebknecht and Jaurès, two of the ablest parliamentary leaders the socialist movement has produced, have again and again spoken of the necessity for gaining a considerable majority of the people before attempting to put socialist principles into operation. Liebknecht says: " It would be both stupid and ingenuous to exact that we should have a majority sealed and ready in our pockets before we began to apply our principles. But it would be still more ingenuous to imagine that we could put our principles into practice against the will of the immense majority of the nation. This is a fatal error, for which the French socialists have paid dear. Is it possible to put up a more heroic fight than did the workmen of Paris and Lyons? And has not every struggle ended in a bloody defeat, the most horrible reprisals on the part of the victors, and a long period of exhaustion for the proletariat? The French workers have not yet fully grasped the importance of organization and propaganda, and that is why up to the present moment they have been beaten with perfect regularity. . . . Not to contract, but to expand," he continues, " should be our motto. The circle of socialism should widen more and more *until we have converted most of our adversaries to being friends*, or at least disarmed their opposition. And the indifferent mass that in peaceful days has no weight in the political balance, but becomes the decisive force in times of agitation, ought to be so fully enlightened as to the aims and essential ideas of our party, that it will cease to fear us and can no longer be used as a weapon against us. All the legislative measures which we shall support, if the opportunity is given us, ought to have for their object to prove *the fitness of socialism to serve the common good.*"

This is very much the line of argument taken by the leaders of the movement. There is not a single socialist of prominence who believes that a change in conditions can be forced upon society contrary to the inherent social forces and the natural evolutionary processes working out in society. For the first time perhaps in the history of the world a constructive revolutionary movement is forming that is based upon a definite doctrine, scientifically deduced from the facts of history and social evolution. Far from advocating violence, socialism realizes, even more than its opponents, that it has all to gain and nothing to lose by the peaceful method. It already has adherents numbered by the million, its representatives in parliament, its exponents in literature, and its friends in every class of society. It is intelligently led and organized in almost every industrial centre of Western Europe for study, propaganda, and political action. And it is daily increasing in strength. Why, therefore, should it seek to use violence or to encourage insurrection, both of which means are to a certain extent even contradictory to its principles and its method of organization?

So much for the methods of contemporary socialism. In order to make clear the basis of its program it is

A Few Socialist Newspapers.

necessary briefly to review modern industrial history, as the entire socialist doctrine is based upon the economic evolution of the last century and a half. It is well known that the last great revolution placed in power the capitalist class. Previous to that time, the trader, the man of commerce, the capitalist, was looked down upon by the landed aristocracies and feudal lords as a person of inferior estate. Men of business had practically no political standing, and the old aristocracies, in order to maintain their privileges and unearned incomes, placed many intolerable restrictions upon trade, commerce, and industry. In the face of these restrictions capitalism could make no headway, and in order to gain freedom of commerce and a fuller development of industrial life, the capitalists, with the help of the masses, broke the political power of the landed aristocracies. The result of this revolution was a marked change in the relative positions of the various classes; and nearly everywhere the landed class are to-day less powerful in government than the trader, the man of commerce, and the capitalist, all of whom they used to look down upon and despise.

With the advent of modern capitalism there came into the world a new class called wage-workers. Their condition differs fundamentally from that of the working-classes in the earlier periods of history. The workers were first slaves, later serfs, and just before the introduction of capitalism, the main body of them were peasants, artisans, and craftsmen. The artisans and craftsmen mostly worked in their own homes, with their own tools, and the product of their labor was almost entirely their own. Excepting for such rates, rents, and dues as were paid to the upper classes and to the government, the workers were largely free from exploitation. They produced mainly for their own use, and it was common in those days for all members of the family to work together in the home, — brewing, baking, dyeing, weaving, and spinning. On a bit of soil attached to the cottage many of the neces- saries of life were grown, and only the most wretched of the populace were without livestock. This simple form of production could not realize great wealth, but there was little starvation, no unemployment, and, ex- cepting when the crops were destroyed through natural causes, the people were able to live tolerably comfort- ably. The peasant sold to the artisan agricultural produce, and bought from him the products of his handicraft.

At the end of the eighteenth century the advent of steam power altered the whole method of production. This period is called in history the industrial revolution. The spinning-wheel, the hand-loom, the blacksmith's hammer, were replaced by the spinning machine, the power loom, and the steam hammer. The individual workshop was replaced by the factory. Industrial cities came into being, and millions of people in Western Europe left their small homes, abandoned their cottage industries, to live in great tenements and to work in great factories. A mighty change took place in the industrial life, and the old individual form of production was replaced by a social form in which masses of men coöperated.

This gave rise to modern capitalism. It was im- possible for the individual workman to own the new tool. It was large and costly in the beginning, and with every new decade it grew larger and more costly. To-day the tool is a vast machine run by steam or electrical power, and enclosed in great buildings. In the early days of this new form of industry there were crying social abuses. The people were herded together in the worst quarters, in great and insanitary barracks. All the traditional moral bonds of the old order were burst asunder. Women and children worked underground and overground like beasts, and the working-class in general was reduced almost to a state of savagery.

These industrial changes revolutionized the face of the world. Gigantic wealth was made possible. Production for domestic use was replaced by production for national and international markets. It was a period of feverish competition, of stupendous labor, of gigantic commercial undertakings, and of big industrial horizons. At a mighty bound the capitalist class rose to a dominant position in modern life. At the same time there came into the world newer and intenser forms of misery.

Under the old domestic system the workman could, so long as he had health, provide himself and his family with the necessaries of life. If his skill was not great, he remained poor; but at any rate he earned a living. He was not employed or unemployed according to the will of another. Under the new régime he worked only when the great machine worked. He sold himself day by day to an employer. He became propertyless, as he could neither own his tools nor his tenement. In other words he became dependent, first upon an employer, second upon a machine, and then upon the state of the markets. When the machine stopped working, he was instantly deprived of the means of life. Without fields in which he could work, or the individual tools of the old order, he was precipitated into pauperism by the slightest industrial derangement. His wages were little more than sufficient to keep him and his family while he was at work, and when illness, accident, unemployment, or death occurred, the family was face to face with misery. In the old order there was a certain security of existence; in the new order there was none.

At certain periods the distress of the working-classes became acute. Great commercial crises and financial convulsions paralyzed all industry. "Since 1825, when the first general crisis broke out," says Frederick Engels, "the whole industrial and commercial world, production and exchange among all civilized peoples and their more or less barbaric hangers-on, are thrown out of joint about once every ten years. Commerce is at a standstill, the markets are glutted, products accumulate, as multitudinous as they are unsalable, hard cash disappears, credit vanishes, factories are closed, the mass of the workers are in want of the means of subsistence, because they have produced too much of the means of subsistence; bankruptcy follows upon bankruptcy, execution upon execution. The stagnation lasts for years; productive forces and products are wasted and destroyed wholesale, until the accumulated mass of commodities finally filter off, more or less depreciated in value, until production and exchange gradually begin to move again. Little by little the pace quickens. It becomes a trot. The industrial trot breaks into a canter, the canter in turn grows into a headlong gallop of a perfect steeplechase of industry, commercial credit, and speculation, which finally, after breakneck leaps, ends where it began — in the ditch of a crisis. And so over and over again. We have now, since the year 1825, gone through this five times, and at the present moment (1877) we are going through it for the sixth time. And the character of these crises is so clearly defined that Fourier hit all of them off, when he described the first as '*crise pléthorique*,' — a crisis from plethora."

These industrial paralyses forced the attention of the capitalists to the dangers of unrestricted competition. It was a new kind of warfare in which capitalists destroyed each other in commercial and industrial battles. At times, the whole nation stood amazed in the face of these appalling crises. With no lack of natural opportunities or resources, with no adverse natural conditions, with superb machines and great factories, with an earnest and laborious working-class, the empty factories and silent machines facing millions of unemployed and starving men, proved above all the necessity of ending the competitive warfare. Thus competition gradually gave way to monopoly. One capitalist, it is said, destroys many, and the smaller were eaten up by the larger, until to-day in all the great countries many of the most important industries have been combined into trusts. The very conditions of modern life forced it; the crises, the panics, the bankruptcies, the fearful periodic disturbances of economic life.

Out of this anarchy of industry developed great organizations of capital, and with them there appeared a new class. In the early days the capitalists were mainly skilled workmen or managers possessing a small amount of capital, or in a position to borrow capital. They were often the hardest and most capable workers; but with the new organization of industry, and especially with the enormous increase of wealth, the capitalist became more and more divorced from actual manage-

M

ment, and more and more merely the owner of stocks and bonds. With each generation this evolution is more marked, and as the property leaves the hands of the old captains of industry it passes into the hands of sons and relatives who do not themselves actively participate in industrial operations. A new class begins to emerge, similar in many respects to the privileged classes of the old feudal régime, and more and more it becomes true that from the moment when you become a proprietor of land, of houses, or of the machinery of production, you may, as Henry George says, " sit down and smoke your pipe ; you may lie about like the lazzaroni of Naples or the lepers of Mexico ; you may go up in a balloon or dig a hole in the ground, and all the time, without any act of yours, the rent of the house and farm, and the interest on your other capital, will keep dropping steadily into your hands."

On this industrial history of the last century the socialist program is based. In the Communist Manifesto, published in 1848, Marx gives a masterly survey of the industrial revolution then reaching its culmination in a society dominated by capitalism. He gives full credit to the vast accomplishments of the new order when he says that during its rule of scarce a hundred years it " has created more massive and colossal productive forces than all the preceding generations together. Subjection of Nature's forces to man, machinery, application of chemistry to industry and agriculture, steam navigation, railways, electric telegraphs, clearing of whole continents for cultivation, canalization of rivers, whole populations conjured out of the ground — what earlier century had even a presentiment that such productive forces slumbered in the lap of social labor?"

At the same time Marx points out that modern society, which has conjured up such gigantic means of
production and of exchange, is like the sorcerer who is
no longer able to control the powers of the nether
world which he has evoked by his spells. Like the
prince in the fable, another writer has said,* capitalism
seems to have released from his prison the genie of
competition, only to find that he is unable to control
him. The poor, the drunk, the incompetent, the sick,
the aged, ride modern society like a nightmare, and the
legislation of the past hundred years is a perpetual and
fruitless effort to regulate the disorders of the economic
system.

In the midst of this chaos Marx saw that a new class
was being formed, the modern wage-workers, which was
performing all the important industrial functions, while
the capitalists were becoming less and less important
to industry. From a purely scientific point of view it
was natural that the useful class should persist and the
useless class be thrown aside. At least it was incon-
gruous that the useful class should continue to be the
poorest class, and especially that it should be content
to suffer the insecurity of livelihood made inevitable
by the capitalist system. That men should consent to
be employed or unemployed at the caprice of a class
which produced for the sake of profit only, and which
stopped all production when the profits decreased, was
inconceivable. The machine having become a social
necessity must be owned socially. To have the machinery of production continue in the ownership of a
class that did not use it, and used by a class that did
not own it, was not only economically unsound, but so-

* " Letters from a Chinese Official."

cially intolerable. To Marx's mind it was certain that
the wage-workers, the producers, who bore the burdens of modern industry, would in time revolt against
the growing class of parasites who lived upon rents,
interests, profits, and other forms of unearned incomes.
As early as 1848 Marx described the tentative struggles
of the working-class against capitalism. "At first," he
says, "the contest is carried on by individual laborers,
then by the workpeople of a factory, then by the op-
eratives of one trade, in one locality, against the individual bourgeois who directly exploits them. They
direct their attacks not against the capitalist conditions
of production, but against the instruments of production themselves; they destroy imported wares that
compete with their labor, they smash to pieces machinery, they set factories ablaze, they seek to restore
by force the vanished status of the workman of the
Middle Ages. At this stage the laborers still form
an incoherent mass scattered over the whole country,
and broken up by their mutual competition.

"With the development of industry," he goes on to
say, "the proletariat not only increases in number; it
becomes concentrated in greater masses; its strength
grows, and it feels that strength more. The various
interests and conditions of life within the ranks of the
proletariat are more and more equalized, in proportion
as machinery obliterates all distinctions of labor, and
nearly everywhere reduces wages to the same low level.
The growing competition among the capitalists, and
the resulting commercial crises, make the wages of
the workers ever more fluctuating. The unceasing
improvement of machinery, ever more rapidly developing, makes their livelihood more and more preca-

rious; the collisions between individual workmen and individual capitalists take more and more the character of collisions between two classes. . . . Now and then the workers are victorious, but only for a time. *The real fruit of their battles lies, not in the immediate result, but in the ever expanding union of the workers.*"

The fundamental cause of this class antagonism is the individual ownership of the means of production. To eliminate class strife, and to harmonize the interests of society, it is necessary to socialize these means of production. Marx, however, takes a very broad view of the evolutionary process which will end by constituting a new and social form of ownership of capital. He did not believe it would proceed in any foreordained way. In the program of the Social Democratic Party of Germany, which his disciples framed, there is no suggestion of national or municipal ownership. His view was far broader and more comprehensive, based as it was upon scientific and historical principles. First of all he advocated the organization of working men, of a nation within a nation, of the useful class against the useless class. He wanted the working-class to realize consciously their power and the historic rôle they must play in the evolution of industry. To teach the working-class self-reliance and self-respect, to educate them, and to organize them politically and economically in order that they should take into their own hands the administration of the state, are fundamental principles of Marxism. The measures by which socialism would be introduced must vary in different countries in relation to the political and social institutions of the country. Marx, therefore, did not prescribe definitely how the

capital essential to industry should be socialized. The
first and most important step toward that end was
the complete organization of the working-class on the
political and economic fields in order that they might
become conscious of their power, and in truth the
arbiters of their own destiny.

Toward this end all socialist parties are working.
The working-class is developing self-reliance, self-
respect, and political capacity. It has already, as I
have shown, its own press, its congresses or parliaments, national and international, that meet together
to discuss the program and tactics of the party, and
the methods of taking into its own hands modern industrial operations. Besides its political organization,
with its men in parliaments and municipal councils,
it has also organized in all lands its trade unions, which
also have a press, a literature, a program, and parliaments, national and international. In Belgium, England, and elsewhere, great coöperative enterprises are
conducted by the working-class; so that at present the
second largest commercial undertaking in England is
owned by the workers, and one of the largest in Belgium by the socialists. In other words, the movement
is forcing its way, politically, industrially, and commer-
cially, into power. Very much the same methods that
the capitalist class used in the old feudal régime the
rising working-class is using to undermine the principles, privileges, and power of the present order.

At the moment, some of the largest industries in the
world are managed and worked by *paid* presidents,
managers, superintendents, skilled and unskilled machine operators, and general laborers; that is to say,
by the working-class. It would be absurd to suppose

that the Vanderbilts are essential to the conduct of the New York Central Railroad, or that Mr. Astor is essential to the management of his landed property; and Mr. Rockefeller, it is said, confesses to "an ignorance of the affairs of his great concern which should cause his immediate removal by any sane board of directors." Whether the latter is true or not is not important. In the next generation the affairs of this gigantic enterprise will be largely managed by paid employees. The capitalists have organized industry so well that they have organized themselves out of it. They are in most instances no longer essential to it. This industrial evolution which has given to salaried men and wage-workers the management and superintendence of industry will only complete itself when the workers themselves own the capital. Little by little they gain force, and day by day become more fully conscious of their own power and the rôle they are to play in this evolution leading toward the socialization of industry.

This is briefly the historic and economic basis that forms the groundwork of the socialist contention. A similar résumé accompanies all the various national programs, either as a statement of principles, or an introduction to the immediate demands. One can take up the program of any one of the national parties, and find in all very much the same thought expressed. Where there exists a difference, it is not so much due to a critical attitude on the part of the socialists, as it is to the belief that local color will add to the effectiveness of the general statement. I have chosen to take as an example of these official programs the one adopted by the German party, because it has served as the basis of many others. It was the work of the closest friends and most enthusiastic disciples of Marx, and was almost a literal following out of his instructions. It, therefore, has exceptional value from a documentary point of view, and while it is heavy and rather technical, it has the advantage of being authoritative.

It will be seen that the German program epitomizes what I have already said, and it is in fact a condensation of the fundamental position of contemporary socialism. Most of the doctrines were first stated in the Communist Manifesto published in 1848. They were then adopted in 1869 as the basis of the first Social Democratic Labor Party in Germany; but in 1875, in order to achieve unity between the Lassallians and the Marxists the program was altered, and many ideas of Lassalle were accepted in the face of the very vigorous opposition of Marx. Finally, however, in 1891 the German congress revised its program, and adopted a thorough and comprehensive Marxian position. The thought of contemporary socialism has, therefore, remained almost unchanged for over half a century. There has been a good deal of criticism of its main doctrines. The progressive concentration of capital, which is the subject of the first and second paragraphs, has been severely criticised. The increasing misery of the masses has been denied, and the class struggle has been the subject of very lively debates both inside and outside the party. The great discussion which occurred between Kautsky and Bernstein a few years ago was really based upon a consideration of these doctrines of the party, but although the discussion created an immense interest outside of the party, the political organizations in every country have remained faithful to the older views, and there seems to be no disposition on the part of the masses to ask for a revision.

The Erfurt Social Democratic Program of October, 1891

The economic development of industrial society tends inevitably to the ruin of small industries, which are based upon the workman's private ownership of the means of production. It separates him from these means of production, and converts him into a destitute member of the proletariat, whilst a comparatively small number of capitalists and great landowners obtain a monopoly of the means of production.

Hand in hand with this growing monopoly goes the crushing out of existence of these shattered small industries by industries of colossal growth, the development of the tool into the machine, and a gigantic increase in the productiveness of human labor. But all the advantages of this revolution are monopolized by the capitalists and great landowners. To the proletariat and to the rapidly sinking middle classes, the small tradesmen of the towns, and the peasant proprietors, it brings an increasing uncertainty of existence, increasing misery, oppression, servitude, degradation, and exploitation.

Ever greater grows the mass of the proletariat, ever vaster the army of the unemployed, ever sharper the contrast between oppressors and oppressed, ever fiercer that war of classes between bourgeoisie and proletariat which divides modern society into two hostile camps, and is the common characteristic of every industrial country. The gulf between the propertied classes and the destitute is widened by the crises arising from capitalist production, which becomes daily more comprehensive and omnipotent, which makes universal uncertainty the normal condition of society, and which furnishes a proof that the forces of production have outgrown the existing social order, and that private ownership of the means of production has become incompatible with their full development and their proper application.

Private ownership of the means of production, formerly the

means of securing his product to the producer, has now become the means of expropriating the peasant proprietors, the artisans, and the small tradesmen, and placing the non-producers, the capitalists, and large landowners in possession of the products of labor. Nothing but the conversion of capitalist private ownership of the means of production — the earth and its fruits, mines, and quarries, raw material, tools, machines, means of exchange — into social ownership, and the substitution of socialist production, carried on by and for society in the place of the present production of commodities for exchange, can effect such a revolution, that, instead of large industries and the steadily growing capacities of common production being, as hitherto, a source of misery and oppression to the classes whom they have despoiled, they may become a source of the highest well-being and of the most perfect and comprehensive harmony.

This social revolution involves the emancipation, not merely of the proletariat, but of the whole human race, which is suffering under existing conditions. But this emancipation can be achieved by the working-class alone, because all other classes, in spite of their mutual strife of interests, take their stand upon the principle of private ownership of the means of production, and have a common interest in maintaining the existing social order.

The struggle of the working-classes against capitalist exploitation must of necessity be a political struggle. The working-classes can neither carry on their economic struggle nor develop their economic organization without political rights. They cannot effect the transfer of the means of production to the community without being first invested with political power.

It must be the aim of social democracy to give conscious unanimity to this struggle of the working-classes, and to indicate the inevitable goal.

The interests of the working-classes are identical in all lands governed by capitalist methods of production. The extension of the world's commerce and production for the world's markets make the position of the workman in any one country daily more dependent upon that of the workman in other countries. Therefore, the emancipation of labor is a task in which the workmen of all civilized lands have a share. Recognizing this, the Social Democrats of Germany feel and declare themselves at one with the workmen of every land, who are conscious of the destinies of their class.

The German Social Democrats are not, therefore, fighting for new class privileges and rights, but for the abolition of class government, and even of classes themselves, and for universal equality in rights and duties, without distinction of sex or rank. Holding these views, they are not merely fighting against the exploitation and oppression of the wage-earners in the existing social order, but against every kind of exploitation and oppression, whether directed against class, party, sex, or race.

Following the above general statement of principles come the immediate demands. I have not included these because they apply particularly to German conditions, and an American would gain from them little idea of what the socialists are trying to obtain in the way of specific reforms. Naturally these demands vary in each country according to the stage of political democracy, the advance in labor legislation, and the extent of social reform. In Germany autocratic institutions force the party to make demands which it is not necessary to make in England, and in America the party is forced to demand labor legislation which exists already in Germany. For this reason no one program conveys a complete idea of this phase of socialist activity. This objection applies with considerable force to the Belgian program, which I have thought advisable to use, but as it is in many ways the most perfect in structure and completeness that

I have happened to see, it will serve as a very useful guide to the reader.

POLITICAL PROGRAM OF THE BELGIAN LABOR PARTY

Electoral Reform. — Universal suffrage without distinction of sex for all ranks (age limit, twenty-one ; residence, six months) ; proportional representation ; election expenses to be charged on the public authorities ; payment of elected persons ; elected persons to be bound by pledges according to law ; electorates to have the right of unseating elected persons.

Decentralization of Political Power. — Suppression of the Senate ; creation of legislative councils, representing the different functions of society (industry, commerce, agriculture, education, etc.) ; such councils to be autonomous, within the limits of their competence, except from the veto of parliament ; and to be federated for the study and defence of their common interests.

Communal Autonomy. — Mayors to be nominated by the electorate ; small communes to be fused or federated ; creation of elected committees corresponding to the different branches of communal administration.

Direct Legislation. — Right of popular initiative and referendum in legislative, provincial, and communal matters.

Reform of Education. — Primary, all-round, free, secular, compulsory instruction at the expense of the state ; maintenance by public authorities of children attending the schools ; intermediate and higher instruction to be free, secular, and at the expense of the state ; assimilation of communal teachers to the state's educational officials ; creation of a superior council of education, elected by the school committees, who are to organize the inspection and control of free schools and of official schools ; organization of trade education, and obligation of all children to learn manual work ; autonomy of the state universities, and legal recognition of the free universities ; university extension to be organized at the expense of the public authorities.

Separation of the Churches and the State. — Suppression of the grant for public worship; philosophic or religious associations to be civil persons at law.

Revision of Sections in the Civil Code concerning Marriage and the Paternal Authority. — Civil equality of the sexes, and of children, whether legitimate or illegitimate; revision of the divorce laws, maintaining the husband's liability to support the wife or the children; inquiry into paternity to be legalized; protective measures in favor of children materially or morally abandoned.

Judicial Reform. — Application of the elective principle to all jurisdictions; reduction of the number of magistrates; justice without fees; state payment of advocates and officials of the courts; magisterial examination in penal cases to be public; persons prosecuted to be medically examined; victims of judicial errors to be indemnified.

Extension of Liberties. — Suppression of measures restricting any of the liberties.

Suppression of Armies. — Organization provisionally of national militia.

Suppression of hereditary offices, and establishment of a republic.

ECONOMIC PROGRAM. — GENERAL MEASURES

Organization of Statistics. — Creation of a ministry of labor; pecuniary aid from the public authorities for the organization of labor secretariats by workmen and employers.

Legal Recognition of Associations. — Especially of trade unions; reform of the law on friendly societies and coöperative societies, and subsidies from the public authorities; repression of infringements of the right of combination.

Legal Regulation of the Contract of Employment. — Extension to all industries of laws protecting labor, and especially to agriculture, shipping, and fishing; fixing of a minimum wage and maximum of hours of labor for workers, industrial or agricultural, employed by the state, the communes, the provinces, or the contractors for public works; intervention of workers, and especially of workers' unions, in the framing of rules; suppression of fines, suppression of workshop savings-banks and benefit clubs; fixing a maximum of 6000 francs for public servants and managers.

Transformation of Public Charity into a General Insurance of all Citizens. — Against unemployment; against disablement (sickness, accident, old age); against death (widows and orphans).

Reorganization of Public Finances. — Abolition of indirect taxes, especially taxes on food and customs tariffs; monopoly of alcohol and tobacco; progressive income tax; taxes on legacies and gifts between the living (excepting gifts to works of public utility); suppression of intestate succession, except in the direct line and within limits to be determined by the law.

Progressive Extension of Public Property. — The state to take over the National Bank; social organization of loans, at interest to cover costs only, to individuals and to associations of workers; abolition on grounds of public utility, of private ownership in mines, quarries, the subsoil generally, and of the great means of production and transport; nationalization of forests; reconstitution or development of common lands; progressive taking over of the land by the state or the communes.

Autonomy of Public Services. — Administration of the public services by special autonomous commissions, under the control of the state; creation of committees elected by the employees of the public services to discuss with the central administration the conditions of the remuneration and organization of labor.

Particular Measures for Industrial Workers: —

Abolition of all laws restricting the right of combination.

Regulation of Industrial Labor. — Prohibition of employment of children under fourteen; half-time system between the ages of fourteen and eighteen; prohibition of employment of women in all industries where it is incompatible with morals or health; reduction of working-day to a maximum of eight hours for adults of both sexes, minimum wage; prohibition of night-work for all categories of workers and in all industries, where this mode of working is not absolutely necessary; one day's rest per week, so far as possible on Sunday; responsibility of employers in case of accidents, and appointment of doctors to attend persons injured; workmen's memorandum books and certificates to be abolished, and their use prohibited.

Inspection of Work. — Employment of paid medical authorities, in the interests of labor hygiene; appointment of inspectors by the councils of industry and labor.

Reorganization of the Industrial Tribunals and the Councils of Industry and Labor. — Working women to have votes and be eligible; submission to the courts to be compulsory.

Regulation of work in prisons and convents.

Particular Measures for Agricultural Workers: —

Reorganization of the Agricultural Courts. — Nomination of delegates in equal numbers by the landowners, farmers, and laborers; intervention of the chambers in individual or collective disputes between landowners, farmers, and agricultural laborers; fixing of a minimum wage by the public authorities on the proposition of the agricultural courts.

Regulation of Contracts to pay Farm Rents. — Fixing of the rate of farm rents by committees of arbitration or by the reformed agricultural courts; compensation to the outgoing farmer for enhanced value of property; participation of landowners to a wider extent than that fixed by the Civil Code, in losses incurred by farmers; suppression of the landowners' privilege.

Insurance by the provinces, and reinsurance by the state,

against epizoötic diseases, diseases of plants, hail, floods, and other agricultural risks.

Organization by the Public Authorities of Free Agricultural Education. — Creation or development of experimental fields, model farms, agricultural laboratories.

Purchase by the commune of agricultural implements to be at the disposal of their inhabitants ; assignment of common lands to groups of laborers engaging not to employ wage-labor.

Organization of a free medical service in the country.

Reform of the Game Laws. — Suppression of gun licenses ; suppression of game preserves ; right of cultivators to destroy all the year round animals which injure crops.

Intervention of Public Authorities in the Creation of Agricultural Coöperative Societies. — For buying seed and manure ; for making butter ; for the purchase and use in common of agricultural machines ; for the sale of produce ; for the working of land by groups.

Organization of agricultural credit.

COMMUNAL PROGRAM

Educational Reforms. — Free scientific instruction for children up to fourteen ; special courses for older children and adults ; organization of education in trades and industries, in coöperation with workmen's organizations ; maintenance of children, except where the state intervenes to do so ; institution of school refreshment rooms ; periodic distribution of boots and clothing ; orphanages ; establishments for children abandoned or cruelly ill-treated.

Judicial Reforms. — Office for consultations free of charge in cases coming before the law-courts, the industrial courts, etc.

Regulation of Work. — Minimum wage and maximum working day to be made a clause in contracts for communal works ; intervention of trade associations in the fixing of rates of wages, and general regulation of industry ; the *echevin* of public works to supervise the execution of these clauses in contracts ; appointment by the workmen's associations of inspectors to supervise the clauses in contracts ; rigorous application of the principle of tenders open to all, for all services which, during a transition period, are not managed directly ; permission to trade unions to tender, and abolition of security-deposit ; creation of *Bourses du Travail*, or at least offices for the demand and supply of employment, whose administration shall be entrusted to trade unions or labor associations ; fixing of a minimum wage for the workmen and employees of a commune.

Public Charity. — Admission of workmen to the administration of the councils of hospitals and of public charity ; transformation of public charity and the hospitals into a system of insurance against old age ; organization of a medical service and drug supply ; establishment of public free baths and washhouses ; establishment of refuges for the aged and disabled ; night-shelter and food-distribution for workmen wandering in search of work.

Complete neutrality of all communal services from the philosophical point of view.

Finance. — Saving to be effected on present cost of administration ; maximum allowance of 6000 francs for mayors and other officials ; costs of entertainment for mayors who must incur certain private expenses ; income-tax ; special tax on sites not built over and houses not let.

Public Services. — The commune or a federation of communes composing one agglomeration, to work the means of transport, tramways, omnibuses, cabs, district railways, etc. ; and to work directly the services of general interest at present conceded to companies, lighting, water-supply, markets, highways, heating, security, health ; compulsory insurance of the inhabitants against fire, except where the state intervenes to do so ; construction of cheap dwellings by the commune, the hospices, and the charity offices.

N

CHAPTER VII

SOCIALISM AND SOCIAL REFORM

IT is difficult nowadays for socialists to keep the details of their immediate program in advance of legislation. For more than a half century socialist and labor programs advocated the abolition of child labor without finding any considerable sympathetic response on the part of the general public. Only a few years ago a child-labor law was considered an unwarrantable interference with the free conduct of capitalist enterprise. To-day the legislation in some countries is in advance of the specific demand made by one or two of the socialist parties. There was a time when the socialists alone advocated national and municipal ownership of public utilities; to-day it is advocated by all the more advanced parties. A few years ago land municipalization would have been hailed as a revolution of the first order. To-day there are few municipalities in Europe that do not see the necessity for radical reform in the ownership of land if slums are to be abolished. There are various causes for this extraordinary change in public policy, but few will deny that the credit for it belongs mainly to the growing socialist movement.

The old parties quite naturally combat the intrusion of the new ideas. When the socialists in the legislative bodies endeavor to carry out their program, their measures are bitterly assailed by the opposition; but the socialists use such opportunities to review the evils of existing conditions and the necessity for reform, with the result that the community becomes aroused. The opposition, who first attack a socialist measure as criminal and vicious, then as well-intentioned but impractical, finally, after as much delay as possible, reintroduce the measure in as weak a form as they dare submit it, and pass it as a great and virtuous public act. It is not, I think, an exaggeration to state that on the continent of Europe, this is the legislative history of most of the important measures in the interest of labor passed during the last twenty years. The socialists are rarely permitted to pass legislation, but in the way described they are really the directing force in nearly all the continental legislative bodies. In other words, the old parties are gradually being forced to follow the line of the immediate demands of the socialist program.

But quite aside from this influence over the course of legislation the socialists are doing a notable work in gradually breaking down that ancient and honorable form of political corruption which is inherent in class government. The patriotic citizens of foreign countries will tell you that corruption does not exist, and one must admit that there is a difference in the corruption abroad and that which obtains with us. Legislators are rarely bought. But then it is unnecessary, as in most cases the "traction magnates," the "gas thieves," etc., — as we are disposed to call them, — where there are any left, are themselves members of legislative bodies. It is obviously unnecessary to buy themselves. The difference between corruption there and here is that we elect Tim Sullivan, Hinky Dink, and Johnny Powers to our municipal councils.   No power on earth could induce us to elect Thomas F. Ryan, August Belmont, or Yerkes.   But unfortunately Ryan and his friends have as their personal representatives Sullivan and his friends, and the latter turn us — the people and "our" government — over to their corporate masters.   Nothing like that is to be found in England or on the continent.   It would be impossible to induce the people of those countries to vote for their Sullivans; they elect their Ryans.   A prominent socialist in the Berlin municipal council told me recently that the greatest difficulty they meet with in their efforts to deal with the traction monopoly arises from the fact that several directors of the company are on the council. Nothing, therefore, can be done without the traction monopoly knowing instantly the facts.   Something of that sort exists nearly everywhere in Europe; the vested interests represent themselves.

It is corruption, but it is a higher type of corruption, unaccompanied by all the inelegant features associated with American politics.   One must admit it is also a preferable form, as it exists in the open.   It is not always easy for the public to know that Sullivan, Hinky Dink, and Johnny Powers, or the thousands like them without their notoriety, represent purely private interests and not the interests of their constituents.   Abroad it becomes clearer, day by day, that the nominees of the vested interests represent those interests.

As a result, the workers in Europe are beginning to send to the municipal councils and to parliament their own representatives, and we find the conflict between the workers and the capitalists sharply defined.   I saw it once strikingly illustrated during a parliamentary de-

bate upon a bill for compensating workmen injured in
the mining industry. A socialist miner, pleading for
more liberal compensation, had delivered a terrible
arraignment of the conduct of the industry. When he
sat down, another member arose. He said he was a mine-
owner, and would like to give notice that he would
answer "the honorable gentleman" on the following
day. In this instance, the miner, representing the
working people, and the mine-owner, representing the
capital employed, stood face to face before the country
in a debate upon the conditions prevailing in that
industry.

This was a dramatic instance of what is occurring
throughout all Europe, as a result of the participation
in politics of independent working men's parties. Class
government, which seemed at first only strengthened
by the extension of the suffrage, is breaking down.
The workers are learning that it avails nothing to vote
the conservatives out and the radicals in, or vice versa.
In either case the upper class remains in complete
control. Only a few years ago the situation in Europe
was almost as bad as it is with us, and we seem unable
to uproot our corruption, to prevent our insurance
scandals, and to eliminate corporation control of our
political parties. In Europe exposures of a similar
character would now destroy any political party involved. The socialists of Italy, for instance, did not
face conditions quite as black as ours, and yet they so
effectually followed up exposures of corruption that
many prominent persons were driven from public life.
The power to accomplish this remarkable work resides
in this independent political movement, this party of the
workers now forcing its way into power. In the face

of its criticism the old order dare not press the kind of class legislation which was so common a few decades ago. It dreads the criticism of the new party, which appears as the expression of the exploited and disinherited, produced largely by the iniquitous legislation of the past. It realizes that any serious blunders on its part, any corruption, any favors to private interests, means the strengthening of this active and subversive group of socialists.

The influence of the socialist party is even more clearly shown by the manner in which it obtains the enforcement of law. It is an old political game to pass laws not intended to be enforced. Having control of the executive as well as the legislative departments of government, the parties in power sometimes find this the easiest way to defeat popular clamor. But even this undignified course is impossible where the socialist party is active. The socialists realize that if present laws were only enforced, they would considerably improve existing conditions. In the German municipalities and elsewhere they taunt the parties in power with the squalor, the vile tenements, the high death-rates, the adulterated food, and the other evils resulting in part from a lax administration. The effectiveness of these stings cannot be overestimated, and one of the most striking changes of the last few years is the increase in efficiency of the municipal administration in the continental cities. In three ways, therefore, the socialist movement exercises an important influence upon European political policy : first, upon legislation itself ; second, in making almost impossible the older form of political corruption residing in class rule ; and third, in compelling the enforcement of existing laws.

Socialism does not set out to occupy itself merely
with political reforms.   It is based upon economic
principles, which emphasize the necessity for industrial
reconstruction.   But one insurmountable political obstacle stands in the way of its advancement as a party.   In
many countries the suffrage is so restricted that it gives
the propertied classes a position of advantage.   A fundamental political demand, therefore, upon which all
socialists agree, is universal and equal suffrage without
distinction of sex.   In Belgium during the last twenty
years enormous pressure has been exercised upon the
government to force it to grant this political right.
Deprived of other means of expressing their will, the
people have had to resort to general strikes and even
to riots.   Several times the electoral law has been
altered, but the governing classes in Belgium fear to
grant universal and equal suffrage, as the growing popularity of the socialists would then make probable their
early advent to power.   Other European governments
face a similar situation, and it becomes increasingly
difficult to obtain universal suffrage.   The danger to
the present order is illustrated by two recent events.
In Austria, after a series of general strikes, and a period
of threatening agitation, universal manhood suffrage
was granted, and the socialists instantly increased their
parliamentary representation from 11 to 87 members.
In Finland the social democratic agitation was even
more successful, and women were admitted along with
men to the right of suffrage.   At the first election
under the new law 80 socialists were sent to parliament,
of whom nine were women.   Coincident with this desperate struggle to win universal suffrage an effort is being
made to obtain the referendum and initiative, and in

many countries the old parties have been forced in self-protection to establish proportional representation. That it should be left to the socialists alone to fight these battles of political democracy shows to what extent the old liberal parties, whose glory it once was to widen the suffrage, have degenerated since they came into power.

In the field of public finance a graduated income tax, and the abolition of all indirect taxes, customs, and other politico-economic measures, which sacrifice the interests of the whole community to the interests of a favored minority, are demanded in all socialist programs. The Germans ask for an obligatory graduated tax upon inheritance, and the Belgian party seeks the suppression of intestate succession except in the direct line. The English Independent Labor Party stands for the gradual transference of all political burdens to unearned incomes, and the Italian party advocates the taxation of unearned increment from land. England and Germany already have an income-tax, and France is at present in the midst of drafting important legislation in the same field. The present legislation, however, does not satisfy the socialists, as it is their avowed purpose to shift the entire burden of taxation on to unearned incomes. The enormous budgets of the European countries, made necessary in part by stupendous annual expenditures for naval and military purposes, have forced the governments to place a part of this heavy burden upon the wealthier classes; but the burden upon the workers is nevertheless crushing. Consequently the socialists are exercising their utmost power in every country to relieve the workers by shifting these taxes upon those classes for whose benefit naval and military expenses are incurred.

The German cities have taken an important advance step in the taxation of unearned increment arising from the sale and transfer of land. The object is to absorb the profits of the speculator. On every change in ownership an increasing tax is placed in a shifting scale in relation to the selling price. The introduction of the new rating forced the Breslau speculators in land to pay in 1900 an increased taxation of $76,250. Frankfurt was the first town to undertake legislation in this direction, and the socialists in all parts of Germany are pressing measures of a similar character. In Berlin they recently introduced an extreme measure, and while it met with defeat, it will doubtless in a year or so be presented in modified form and passed by one of the conservative parties. Many of the German Town Councils also rate unimproved land on the amount for which it could be sold. Crefeld, Breslau, Aachen, Düsseldorf, Elberfeld, Charlottenberg, Kiel, Wiesbaden, and other towns have already adopted the new method and all German towns are urged by the Prime Minister to follow their example. These new forms of land taxation have not yet been sufficiently developed in Germany to show very important results; but under socialist pressure they are certain to be gradually extended until the cities will absorb the entire unearned increment arising from land. So much for the attitude of the socialists in the field of public finance.

A most important change has taken place of recent years in European political thought concerning factory legislation. The old ideas of *laissez faire*, which are still potent in America, are rapidly being abandoned on the other side of the Atlantic. During the last twenty years there has been a steady growth of state intervention, until now there are laws regulating almost every phase of the competitive system. The relation between labor and capital, the conduct of factories, mines, and other industrial enterprises, and the sanitary condition of tenements and workshops are more and more regulated by law. The old political principles allowed complete freedom of contract, neglecting to make any provision for the necessary basis of equality in condition. State intervention is a tardy and indeed vain effort to equalize conditions and to put labor upon an equal footing with capital.

The socialists in forcing labor legislation work as the direct representatives in parliament of the trade-union movement. They are constantly agitating for laws giving greater freedom of action to the unions. Even before the organization of their political parties, the working-class had gained in most countries the right to unite and the right to strike. In some countries the right of peaceful picketing is now guaranteed to the workers. Usually this is a result of an administrative measure, but the English parliament, during its last session, specifically granted the right in the Trades Disputes Bill. Injunctions are rarely used in Europe against labor organizations; but in case any court should be unwise enough to grant one, it would seldom be sustained. In some countries the use of the army and police against strikers is still common, and of course in all demonstrable instances of violence the intervention of the authorities is certain. Nothing, however, in Europe compares with the use commonly made of the army in America, and it is doubtful if anywhere else employers would be permitted to hire "Pinkertons"

to shoot down or to intimidate starving workmen.   As
a matter of fact, things have changed greatly in most
European countries during recent years.   The socialist
municipalities of Italy and France sometimes supply
strikers with food and shelter, and in all cases they
see that the children are cared for.   In these instances
the old order is completely reversed, and instead of
the employer being given governmental aid to break
strikes and to crush the workmen, the men are rendered
assistance to the extent sometimes of direct contributions to their funds.   The French chamber itself has
many times, after the conclusion of a strike, voted
financial aid to the families of the working men.

It is impossible to give an adequate review of the
progress of factory legislation.   As I have said before, there was practically no such legislation in Belgium previous to the formation of the Labor Party.
The reader will have observed in its program, that
among other things it demands the prohibition of the
employment of children under 14; a half-time system,
that is to say, half a day at work and half in school,
for workers between the ages of 14 and 18; the prohibition of the employment of women in all industries
where it is incompatible with morals or health; the
reduction of the working day to a maximum of eight
hours for adults of both sexes; a minimum wage; the
prohibition of night-work for all categories of workers
in all industries where this mode of working is not
absolutely necessary; one day's rest per week, so far
as possible on Sunday; responsibility of employers in
case of accidents; and the appointment of doctors to
attend persons injured; the employment of medical
authorities to work in the interests of factory hygiene,

and the appointment of all inspectors by joint committees of employers and employed. Some of the other national programs advocate more stringent measures, and the Fabians demand for women workers that for equal work they should receive equal pay with men. Nearly all the programs demand a general compulsory insurance of citizens against unemployment, disablement, and death. The Fabian program also advocates the eight-hour day, the prohibition of the employment of children under 16, the undertaking of useful public works in special cases, and a general extension of governmental ownership of industrial operations: all for the purpose of doing away with unemployment. As a result of constant pressure exercised by the socialists every country in Europe has sensibly increased, and in some cases initiated, legislation protecting workmen against insanitary conditions, dangerous trades, and other evils incident to industry which undermine the health and vitality of the working-class. France is one of the first countries to establish *le repos hebdomadaire* — one day's rest in seven.

Perhaps the most important legislation that has been passed in the interest of labor is the compulsory insurance of working men, now spreading all over Europe. It is mainly an effort to render tolerable the present economic system, and to give to the working-class some security in life. The German empire was the first country to realize the widespread discontent of the workers which resulted from their uncertainty of livelihood. England and America still persist in throwing upon the poor law, and degrading to the position of paupers, the aged, the sick, and the unem-

ployed, as well as the families of those who have sacrificed their lives to industry. In Germany, where the
insurance system is best developed, every employee
receiving less than $500 a year in wages must be in-
sured against accident, sickness, invalidism, and old age.
Practically every workman in the German empire is,
therefore, assured of an economic existence, when he
is unable to continue at work. One no longer finds
broken-down workmen, suffering from tuberculosis,
chronic rheumatism, or other forms of invalidism, or
maimed and injured so as to be incapable of further
labor, or weary and exhausted veterans, still forced to
maintain a tragic and futile struggle to earn the necessaries of life. To all these unfortunates, pensions
are granted at a cost of over $100,000,000 a year. In
Austria, insurance against accidents, sickness, and old
age is obligatory for practically the entire laboring
population. Compulsory insurance has also gained a
foothold in France and Roumania, while for fifty years
there has been a system in Belgium of miners' insurance which is practically compulsory upon mine-own-
ers. The best examples of state voluntary insurance
are found in France, Belgium, and Italy. The first
country has had in existence for many years three independent departments for accidents, old age and
invalidism, and death. Belgium has a similar institution for old-age insurance, while Italy has established
a national bank for insurance against accidents. The
English employer is now forced by the Workmen's
Compensation Act to indemnify injured workmen, a
more complete form of the law having been recently
passed under pressure from the Labor Party.

The system of governmental insurance, however,

does not include insurance against unemployment. There is a scheme for pensioning the unemployed, which was started a few years ago in Ghent, and is gradually being adopted by other cities throughout Europe. The working method is for the unions to establish an insurance fund against unemployment, to which every member subscribes a certain sum weekly or monthly ; and for every dollar contributed by the workmen an equal sum is usually contributed by the municipality. The unions, being financially responsible to the same extent as the municipalities, undertake to see that no idlers shall be supported from the funds. In this way society is beginning to assume a part of its responsibility for unemployment, instead of throwing the burden entirely upon the workmen. In nearly all the socialist municipalities of France a similar system has been developed, and the French chamber recently acknowledged the principle of society's responsibility for unemployment, by making a subvention to these funds.

A step in advance of governmental regulation and even of governmental insurance is national and municipal ownership. It is unfortunate that no general figures exist giving the extent of public property, but in every country in Europe during the last twenty years there has been an astonishing growth of state socialism. Many countries have nationalized the railways, and there is a growing tendency to own nationally all the great natural resources, such as coal and iron mines, etc. Switzerland is considering a proposition to keep under national control the immense power which lies in her mountain streams. There is a possibility that Great Britain will nationalize the railroads in Ireland, and there is considerable agitation for the nationalization of all British railways. Public enterprise is, of course, most extensive in the cities. Hardly a franchise expires in any European city that is not immediately taken up by the municipality. In many places no new franchises are granted to private companies, and little by little all public services are coming into the hands of the government.

In Great Britain this movement has taken on an enormous development, so that now most of the municipalities own the water, gas, and electrical supplies, trams, baths, wash-houses, libraries, and of course the public schools, parks, playgrounds, etc. Many of the cities have entered the field of municipal housing, and some have undertaken to demolish large areas of slums, replacing them by municipally owned tenements. For many years past a number of cities have had a municipal telephone service, and the national post-office has recently made arrangements looking to the nationalization of all telephones as soon as the existing licenses expire, expecting a complete national ownership by 1911. Some of the cities have also instituted municipal slaughter-houses and sterilized milk-supplies. Nearly everywhere there has also been a great extension of municipal institutions for the intellectual development of the community, such as museums, art galleries, and libraries; and for the physical development, such as parks, playgrounds, and recreation fields.

One of the strongest influences in the recent growth of this enlightened public policy throughout England is the work of the Fabian Society and similar bodies, whose members have carried on an extraordinary propaganda and have constantly urged their practical municipal program. The Independent Labor Party in the provinces has exerted a powerful influence in the same direction, and upon nearly all the councils in the industrial districts the fighting has been led by its representatives. It cannot, however, be said that British municipal socialism is the result of an organized and threatening movement of the workers. For this reason many of the reforms have been more for the benefit of the entire community than for the working-class in particular. Certain collectivist ideas appeal to all, as for instance the municipalization of such public services as are essential to the comfort of all. It is possible for a city to own practically all of these public services without greatly improving the life of the masses. The pressure for reform has come mainly from the middle class instead of from a politically organized working-class, and the difference between the results obtained in England and those obtained on the continent by the socialist parties is the English slums, the most abominable of Europe.

In the continental countries the trend toward municipal socialism is, on the other hand, mainly the result of an organized working-class movement. Certainly the infiltration of socialist ideas throughout all classes of the community, and the labors of that considerable class who now call themselves state socialists, have not been without effect; but the influence of the latter is often limited to forms of collectivism which do not always directly benefit the poor, while the socialist party itself has forced a whole series of measures materially ameliorating the condition of the workers. It is actually in control of a large number of cities, and there is hardly a municipal council without its representatives. In France the party elects the mayors of over a hundred cities, and in Belgium and Italy it controls some of the most important of the secondary municipalities. But unfortunately in these countries there is a highly centralized government which prevents the socialists from carrying out their ideas, and often forces them to grant to private interests the conduct of public utilities. Although they have fought valiantly for increased power, it has thus far availed little. Here and there they have established municipal pharmacies, new and improved hospitals, and nearly everywhere they have a sufficiently free hand to establish school restaurants for the feeding of the children.

Curiously enough, the most important results of the socialist movement are to be found in Germany. In France, Belgium, and Italy their electoral strength places them in possession of the municipal government, but the centralized powers prevent them from carrying out their policies. In Prussia the law does not permit them to control a municipality, but they can and do direct its policies. The electoral law provides that the non-propertied classes shall only elect one-third of the municipal council. In nearly every city the socialists elect the full third, and in many industrial cities their vote is larger than that of all other parties. The moral power which this electoral strength gives to the socialist minority enables it to exercise enormous pressure upon German municipal policy. The position of the socialists may be merely that of critics, but their activity in placing before the councils measures for the improvement of the conditions of the workers, the sanitary renovation of the poorer quarters, the building of model tenements, the municipalizing of public utilities, and countless other measures for municipal improvement, make them a source of perpetual irritation to the old parties. They drive the conservative majorities to more and more extreme measures, until Germany has now the most enlightened municipal policy in Europe. Twenty years ago her slums were notorious. There was hardly a great city which did not have conditions rivalling those still prevalent throughout Great Britain. To-day there is hardly a poor district in Germany that can justly be called a slum.

The German cities have developed municipal ownership to a greater extent than perhaps any other cities of Europe, and in addition they have for years pursued a policy of extensive land ownership. Since 1890 Cologne has increased its public land by over 1000 per cent, Chemnitz by over 600 per cent, Munich by over 300 per cent, and so forth. Strasbourg has over 350 square yards of land for each inhabitant. The town of Ulm owns over 80 per cent of the land within its boundaries. It buys and leases land daily, and by its power as landowner it prevents all land speculation. It is now the general policy of all German towns not to sell any land.

To review the extent of municipal enterprise at present would exhaust the pages of a very large book, and it is only possible to mention its increasing development in the above general way. It is unnecessary to say that national and municipal ownership is advocated in nearly all socialist programs, but even where it is not a formulated demand, the socialist parties have usually supported any effort in this direction. They, however, place greater emphasis upon those forms of municipal or national ownership which tend definitely to relieve or abolish the exploitation of the workers. Among the first measures they press are those for municipal housing, and the control of the food, clothing, and fuel supplies. It is their primary effort to take the necessaries of life out of the field of capitalist exploitation. But even where municipal or national ownership is gained, they do not consider their end attained. Nearly all socialists would agree with Wilhelm Liebknecht, who said, "The state when it assumes control in place of the private entrepreneur carries on the capitalist exploitation exactly as the private entrepreneur. It can in fact exercise yet greater oppression." This leads the socialists to make strenuous efforts to obtain better hours, wages, and conditions for government employees. The London County Council have endeavored to follow out this socialist policy, and in all public work they have established among other things the eight-hour day, trade union wages, one day's rest in seven, and the employment by the municipality direct of all classes of workmen engaged upon public works. In many German cities like conditions have been established, and wherever the socialists have been in control, in France, Italy, or Belgium, a similar program has been put into operation.

It was pointed out a moment ago that the centralized government of France prevents the socialists from carrying out a general policy of municipalization. It may be interesting, therefore, to mention some of the work they have been able to accomplish. It is sometimes said that socialism will destroy the home, and some of its opponents have been unscrupulous enough to attack socialists as advocates of free love. In answer to such accusations perhaps nothing could be more conclusive than what the socialists actually do when they come into power. It is known that illegitimacy is common in France, especially among the poorest people. To what extent it is due to poverty, and the inability of the poorest workmen to pay fees for the marriage service, is not known; but when the socialists came into control of the city of Lille, they established a free marriage service, the fees to the pastor being paid directly by the municipality. Thousands of marriages have been sanctioned under this new act, and a great number of children who would otherwise have been classed as illegitimate are now legalized. The work of the socialists in the same city is sufficient to answer the other accusation.

It is a theory that socialism will destroy the home; it is a fact that for millions of the poor capitalism *has* destroyed the home. Go through any great centre of industry, and see the mothers who are forced to give their children to the street and themselves to the factory. Literally speaking, millions of women, how many with children one cannot say, leave their homes at dawn, and return to them only at nightfall. Some of them hardly have time to give birth to their babies before they are called back to the mills. These facts make little impression upon those who are not working people; but can any one really think for a moment that the poor suffer without complaint this destruction of home life? Can any one believe that when the mothers and fathers rise in the morning before dawn, and leave their children to the care of an older child or upon the streets, and go themselves to toil for ten, twelve, or fourteen hours in the factory, they are without feeling in the matter? If that is the impression, the pathetic efforts of these French working men when they come into power are a sufficient answer. Amidst the greatest imaginable difficulties they strive to retrieve something of the social advantages lost to them through the industrial revolution. They establish public kitchens so that soups, meats, and vegetables can be obtained warm when the people return from their work. They establish *crèches* for the babies of working mothers. The *cantine scolaire*, or school restaurant, is but another effort to reëstablish in some manner the social institutions lost by the destruction of the home. So long as the present system lasts, or at least so long as socialists remain in a minority, it is impossible for them to free from toil the mothers of their children. But they can save the babies from neglect, the children from the streets, and all from actual hunger. There are few workmen who would not, if they could, destroy all the *crèches* and *cantines scolaires* and *écoles maternelles*, if at the same time they could reëstablish the home and give back to the babies their mothers. This, however, being impossible, it will be a curious and perhaps interesting fact to the prosperous classes that, among the first things to which the socialists turn their attention when they become charged with the responsibility of municipal government are these very problems of the family and the home.

This is typical of the activity of the socialists in France, Italy, Germany, and Belgium, whenever they obtain control of a municipality. The feeding of the children in school restaurants is rapidly spreading throughout all Europe. Where the Italians have gained control, they have immediately established the system and in some cases in order that there shall be no distinction between poor and well-to-do children, attendance at school meals is made compulsory for all children. In Norway the municipalities provide a nutritious midday meal regardless of whether the children can pay or not, and this is also true of a number of Belgian cities. In France the children usually pay where possible, but no one knows which of the children pay and which do not.

Probably the most interesting development in the care of the children is that of the forest school near Berlin. The German cities, having generally provided school physicians, found a large percentage of the children of such delicate health that there was no likelihood of their growing into strong men and women. Bad food and insanitary homes, added to general tendencies, were producing a class of children who must in time become a burden upon the community. Merely as an experiment a forest school was established, to which several hundred children were sent. They are fed; nurses and doctors attend them; their lessons are given, as far as possible, in the open air; and every effort is made to build up a strong physical constitution. It has proved an amazingly successful experiment, and after a year or two of attendance practically all of the delicate children return to the ordinary schools in robust health. The food, the doctors, the nurses, and the medicine, as well as the teaching, are supplied at the expense of the community. Other similar schools are now being established, and it is reasonable to hope that within a few years they will have spread all over Germany, with the result that there will be few weak and delicate children at the end of the school period. The socialists of Lille have undertaken a somewhat similar experiment, and the municipal control of the milk-supply, which is now becoming general, is having an excellent effect upon the babies.

In line with these efforts to solve some of the problems of morals and health is the war upon alcoholism.
It is one of the most important problems that now
confront the socialist party. Aside from the purely
humanitarian motives which influence the socialists to
attack alcoholism, there is also a party motive. They
fully realize that one of the greatest enemies to the
propaganda of their ideas is drunkenness. In many of
the European countries almost the only strength remaining to the old political parties among the working-class
is the support of the shiftless and drunken elements
in the large towns and industrial centres. In Belgium
the socialists own a large number of club-houses or
Houses of the People, all of which are based upon extensive cafés patronized solely by the working-class.
Regardless of the financial loss entailed, alcoholic drinks
are no longer sold in many of these coöperatives,
and the Belgian party is gradually developing a definite
political policy against the entire drink traffic. One of
the most significant things that has recently happened
in Europe is the resolution against alcoholism passed at
the last German national congress. In Sweden and the
northern countries the socialists have used their influence to promote the Göthenburg system of controlling
the drink traffic. A law prohibiting all traffic in drink
was recently passed in Finland, although there is a
doubt whether the existence of certain international
fiscal treaties will not render it to a great extent inopera-
tive. The Fabians in London advocate the municipalization of the industry in order to abolish the private
interest in the making of drunkards. In Switzerland
the drink traffic has been nationalized. In Russia the
state monopoly of spirit retailing was established solely

for fiscal purposes and not to decrease drunkenness. The problem is a new one for the socialist movement, but nearly everywhere in Europe it is beginning with characteristic energy an active campaign against the liquor traffic, and using its tremendous moral power among the masses to combat alcoholism.

I shall not attempt here to give the attitude of the party upon militarism, the colonial question, and agriculture, — all questions of fundamental importance to the European movement. They are extremely complicated, and the party has not yet adopted a policy that may be considered final. Not only have the national congresses given serious consideration to these problems, but the several international gatherings have passed resolutions, trying to define the position of the movement. Thus far there has not been an agreement reached which meets the approval of all the national parties. But in passing over these difficult questions, there still remains one matter of too great importance to go without consideration, and that is the tactical attitude of the party toward social reform. Socialism is a movement for radical and revolutionary change in the constitution of society, and its policy in regard to reforms and ameliorations in the present order cannot be ignored.

There are two groups in the socialist movement which advocate different political tactics in regard to social reform. A few years ago there was no end of discussion within the organization, and the debates between the two groups became bitter, until finally the strife was brought to the attention of the outside world by a public controversy between Kautsky, "the Marxist," and Bernstein, "the Revisionist." The press heralded the discussion with sinister delight, and Bernstein became for a time an international figure. It was thought at first that the difference between the two tendencies was limited to Germany, but as the discussion progressed it was found that the party was divided in nearly every country into two camps — on the one hand, reformists, revisionists, moderates, possibilists, and ministerialists, as the opportunists are called; on the other, impossibilists, Marxists, and revolutionists. These various designations were often used in contempt, and in all the more important countries of Europe the two factions were struggling to impress upon the party a political tactic in accord with their own particular view.

I have already given the unhappy history of the schisms in the French party. In the very beginning there was a division between the possibilists and the impossibilists, and only a few years ago there occurred the critical and passionate struggle between Guesde and Jaurès. The English movement is divided on somewhat the same lines, the Fabians going to the most extreme limit of the reformist tactic, and the Social Democratic Federation going to the other extreme. In Germany the struggle between the two factions has been almost continuous since 1891. Vollmar, the leader of the Bavarian section of the movement, was one of the first in the German party to take issue with the Marxian tactics of Bebel, Liebknecht, and the North Germans. Bernstein followed with his polemics upon the subject, and at nearly every congress for ten years the matter was brought up in some form. In Italy the quarrels have been more serious even than in France. The reformists definitely allied themselves with the two ministries of Zanardelli and Giolitti. Throughout the north they have pursued everywhere a policy of compromise.

Again and again in the Italian congresses this question threatens the very existence of the movement.   Austria has not been without a similar struggle, and in Belgium the reformist policy prevails.

The reformists believe that the movement should use all its effort to accomplish certain definite reforms, and in this manner gradually alter the whole constitution of society.   They are not agreed as to the extent to which they would go for the sake of specific reforms.   Some believe in coöperating with the parties in power; some, in electoral alliances with the more advanced parties; some, that the members of the party should accept posts in the cabinet; others go so far as to say that "the movement is everything; the aim nothing."   They do not, however, disagree with their adversaries as to the end.   They are all in a sense revolutionists; but they are convinced that we shall arrive at socialism more quickly by specific reform, and collaboration with other political parties, than by an attitude of uncompromising hostility.

The Marxists believe that no fundamental alteration will be made in society except by working-class unity and action.   The education and organization of the workers is, therefore, their chief aim.   To them parliament is largely a place for propaganda and agitation. Reforms gained are looked upon in the light of strengthening the working-class revolt.   They do not deny the value of reform, but they do not want the end and aim of the movement to be confused with what they consider as only temporary ameliorations in the capitalist system. Furthermore, they claim, and this is their chief argument, that reforms are more easily gained by a hostile group of working men in parliament, jealously maintaining its isolation, than by compromise and collaboration with the old parties. In other words they set out to organize the people, and to impress upon them the principles of socialism, fearing to obscure their ideals by an appeal based upon the immediate program alone.

The battle between these two tendencies raged inside and outside the party until the Amsterdam Congress, when the Marxists won a signal victory. The latter proved that in those countries where the party had been the most uncompromising the reforms gained are most numerous. For instance, in Germany the movement as a whole, despite Bernstein, Vollmar, and other reformists, has pursued a policy of continuous and bitter hostility to all other parties. And it is in Germany that the most important and fundamental reforms have been obtained. It is not to Italy, France, or Belgium, in all of which countries the socialists have allied themselves with the radical parties, that one goes to find the most advanced reform legislation. In all these countries, the conditions among the masses are abominable. Despite the fact that the socialists have been sufficiently powerful in the first two countries to decide the fate of nearly all the recent ministries, they have not been able to obtain freedom for socialist action, even in those municipalities of which they have control. Millerand was certainly responsible for some important legislation, but it is not to be compared with that of Germany. The fact that the working-class of Europe altered the whole political outlook as soon as it became a party working in open hostility to the other parties is also proof of the soundness of the Marxian tactic.

The Fabian and reformist tactics are often thought to be the same, but there is, it must be said, a vital differ-

ence between the two policies. The Fabians steadfastly
decline to adopt the party idea. For years they have
pursued an adroit and effective policy in permeating the
liberal party, and especially the progressives of London, with collectivist views. It would be difficult to
overestimate the practical value of the work of Sidney
Webb, Bernard Shaw, and others, who have for more
than twenty years carried on a campaign for municipal
ownership. The Fabian essays and tracts have unquestionably revolutionized the ideas of the younger generation. Sidney Webb's "The London Program" and
" London Education," and Bernard Shaw's "The Com-
monsense of Municipal Trading," are outlines of a fundamental municipal policy. In London the Fabian
policy has been extremely successful, and as early as
1888 Bernard Shaw says: "We counted the solid advantage of a progressive majority full of ideas that
would never have come into their heads had not the
Fabians put them there. The generalship of this
movement was undertaken chiefly by Sidney Webb,
who played such bewildering conjuring tricks with the
Liberal thimbles and the Fabian peas, that to this day
both the Liberals and the sectarian socialists stand
aghast at him." Wholly without an organized movement the Fabians have almost from the beginning been
the brains, conscience, and will of the progressive
majority in the London County Council, and the results
they have attained are not to be despised. But to say
this is not to ignore the dangers of their policy. The
progressives at the last election were defeated, and the
socialists of London are left in an almost helpless position, entirely without a political organization. As a
contrast, we find that in Berlin, Paris, Brussels, and

G. Bernard Shaw.

Vienna the socialists have their strongest organizations. In Berlin, the party polls a large majority of all votes cast. It would be impossible for it to be disorganized and rendered helpless by a single defeat. It is a question, therefore, whether the Fabian policy has really been successful from the larger point of view. To have a history of agitation in London extending over twenty-seven years, and to show at the end of that period no definite political organization of the working-class, is perhaps the most damaging evidence against the Fabian policy. The Fabians can, of course, answer that they never intended to form a political party, which is perfectly true; and in that lies the difference between Fabianism and reformism.

The reformists on the continent have invariably worked inside the party, and they have often been most effective in building up the political organization, while the Fabian policy takes us back to the tactics of the French socialists before 1848, who had no thought of organizing politically the working-class. They were endeavoring to convert the middle class, and without organization to capture the government. It was the opinion of nearly all socialists of that period that social reorganization must come from above, and there were those who believed that the advantages of socialism could be made so clear to every rational mind that it only needed an intelligent statement to convince mankind. That was the view of St. Simon, Fourier, and Robert Owen; and Louis Blanc, Vidal, and Pecqueur endeavored to persuade the governing classes to abolish themselves. To Blanc and his friends socialism was governmental ownership, or if you please, the ownership by the people of certain or all forms of industry. They portrayed the evils of our present system; they sought to abolish competition and capitalist institutions. They were all brilliant men, to whom modern socialists owe an infinite debt of gratitude; but Marx called them Utopians because they failed to realize that the sole means of obtaining their end was the organization of the working-class. The present-day socialists who hold to this utopian view often leave the party because they feel they can do more effective work for socialism through liberal or radical organizations. This seems to be the view of Burns, Millerand, Viviani, and Briand. It is absurd to question their sincerity without more direct and damaging evidence than is now possessed by socialists who attack them, but if they retain their socialist views, they should certainly be classed among the Utopians.

We shall see in a later chapter how Marx condemned and finally destroyed the earlier Fabianism, and no finer tribute has ever been paid him than that of Jaurès, who was for a time the foremost reformist on the continent, and often an unsparing critic of the Marxists. "To Marx belongs the merit, perhaps the only one of all attributed to him that has fully withstood the trying tests of criticism and of time, of having drawn together and unified the labor movement and the socialist idea. In the first third of the nineteenth century labor struggled and fought against the crushing power of capital, but it was not conscious itself toward what end it was straining; it did not know that the true objective of its efforts was the common ownership of property. And, on the other hand, socialism did not know that the labor movement was the living form in which its spirit was embodied, the concrete practical force of which it stood in need. Marx was the most clearly convinced and the most powerful among those who put an end to the empiricism of the labor movement and the Utopianism of the socialist thought, and this should always be remembered to his credit. By a crowning application of the Hegelian method, he united the Idea and the Fact, thought and history. He enriched the practical movement by the idea, and to the theory he added practice; he brought the socialist thought into proletarian life, and proletarian life into socialist thought. From that time on, socialism and the proletariat became inseparable. Socialism can only realize its ideal through the victory of the proletariat, and the proletariat can only complete its being through the victory of socialism. To the ever more pressing question, 'How shall socialism be realized?' we must then give the preliminary answer, 'By the growth of the proletariat to which it is inseparably joined.' This is the first and essential answer; and whoever refuses to accept it wholly and in its true sense, necessarily places himself outside of socialist life and thought." It would be impossible to state more clearly the distinction between reformism and Fabianism.*

That socialism cannot be realized so long as labor remains disorganized and unconscious of its power both the Marxists and the reformists are agreed, and it is this consideration that led three of the ablest politicians in the socialist movement to place higher even than doctrine the unified organization of the workers. Liebknecht, de Paepe, and Hardie have all sacrificed the program in the interest of solidarity. It is unnecessary to dwell

---

* Of course I am using the term only as it applies to political tactics. The Fabian Society as a force in socialist education and propaganda cannot be overestimated.

upon the difference between these tactics and those of the Fabians. In the one case the workers are left unorganized, unconscious of their strength, and incapable of exercising their will or of fulfilling their immense obligations to society. In the other they are taught self-respect, independence, and responsibility. They acquire a knowledge of their tremendous power when united. They become conscious of their moral obligation to each other and to society, — an obligation which they cannot throw on to other shoulders. Above all they are taken out of the corrupting and demoralizing atmosphere of Liberal and Tory party patronage which enervates when it does not destroy all manly qualities. Fabianism sacrifices all this for the sake of specific reforms, perhaps extremely important in themselves and of great social value, but they will be obtained fast enough when the workers are once organized politically.

Fortunately there is no disagreement of this sort on the continent, and in the sense I have used the term, there are few Fabians outside of England.* Reformism is a different tactic altogether, as it presupposes a party. It is a policy to be pursued by the party as a whole. It has the same confidence in the conscience of the party that the Fabians have in individuals, and is without fear that its solidarity will suffer or its social-

---

* Perhaps there should be one reservation made to this statement. In America there are many socialists and single-taxers who have long pursued the Fabian policy. The most striking instance is the brilliant fight of Tom Johnson in Cleveland. He has the almost unique distinction of having used these tactics with success. But in winning a three-cent fare he has done no more than the socialists of Milwaukee, and in addition they have built up a great party that has already forced through the legislature and city council many important reforms, and promises to become a controlling influence in Wisconsin politics.

ist aim be obscured by the adoption of a more genial and compromising attitude toward the old parties. It urges agreements and affiliations before election, and in the legislative chambers coöperation with the other advanced parties to the extent of forming blocs, and any other agreements that will advance reform legislation. It considers that there are two distinct parts to every socialist program : one essentially reformist, the other essentially revolutionary. For the time being it would present to the governing classes that part which is most easily accepted, and work together with them upon that basis, leaving the other part, which exceeds the bounds of what is immediately realizable, to the future.

Reformism as a political policy seemed to reach its climax in Europe before the international congress at Amsterdam, but the Titanic struggle between Jaurès and Bebel settled the matter for the time being. Some details of that debate have already been given in another chapter, and there is no necessity for considering it further. Its importance lies in the fact that Marxism, which had built up modern socialism and had for over forty years been the basis of the doctrine and program of the party, was definitely established as the political tactic of the international movement. Of course this does not mean that the party has abandoned efforts for immediate reform. It simply recognizes the indisputable fact that the socialist movement cannot help being a stupendous reform force, and that no matter what course it pursues the mere fact of its existence obliges the governing classes to ameliorate the conditions of the workers.

P

CHAPTER VIII

SOCIALISM IN THE PARLIAMENTS

THE parliaments of continental Europe are not mere legislative bodies : they exercise a profound influence upon thought and life. The newspapers give first place to parliamentary news, and during the progress of a great debate every detail is followed with interest. The entire conversation in cafés, clubs, and even at private dinners, is often devoted to the parliamentary events of the day. The " full-dress " debates are numerous, and resemble in many ways great battles. The chief debaters are like generals, each with an enthusiastic and devoted following. The parliaments are, therefore, not dull and methodical as with us, discussing mere details of legislation; they are in a sense the centre of the intellectual life of the community. The discussions cover a wide range of subjects. Days and days are spent in fighting out questions of principle, and the policies of the government are considered both from the theoretical and practical standpoint in relation to the welfare of the people. It is surprising how little there is of moment that does not find its way into parliamentary debates, and one who follows the proceedings day by day will find himself *au courant* with nearly all events of national or international importance.

One reason for this breadth of thought and influence upon life is that the European parliaments are in every way more powerful than our own. Historically the lower houses have come to be thought the direct representatives of the people, as opposed to the hereditary power of the monarchy or the upper houses. They are thus looked upon as nuclei of concentrated public opinion. To a degree, therefore, quite unknown to us their decisions are considered final; and only in case of serious danger to the established order do the upper houses or monarchs attempt to interfere. The latter, as a result of the amazing growth of democracy throughout Europe, feel increasingly their precarious position, and they rarely interfere when the lower assembly shows a determined and hostile spirit. The long years of struggle between democracy and autocracy have gradually crippled the power of the latter in many European countries. In republican France the executive has very little power. " There is," Sir Henry Maine says, " no living functionary who occupies a more pitiable position than the French president. The old kings of France reigned and governed, the constitutional king reigns but does not govern ; the president of the United States governs but does not reign. It has been reserved for the president of the French republic neither to reign nor yet to govern."

And notwithstanding the increasing helplessness of the European executive, there is no judiciary to defeat the will of the people as expressed in their legislative assemblies. The power of the French parliament is almost omnipotent, or at least little less so than the British parliament. As there is no written constitution in England, the law of the legislative assembly is considered final. In France it is intended that the constitution shall not be changed by the ordinary statute, but if

the chambers should decide to pass a law that was obviously unconstitutional, no court or official could legally
prevent its application.   In Italy there has long been a
dread of judge-made law, and the courts have been
gradually rendered impotent to thwart legislative decisions.   There is some difference of opinion in Germany
as to the power of the courts to pass upon the constitutionality of an imperial law, but it is not at all likely that
the courts will ever venture to set aside statutes passed
by the legislature of the empire.   In Austria the courts
can pass upon the validity of ordinances, but are especially forbidden to inquire into the constitutionality of
statutes.   Even in Switzerland the legal tribunals must
enforce without question the laws of the federal assembly.   In none of these countries is there a body vested
with the supreme authority that rests in our higher
courts.   Both, therefore, in the absolute power of final
legislation, and in their moral power as representatives
of the people, most of the lower houses of the parliaments
of Western Europe exercise a dominant influence upon
the course of progress.

Even this does not exhaust the constitutional rights
of the European legislators.   They also exercise an
effective control over the policy of the administration.
It is thought that to have the power to pass laws without
being permitted in any sense to control their method of
enforcement is to render the popular assembly well-nigh
helpless.   Little by little, therefore, the lower houses
have brought under their control the ministers in charge
of the various executive departments; and in nearly
every country in Europe they are now directly responsible to the lower house.   When the government is a
highly centralized one, this power of supervision and of

effective criticism is perhaps as important as the legislative work itself.

In all European parliaments the legislators have the right to question the administration upon its acts, and even in advance upon its policies. In England this rarely goes beyond questions, but in France, Italy, and Belgium, the custom has grown into extended interpellations. In Germany this right of questioning the government is invaluable, as the legislative power of the Reichstag is limited, and the lack of ordinary political rights would otherwise prevent the socialists from exercising any considerable influence. This privilege enables the socialists to use the Reichstag as a platform for speaking to the people. It is customary in some countries to limit the use of questions, and often they may be addressed to a minister only with his consent. But the interpellation is a matter of right, which any representative may exercise irrespective of the wishes of the cabinet. Thus it is often the vehicle for the severest criticism of the government; and as any section of parliament may exercise it at will, it gives that section, no matter how small, an exceptional opportunity to place its views before the country.

It would be impossible to overestimate the value to democracy of the right of interpellation. It is an invaluable aid to those whose rights are jeopardized by official violence or by any form of governmental injustice. Except in Russia, and a few of the more backward countries, it is inconceivable that in Europe men should be shot, deported from their homes, denied every constitutional protection, and put at the mercy of martial law, — as happened for a period of many months a year or so ago in Colorado, — without the entire country knowing both

sides of the case.   And it is for exactly this reason that
the right of interpellation is regarded in Europe as one
of the main bulwarks of political liberty.

A dramatic element adds to the influence of European
parliaments.   A section of a legislative body may at any
moment overturn an unpopular administration.   Again
and again cabinets are forced to resign as a result of
acts which, if committed daily by American executives,
would go unquestioned.   In watching the French
chamber at work for a few weeks I saw the socialists
several times give the government a thoroughly un-
pleasant trouncing : twice upon its policy in dealing
with two serious strikes, and once it was put in danger
over the administration of the law defining the relation
of the church to the state.   Upon these occasions the
debates were of intense interest, and it seemed as if all
Paris were watching the outcome.

But the debates in the European legislatures are not
limited to specific questions of administrative policy.
There is no hesitancy whatever to grapple with great
and fundamental social, economic, and political principles.
In fact, nearly all questions having to do with administrative policy present themselves, in one way or another,
either as the working out or the violation of some general
principle which is supposed to underlie social institutions.   During the last decade the socialists have led
most of these battles ; and naturally, as their attitude is
severely critical of the principles underlying the present
order, they have again and again drawn the representatives of the majority into heated discussions upon funda-
mentals.   In this way Bebel used to be pitted against
Bismarck, and is now carrying on, from day to day, a
running parliamentary battle with von Buelow.   In

France, it is Jaurès against Clémenceau, in Belgium Vandervelde against de Smet de Neyer, and in Italy Ferri against Giolitti. On the occasions of these great debates the galleries are crowded, and thousands fail to obtain seats, while the people generally display an un-flagging interest.

This is all in extraordinary contrast to our own parlia-mentary life, which passes on from day to day without raising a single ripple of excitement. One can even read the papers diligently and not obtain any consecu-tive notion of what is happening in the chief legislative body of the nation. The people know that nothing of any importance is going to happen, and they fully real-ize that the legislature has little power, and almost no desire to exercise that power in the interest of the com-munity. As there exist only two parties, there is nearly always a permanent majority during the legislative session ; and while in other countries this would give the party in power an opportunity to carry out its policy unhindered, it seems to be with us an opportunity to prevent the passage of any measure of national interest. The body is strictly limited to legislative work, and the ministers and executive are in no wise responsible to it. Decentralized government puts quite out of the reach of our legislators some of the most important executive departments; and no matter how badly, unjustly, or even autocratically the law is administered, the legisla-ture has no power to interfere; it can only retort by some change in the law. Our parliamentary work, therefore, consists largely in passing laws which are soon repealed, and then with the growth of abuses passed again. Our executive is only less powerful than our judiciary, which in America exercises an autocratic influence over the course of legislation; so that, instead of being governed by popularly elected representatives, we are the subjects of a judiciary which wields a greater power than that vested in any monarch or upper house of Western Europe.

In addition to these constitutional disabilities we suffer from the fact that our electoral power is in the hands of two political parties, while in nearly all continental countries there are many parties. It is an old custom among the Anglo-Saxons for two parties to battle for supremacy. The institution is being mutilated at present in England, but in America it remains unimpaired. To a certain extent both parties exist without principles, and the main distinction between them is that one is out and the other is in. On the continent the various parties represent widely different principles and interests, perhaps as a rule the latter more than the former. Thus in nearly every country there are political groups representing royalty, the landowning interests, the capitalists, and the workers. In some cases, however, the parties avow certain principles; and, of course, in all countries the socialist party rests its entire campaign upon a definite program, fully stating its fundamental principles and doctrines. Instead of two parties, therefore, the political forces are broken up into numberless groups representing almost every phase of national life; and when a government comes into power, it is confronted by the difficult problem of trying to harmonize the interests of a sufficient number of representatives to form a working majority.

This splitting up of the political forces into groups is largely due to the system of voting. The second ballot is in almost general use. The theory is that where three or four candidates are in the field, one may be elected without having obtained the support of an actual majority of the constituents. The first ballot enables all the various groups to vote for a candidate directly representing their own interests ; but at the second election only the two candidates that received the highest number of votes remain in the field. This electoral method enables the various sections to test their strength at the first ballot, knowing that if they fail in electing their own representative, they have still an opportunity to elect the one who seems to them the better of the two candidates remaining in the field. As a result it is possible for the voters on the continent to maintain a party with principles, instead of being forced to vote at all times for the one whom they consider the better of two candidates put forward by the opposing political machines. However inefficient or dishonest the candidates may be, no other choice exists where only two parties battle for supremacy.

This is, of course, what happens repeatedly in America. Except for an occasional independent campaign, and the nominees of the prohibition and socialist parties, the voters are forced to select one of two candidates, both of whom may be unprincipled and inefficient. When it occurs, as it does frequently, that the two main political organizations are secretly united for the purpose of betraying the people, representative democracy becomes a farce, and government by the people degenerates into government by two unprincipled and predatory machines. The evil is not a new one, and various independent political parties have been alive to its dangers. In 1874 a party was formed in California, which denounced in its program the doctrine of party fealty and the tyranny of party discipline as the greatest political evils of the time. Twenty years later the Populist party declared that the nation had been brought to the verge of moral, political, and material ruin by the corruption which dominates the ballot-box, the legislatures, the congress, and the judiciary. " We have witnessed," the program says, "for more than a quarter of a century the struggle of the two great political parties for power and plunder."

Again and again these independent movements have arisen with the idea of breaking down machine rule. Both the Greenbackers and the Populists obtained the rank of national parties, with seats in Congress, and even in the Senate ; but as soon as they began to exercise a really important influence one of the old parties adopted their program or some of their candidates, with the result in every case of destroying the organization. The first campaign of Henry George in New York and the recent one led by William R. Hearst were destroyed in a similar manner. There is no question but that it would have been easier for these movements to have continued independent if the second ballot had been in use; but even without the second ballot a party with the highest principles, and with a consciousness of the power which a hostile third party can exercise, even in the face of formidable opposition, might have come to occupy a position similar to that held by like parties in Europe. Unfortunately the Americans seem not yet to realize that an independent movement, which can force one of the old parties to adopt its program, might exercise a similar power in other directions by continuing its independent methods. In nearly every country of Europe the old parties have pursued the tactic of partially adopting the socialist program for the purpose of destroying the movement, but in each case the attempt has failed. The socialists have considered this as only the beginning of their influence as an independent political force.

The lack of principles and political foresight, and especially the overwhelming desire to win power immediately and by strategy, which often distinguish the " reform " movements from the socialist movement, have enabled the bosses to outwit and divide every sincere body of radicals, with the result that the corporations are now in complete control of all our law-making bodies, leaving America with the unenviable and unique distinction of being the only large country where working men have no representation in its chief legislature. The House of Representatives is a striking instance of the dominant power of capitalism. Neither the farmers nor the working-class as such have any directly controlled representatives. The Senate is largely a body of millionaires and their legal retainers. As a rule over 60 per cent are lawyers, and the rest are nearly all capitalists, without the slightest interest in or sympathy with the workers. It is the same in the House, where again not less than 60 per cent are also lawyers; that is to say, railroad attorneys and the representatives of the great monopolies and favored business interests. In case "a friend of the Peepul," as he would be called in Washington, happens to get into the House or the Senate, the legislative machines are so strong that they effectually prevent the recalcitrant individual from being heard. The speaker of the house is often referred to as a Czar, and he exercises a tyranny over the representatives which would not be tolerated in any other parliament. The United States Congress is, therefore, the least democratic legislature in any advanced country; and for this reason we are the most backward in all forms of legal protection of the life and interests of the masses.

Passing from these striking contrasts between the parliamentary situation with us and that existing in Europe, we find that the socialist groups in the various parliaments occupy a peculiar position among the other political representatives. To begin with they are controlled by a large party membership, which, through its representatives, has agreed upon a complete political program and devised a conscious and definite parliamentary policy. The other parties of Europe are ordinarily without organization, sometimes consisting of little more than electoral groups or national clubs. The parliamentary representatives are, therefore, not as a rule bound to any program. In the case of the socialists the parliamentary group is always under the direct control of the party, and this constitutes a rather striking innovation in political methods. The general scheme of political organization was worked out first by the Germans, whose socialist party is older by far than that of any other country. As early as 1867 there were eight representatives in the Reichstag, and by 1884 there were twenty-four. So that the Germans began to exercise a parliamentary influence nearly twenty years before the socialists of any other country. France did not win any seats until 1887. The Belgians obtained representation first in 1894, and the Italians, while winning their first victory in the early eighties, exercised no influence until 1895. The German movement, therefore, was early forced to meet problems unknown to the workers of other countries, and to fight out its parliamentary policy and electoral tactics without precedents to be guided by.

It was natural that there should have been some confusion during the early days, and indeed the leaders were greatly divided as to what policy the party should pursue in parliament. The Lassallians were willing to make the most of parliamentary alliances in order to obtain an amelioration in the condition of the workers, while Liebknecht was at first violently anti-parliamentary, fearing lest the energies of socialism should be engulfed in the swamp of *parliamentarism*. He wished to go to the Reichstag merely to protest against the capitalist régime, and especially against the "blood and iron" policy of Bismarck, and after protesting, to leave without resigning his seat. It was a rather melodramatic method for a party to pursue, but it must be remembered that the government was then carrying on a ferocious policy of persecution against socialists. The organization itself was illegal, and it was next to impossible for its leaders to entertain the idea of a working arrangement with anybody not actually a member of their secret organization. It was Bebel who first broke away from this negative policy, and when in 1869 he took an active part in the discussion upon the revision of the industrial laws, and even took a place upon the commission instituted to study the question, Liebknecht at a public meeting pronounced a severe criticism of his action. He maintained that it was impossible to obtain anything except by force from a parliament made up of the enemies of labor. "What practical object have we then," he asked, "in making speeches in the Reichstag? None whatever; and to speak without an object is a fool's pleasure."

It was not long, however, before Bebel and Liebknecht came to an understanding, and at the congress of the Social Democratic Party in 1870 the delegates, after discussion, adopted a definite parliamentary policy. They agreed that the main purpose in taking part in elections was to carry on the socialist propaganda, but that the parliamentary group, while maintaining in general a strictly negative attitude, should nevertheless take part in all discussions of proposed legislation affecting the interests of the workers. But even this policy, while more advanced than the other, became inadequate as the party grew in power. At nearly every election their votes increased, and from little more than 100,000 in 1871 the number increased to over 2,000,000 in 1898. As its following became greater, its responsibilities grew heavier, and every one saw that a broader parliamentary policy was necessary. At the national congress in 1897 Liebknecht himself took the initiative, and frankly stated that events, and especially the growth of the party, had forced him to alter radically his theory of parliamentary tactics. He criticised unsparingly his own former policy of anti-parliamentarism, which he called contemptuously the tactic of talk; and advocated with eloquence and power a complete and practical parliamentary policy with all liberty to the party's representatives in working for specific legislation intended to ameliorate the condition of the workers. "That is the necessary tactic of the party, a tactic infinitely more revolutionary than the tactic of talk," he said amidst tremendous applause. "Yes, comrades, he who does nothing at all except to mouth revolutionary phrases is at his ease to judge and to condemn; he who does nothing can make no mistakes. But he who acts, he can easily make mistakes; but he is in the struggle, and that is of much more account than the making of beautiful phrases."

But despite the fact that the party did not revise its parliamentary policy until the nineties, the movement itself was exercising a profound influence upon the course of legislation. As early as the seventies the German government began to fear the rising tide of socialism, and in 1878 Prince Bismarck told the Reichstag: "I will further every endeavor which positively aims at improving the condition of the working-class. . . . As soon as a positive proposal comes from the socialists for fashioning the future in a sensible way, in order that the lot of working men may be improved, I will not at any rate refuse to examine it favorably, and I will not even shrink from the idea of state help for those who have the disposition to help themselves." Along with this statement came the proposal for the compulsory insurance of the working-class. A few years later Bismarck proclaimed his belief in the justice of the socialists' contention that every man should have the right to work; and in comment he said: "Give the working man the right to employment as long as he has health. Assure him care when he is sick, and maintenance when he is old. If you will do that without fearing the sacrifice, or crying out 'state socialism' directly the words 'provision for old age' are uttered, . . . then I believe that the gentlemen of the Wyden (Social Democratic) program will sound their bird-call in vain; and as soon as the working men see that the government is earnestly concerned for their welfare, the thronging to them will cease."

These two quotations from Bismarck's speeches in the

Reichstag show the already great influence of the socialist movement. Even the socialists were astonished at the change in the attitude of the government; and it seemed a remarkable victory to have forced autocratic Germany to revolutionize its economic policy. If the government had ceased persecuting the socialists, while granting these concessions to their program, it might have disarmed them. But as it was, the socialists and not the government obtained the entire credit. Bebel said at the time, in the humorous and confidential manner he occasionally assumes toward his opponents in the Reichstag: "I will frankly tell you something. If anything has furthered the social democratic agitation and tendency, it is the fact that Prince Bismarck has to a certain extent declared for socialism and social reform; only one must remember that we are in this case the master and he the scholar. People are saying everywhere: When to-day Prince Bismarck with his great authority comes forward and not only acknowledges the existence of a social question, — which only a few years ago was emphatically denied by the ruling authorities, — but even declares for socialism, and regards it as his duty to introduce measures on the subject, then it may well be concluded that social democracy is at bottom right."

At this time the two chief leaders in the German movement were Liebknecht and Bebel. Liebknecht was the older of the two, and a man of exceptional education. "As far back as the beginning of the eighteenth century," Edward Aveling says, "an ancestor of his was professor and rector of the University of Giessen," and in the middle of the sixteenth century a forebear, Martin Luther, "was making some

Wilhelm Liebknecht.

stir in the world." His thorough education and scholarly instincts led Liebknecht to think of a university career, but strong democratic sympathies forced him to take a part in the various revolutionary outbreaks which were occurring in 1848, in all parts of Europe. He lay in prison for nine months as a result of his revolutionary ardor, and finally he was exiled and forced to live in England for nearly thirteen years. There he met Marx, and carried on his studies directly under his influence and tutelage. In 1862 there was an amnesty for political offenders, and Liebknecht returned to Germany. A few years later, having been banished from Prussia, he went to Leipsic, where he met Bebel. The trade unions were then growing in power, and Bebel and Liebknecht joined forces. In 1867 the latter was again imprisoned, but nevertheless in September of the same year he was elected to the Reichstag, where as a result of his superior education he was more than a match for his parliamentary opponents.

Bebel, on the contrary, was a working man, and in the early days of his parliamentary career his language was rough and unpolished. Occasionally he made grammatical errors, and was hooted at by his opponents, who even called out that one who could not speak German properly ought not to pretend to talk to educated people. Nevertheless, Bebel represented infinitely more than Liebknecht, personifying, as it were, the entrance to power of the men of toil. One can understand that it must have been annoying to the aristocrats to have had this rough agitator break into their midst, and at first Bebel had to suffer day by day the ridicule and even the insults of the representatives of the educated

Q

classes.   But Bebel had the natural power of oratory, and even in those days he often humiliated his proud opponents.

Princess Catherine Radziwill gives an interesting picture of Bebel in her recently published memoirs of life at the German and Russian courts.   It was at the time Bismarck was trying to force through the Reichstag the anti-socialist laws ; and she says the debates between Bebel and Bismarck were listened to feverishly by all those who could get access to the house.   " They were opened," she says, "by the Chancellor himself, who spoke for over an hour, and to him Bebel replied in a speech which deserved to go down to posterity as an example of eloquence.   Never were such impassioned accents heard within the walls of the old building; every one felt moved by the strange persuasiveness with which this remarkable man appealed to the sense of justice and humanity of the whole German nation, abjuring it not to make outcasts of thousands of its children.   In listening to those savage accents one seemed to hear, made vocal, the writing on the wall, which amid the splendors of the Persian king's supper appeared to remind him that ' for all these things he would be brought into judgment.'   It is impossible," she continues, " not to be moved by an argument when it comes from the lips of Bebel.   He speaks of poverty, of misery, of vice, as a man who has known and suffered from these things.   He knows how to excite his listeners' pity, not for imaginary facts, but for painful and sad truths.   He knows how to make them touch with their finger all the evils of which he speaks to them, — he surpassed himself, but his efforts were doomed before they were made."

It is a curious example of the irony of fate that the crude, rough working man of forty years ago is to-day one of the greatest powers in Europe. He was always an orator, and to-day he is the ablest parliamentarian in Germany. Now one of the oldest and most experienced men in the Reichstag, his memory and his intimate knowledge of the events of the last half century give to his utterances an authoritative value that is not equalled even by those of the emperor. Despite the fact that he represents in the Reichstag a small minority, no other member exercises a personal influence equal to his ; and one can actually feel a thrill of excitement pass through the chamber when he rises to speak. Professor Theodor Mommsen, the great German historian, once said, " Everybody in Germany knows that with brains like those of Bebel, it would be possible to furnish forth a dozen noblemen from the east of the Elbe in a fashion that would make them shine among their peers."

It would serve no useful purpose to treat in detail one of the many great debates that have occurred in the Reichstag between the socialists and their opponents. Hardly a month passes without one of importance. And I have already shown the immense influence of the movement in obtaining the most revolutionary reform legislation that exists in any country in Europe. The running fire of criticism and the hostility of the socialists have simply broken down and shattered all of the cherished principles of economic liberalism. The government has been driven to abandon one after another, and by the sheer force of socialist opposition it has been obliged to grant a series of fundamental social and industrial rights. Bismarck granted in principle the right to employment, and the imperial legislation grants the right of compensation to the aged, to the sick and infirm, and to those injured in industry. The right of trade union organization, of striking, and of peaceful picketing are also now assured by the law, and the government throws upon the manufacturing classes the entire responsibility for accidents. The right of the community to its natural resources, to its public utilities, and to the unearned increment arising from the sale and transfer of land, have also been won in principle, and in no small degree worked out in practice.

The real significance of the parliamentary victories of the socialists lies in the fact that the workers are no longer at the complete mercy of the capitalists. They have won for themselves important means of defence, and instead of being forced individually to deal with their employers they have acquired entire freedom in their battle to force collective contracts. Some of the worst forms of capitalist exploitation are done away with by labor legislation, which establishes a certain standard of conditions to be observed in industry ; and if an employee is rendered incapable of further labor, he and his family are insured care and protection, instead of being forced to become beggars and paupers. While the socialists are pressing upon the state a higher conception of its social duties, they are at the same time breaking down the polity which acknowledges that all natural resources and all forms of profitable enterprise are divinely established for the benefit of the capitalist ; and as a direct result, the state is taking into its own hands some of the most important and socially necessary of the capitalistic enterprises.

The German party is the oldest, and because of that

it has more to its credit than any other movement, but the influence of socialists is quite as clearly seen in the parliaments of other countries. In the chapter on the British movement some details are given of the power exercised by the Labor Party during the last two years. The gain in legislation is considerable, but the most striking change to be noticed as a result of the advent of labor is the new atmosphere in the House of Commons. What used to be " the most exclusive and interesting gentlemen's club in Europe " has been invaded by working men, and their presence alone has revolutionized the old order. Their election is a direct imputation that the Liberals and Tories have neglected the public welfare, and that the public know it and have lost confidence in them. Probably no other aristocracy in Europe has in the past enjoyed a power so free from restraint and criticism on the part of the lower classes as the British, and it realizes instinctively the fundamental danger of the present situation.

This feeling is entirely a product of the last two years, although Hardie has from the beginning irritated and offended the representatives of the old order. Shortly after his entrance to parliament he found the House one day in the midst of rejoicing because a son had been born in the royal family. There was a great demonstration, and messages of congratulation and felicitation were sent to the mother. At almost the same moment there occurred in Wales a terrible colliery disaster in which many miners were buried alive, and Hardie arose in the midst of the parliamentary rejoicings to ask the House to send to the wives, mothers, and sisters of the miners some expression of its sympathy. It would be impossible to describe the effect of his request. The members of what was supposed to be the nation's house of representatives were so completely bound up in their narrow family circles that to them the death of these workers was no more than a passing newspaper story ; and the mere mention of this terrible accident during the progress of the festivities was an unwarrantable piece of impudence and bad taste. It was certainly awkward and annoying, but it was significant of the broad horizon that the representatives of the working men bring with them when they enter parliament. It seems a breaking down of class lines; but while it does not go as far as that, it has nevertheless worked a revolution in the psychology of the House of Commons.

One day the question of the unemployed was being debated, and Hardie sat alone, stung and embittered by the lack of all consideration or sympathy for the unhappy starving wanderers, until, unable to contain himself longer, he called out, " You well-fed beasts ! " It was not a remark that one expected to hear in the House; but it had its effect on the tone of the discussion. Upon a similar occasion, Will Crooks said with some fire, in answer to the Liberals and Tories who had been saying that the unemployed were lazy, lounging vagabonds who did not want work, that he had observed a goodly number of vagrants about Rotten Row — a fashionable English promenade — dressed in top-hats and spats. On still another occasion, when a bill was before the House for the feeding of school children, the gentlemen of the old parties had been saying over and over again that the children were hungry not so much because of poverty as because their mothers did not know how to cook, or preferred drinking in the saloons, or gossiping with their neighbors, to attending to their household duties. This would have passed without comment in the old House; it would have been thought perfectly proper to have referred in this manner to several million mothers. But in the new order it was taken as an insult by the men on the labor benches, and one can imagine the electric effect on the House when Hardie remarked that it was embarrassing for the labor members to sit quietly in their seats while hearing their wives described as slatterns. These are, of course, the merest incidents of debate, but I cannot help thinking they are more significant than legislation. Instead of merely a few landowners, younger sons of noblemen, barristers, solicitors, capitalists, and other gentlemen spending their time largely in discussing their own affairs, and with some annoyance philanthropically deciding to give an occasional evening to a bill having to do with remedying the frightful abuses of the English slums, and the wretched conditions of a deteriorating populace of some 12,000,000, there are now at least a few representatives of the underworld who have forced their way into the midst of these oligarchs, to insist upon the necessity for social reform.

To say the least, the upper classes do not like it, and being rather put to it to find a way out, they have begun an attack upon socialism which is far from observing that spirit of fair-play upon which the Briton has always prided himself. At every new election fought by labor, and at every sign of its increasing power, the bitterness grows more intense; until now the propertied interests have entered upon a crusade against socialism and are trying to prove that it advocates free love, the destruction of the family, atheism, and the outright confiscation of private property.

Many well-known men, including some prominent nobles, are at present issuing manifestos warning the people of the danger to England of this new movement. At first the campaign was so absurd that the socialists looked upon it complacently, and even considered it a valuable asset to their propaganda, but the din grew, until at present these attacks from thousands of platforms and nearly all the newspapers have become too serious to be ignored. Finally Bruce Glasier, the able editor of " The Labour Leader," like a lion at bay, has turned upon the accusers, and for several weeks has answered their charges by a series of articles so damaging to the Liberals and Tories that they plan already to abandon their method of attack.

In answer to the charge that socialism is spoliation, Glasier has given the shameless facts of confiscation, bribery, and corruption, that have been practised by prominent English families in building up their vast fortunes. In answer to the criticism that socialism wishes to alter the marriage relation and to establish a licentious system of free love, he takes up one after another of the Liberals and Tories who have advocated the loosest of sexual relationships, and lived lives of the grossest immorality. As a testimony upon upper-class ethics, he quotes one marquis to the effect that "There is no law of nature, human or divine, in man's present state which confines him to one woman, and that not one man in ten thousand could on his deathbed swear that he had truly obeyed the marriage law." He prints the infamous memorandum of Lord Roberts, a Tory, issued in June, 1886, which instituted compulsory medical service for the inspection of prostitutes for the Indian Army, and drew from an under officer a request that more young and attractive women should be sent out. In answer to the accusation that socialism is agnostic, Glasier pursues the same policy of proving that for every militant agnostic among the socialists of any importance there are many among the Liberals and Tories. He shows that socialism has nothing in common with confiscation or spoliation, with any change in the marriage relation, or with any alteration in the religious views of the individual. The response of the socialists to these attacks is by no means limited to this effective work of Bruce Glasier in "The Labour Leader." Robert Blatchford and all the other journalists have taken a hand in the fight, and the campaigners of both the labor and socialist parties are addressing enormous audiences at about two thousand meetings every week.

I have dealt at length with this situation in England because it illustrates what occurred in other countries of Europe as soon as socialism began to force its way into parliament. Similar arguments were used against it in Germany during the seventies, when the movement began to be formidable there; and by imputing to it responsibility for some attacks upon the life of the emperor, and repeatedly referring to it as a criminal organization advocating every immorality, Bismarck was enabled to force through the Reichstag his iniquitous measures which made outlaws of all socialists. In France during the eighties and early nineties the same thing occurred, and in Italy, although the socialists oppose the anarchists, they are invariably held responsible for the work of the latter in encouraging insurrection and violence. What is happening at the present moment in England is, therefore, typical, but this form of attack has nowhere in Europe availed to defeat socialism. Indeed, with hardly a single exception it may be said to have aided the movement, for as soon as the people have discovered that the attitude of the upper classes is one of intentional misrepresentation they have turned to the socialists with increasing enthusiasm. And when the upper classes in other countries have learned that misrepresentation and falsehood have only a momentary effect, and are followed by a strong reaction, they have settled down to a policy of social reform.

We are beginning to see the same change in attitude on the part of the British upper classes.* The more far-seeing political leaders begin to realize that the campaign of nastiness and falsehood is not hurting socialism, and they are now exerting themselves to stop this method of attack. Lord Milner openly rebukes the anti-socialist campaigners, and suggests a response similar to that of Bismarck to the rising tide of revolutionary feeling. " The true antidote to socialism," he says, " is practical social reform," and he urges with

---

* There is a faint rumor that many of the sincere radicals in the Liberal Party are becoming convinced that this campaign is a cloak for reaction, and that back of it are men in the Liberal and Tory parties who desire not only to oppose revolutionary socialism, but also every effort to ameliorate the condition of the masses. These reactionaries are notoriously unsympathetic toward every democratic aspiration, and consistently, both in politics and in business, fill their own pockets at the expense of the community. Some of the more high-minded Liberals and Tories find the present situation intolerable; because however much they differ from the views of the extreme socialists they differ as much from the class selfishness and inhumanity of the reactionary elements. Therefore it is rumored that unless a majority is to be found for the support of a constructive policy of social reform, the more public-spirited of the younger men may form a new party resembling in some respects the radical-socialists of France.

passionate intensity the necessity for remedying the wrongs of private property in time to save the country from getting into the hands of the revolutionary elements. Many other prominent leaders are expressing the same views, and it is unquestionable that the present inadvisable method of meeting advancing socialism will be revised. It is not improbable, therefore, that within the next few years we shall see both the Liberal and Tory parties competing with each other to introduce social legislation as radical in character as the state socialism of Germany.

In both Germany and England, therefore, we find that socialism is a powerful parliamentary force, and even occupies a foremost place in the thought of the entire community. And this is not less true of France and Italy. In the Latin countries the fear of socialism on the part of the upper classes has become almost a mania. Two causes lie at the bottom of this dread. The first is the revolutionary tradition among the Latin peoples; and secondly, there is hardly an upper-class man in Italy or France who does not fear that the slightest change in events may bring the socialists into power. In talking with well-to-do men one frequently hears it said, with a kind of despair, that socialism is inevitable. Among the masses it arouses unbounded enthusiasm, and it is unquestionable that it is fast taking hold of the entire working-class. It is sometimes difficult to account for its influence, because as a rule the movement is badly organized in these countries, and most of its adherents rarely read socialist books or pamphlets. It is more of an instinctive movement than one finds in England, which gives an Anglo-Saxon the feeling of unsafe foundations.

In Italy the political leaders of the older parties lack the power to concentrate the propertied classes upon really effective measures of social reform. The reactionaries are extremists with no faith in any other method of dealing with discontent than massacring the people at every sign of an uprising, and limiting the right of free speech, combination, and the suffrage. Their retort to the cry of misery is martial law, a permanent form of which they tried to force through parliament in 1899. The effect of repression is, of course, not what they hope for, as instead of pacifying they inflame the masses until they resort to violence and lawlessness. The parties of the Right will not see that the workers are driven by starvation to bread riots and strikes, and they refuse the demands of the socialists for remedial legislation. As a result a situation is created with which no party is able to cope. Between the reactionaries above and the anarchists below the socialists are the only constructive force in Italy.

The middle parties are weak and wavering. Without principles they seek and obtain power under the cover of one or two leaders of excellent character who are popular in the country. The radicals, the republicans, and the socialists, who form the extreme Left, are unable to come to any permanent agreement because of vital differences in their views. Recent parliamentary history is, therefore, a continuous record of repeated upheavals resulting from these clashing forces. The failure to agree upon any measures for ameliorating the poverty-stricken condition of the masses leads the latter more and more to despair of parliamentary methods. Anarchism is again making headway among the most wretched of the workers, and leading them to desperate revolts and insurrections, which the socialists, with all their power, cannot prevent, or when once started, control.

Recently when a radical ministry came into power, the socialists gave it support upon the assurance that it would carry out a program of social reform. One was actually drawn up that included extremely important and advanced legislation in the interests of the people. The king himself seemed favorable, and it looked for a time as if Italy had settled down to a constructive parliamentary policy which promised relief to the masses; but after a time some strikers were shot. The union between the radicals and the socialists was then broken, and the same old parliamentary antagonisms flared up again.

This is the darker side of Italian parliamentary life, and it is really difficult to see how the situation will work itself out. As I have said in the chapter on Italy, the socialists have performed an enormously useful work in the exposure of corruption. They have unquestionably the ablest leaders in Italian political life. Every fair-minded Italian realizes the moderation of their minimum program, which even Professor Villari, a conservative leader, says every sensible man could indorse almost in its entirety. But there seems no immediate prospect of the socialists gaining a parliamentary majority, and until that is accomplished misery on the one side and brutal reaction on the other make peaceful methods barren, while violence only results in increasing misery and suffering for the unfortunate workers. The situation in Italy presents stupendous difficulties to the socialists, and while no

one can help admiring their parliamentary leaders, and
recognizing the superior ability of Ferri and Turati,
who are so fearless and honest, so passionate in debate,
so careless of consequences to themselves, one cannot
think of the future without some misgiving.

Of all parties the French socialists seem the most
fortunate.   They have many able orators, and both
Guesde and Jaurès are skilled parliamentarians.   Unfortunately, while I was in Paris last winter, ill-health
forced Guesde to be away, so that I did not see him
at work in the chamber; but I heard Jaurès many
times.   It would be difficult to imagine a person who
possessed in a larger degree the necessary qualities of
a parliamentary leader.   He is not a small man among
small men; he is a big man among big men.   I mean
by that that the French chamber contains more brilliant orators and debaters than any other parliament in
Europe.   First and foremost among them is Clémenceau.
He has a remarkable attraction for the French people,
as he is radical and fearless and personally disinterested.   He has fought upon the popular side against
all waves of reaction, including the ones led by Gam-
betta, Ferry, and the Boulangists.   He has upset more
governments than any other man in France.   His
record in the Dreyfus affair was one not to be forgotten.   He has a real sympathy for the aspirations
of the people, although he is a strong individualist.   A
man of high education and cultivation, he is one of the
most formidable debaters in the French chamber; and
his skilful phrase, epigrammatic sentence, and burning
satire make him feared by those who find themselves
in opposition.   His high individualist idealism, together
with a deep-rooted cynicism, lends to his political views

a complexity which is the despair of opponents. He is the kind of man the genial, idealistic Jaurès might be expected to fear, but again and again these two extraordinary men cross swords in battle.

When the radicals came into power early in 1907, it seemed a necessity to the logical French mind clearly to define the difference in policy between the radicals and the socialists. The ministry was nominally under the control of Sarrien, although really completely in the hands of Clémenceau; and between the latter and Jaurès there occurred a significant debate upon fundamental social and political principles. For the first time in the political life of Clémenceau he faced an opposition with views more extreme than his own, and he taunted the socialists with being a party of negation, destruction, and violence. He defied Jaurès to produce anything constructive in their policy. In answer Jaurès delivered what is perhaps the clearest statement that has yet been made in any parliament of the constructive ideas of socialism, and for that reason it deserves special and extended consideration in this place. It was the intention of Jaurès to make an authoritative declaration and as far as possible to express the views of the international party, and he, therefore, quoted decisions made in party council, and the views of the chief leaders. Consequently it can be considered not only as the deliberate statement of an eminent leader of one of the largest national parties in Europe, but also in the main as the view of the international movement.

In the first part of his address he gave a hurried sketch of what he thought would be the main outlines of the new social order under socialism, and he promised, if the chamber would give him time, to place before it a more comprehensive and detailed plan of the legislation which would bring about the transition, and the main institutions which would exist under socialism. As the new social order would have to evolve out of present-day society it would have to be largely influenced by national institutions, and for this reason the first part of his address applies particularly to France. Passing, however, from this consideration, he endeavored to answer the question whether or not the socialist order would be established by the confiscation of capitalist property.

Jaurès confessed that he could not foretell with any certainty what would take place. " It is not because my own thought on this question is uncertain or hesitating," he said. "It is because in these matters programs, even when they are clearly determined and deliberately planned, are subordinate to the force of events. You have had a proof of this during the great French Revolution, which began with decrees of expropriation with compensation, with the thought of purchasing most of the feudal rights; and which afterward, carried away and exasperated by the struggle, proceeded to that expropriation without indemnity. And you now see, gentlemen, at this hour, a similar crisis at the other end of Europe. There is there a great gathering, the first national gathering of the Russian people, which is studying the means of giving the land to the peasants by large expropriations. The leading parties of that assembly propose to give compensation for the large private estates which will be expropriated. Gentlemen, it will not depend upon them whether they can bind the future to this scheme.

It will be realized if freedom is established there by legal evolution; but if the government blindly resist, there will be risings and rebellions, and it is likely that the expropriations will be carried out in a very different manner.

"That is the reservation I wanted to make, and for my part I have no pretension of laying down in advance conditions to the working-class, to the world of labor. I know, and I declare, that the rights of labor are sovereign, and I shall assist with all my heart, and with all my mind, in any effort necessary to establish a new society. But I have the right before parliament, before the working-class, to assume the hypothesis of a legal transformation of a regular and peaceful evolution; for I ardently wish that such a consummation may be realized, and toward its realization I will work, we will all work, my friends and I, with all our strength, for a policy of democratic reforms which will increase the legal power and regular means of action of the working-class.

"It is with this thought, with this hope, that I invoke the authority, freely admitted by our reason, of all the great socialist theorists who have advised, in various ways and in the interest of the social revolution itself, expropriation with compensation. It was Marx who, according to Engels, uttered these words: 'It will still be, if we can proceed by compensation, the cheapest way to achieve the revolution.' He meant that by this means it would not be necessary to suspend for one moment the productive activity of the country. Kautsky, in his commentary on the socialist program of Erfurt, said, 'Expropriation does not necessarily mean spoliation.' Our friend Vandervelde has spoken

R

in the same sense, and I ask of the House permission to read the powerful and beautiful declaration of Lieb-knecht: —

" 'Social democracy is the party of the whole people, with the exception of two hundred thousand great and small proprietors, capitalists, and priests. It ought then to turn toward the people and, as soon as occasion offers, by practical proposals and projects of legislation of general interest, to give positive proof that the good of the people is its only aim, and the will of the people its only rule. It must follow the path of legislation without doing violence to any one, but with a firm purpose and unerring aim. Even those who now enjoy privileges and monopolies ought to be made to under-stand that we do not propose any violent or sudden measures against those whose position is now sanc-tioned by law, and that we are determined, in the interest of a peaceful and quiet evolution, to bring about the transition from legal injustice to legal justice, with the utmost consideration for the individuals who are now privileged persons. We recognize that it would be unjust to hold those who are now privileged by the sanction of bad legislation personally responsible for that bad legislation and to punish them personally. We declare expressly that in our opinion it is the duty of the state to give an indemnity to those whose in-terests will be damaged by the necessary abolition of laws which are detrimental to the common good in so far as this indemnity is consistent with the interests of all. We have a higher conception of the duty of the state toward the individual than our adversaries, and we will not lower it, even if we are dealing with our adver-saries.' "

Following this statement of the views of the leading socialists as to the method the party would pursue in establishing the new order, Jaurès declared that society had reached a stage of development wherein it was no longer of public utility for it to be divided into two classes, the one possessing all the means of production, and the other unable to make use of its labor except on conditions which the first class was willing to concede. He showed that the efforts of some radicals to establish compulsory arbitration would not affect this antagonism; that the present civil war only shows itself on the surface by means of strikes, but is going on at other times as well. It is at the very bottom of the present system of society, of a system of property which gives power to one class and inflicts obedience on the other. This economic civil war will continue, now apparent, now hidden, now loud, now silent; but ever with the same sufferings, the same exasperations, so long as the world of production is divided into two antagonistic camps. He admitted that there were means of softening the shocks, but he declared that this permanent fundamental antagonism results from the very privilege of property, and can never be entirely prevented until the capital necessary to social labor is absorbed by the workers. " There must be but one directive force," he said; " namely, the creative force of labor."

Considering, therefore, that the greatest public necessity at the present moment was to harmonize the relations between capital and labor by making them one in power and direction, Jaurès answered the assertion that if this were accomplished by compensation, there would still exist some rich and some poor and, therefore,

a class antagonism, by saying that the bonds of compensation given to the holders of capital at the time
of expropriation would be limited in their power by the
very nature of the new society. At the present time
title-deeds and bonds enable their holders either to
purchase the means of production and of profit, such as
factories, buildings, shares, etc., or else to purchase
products for consumption. In the new society, when
capital shall have been socialized, when the community
shall have put at the disposal of the organized workers
the means of production, the bonds of compensation
which will be given to the former capitalists will not
enable them to purchase further means of production;
they will only enable them to purchase the products of
labor. Illustrating this argument, he said that when the
law abolished slavery and compensated slave-owners,
the latter were not able to use their compensation for
the purchase of new slaves, and when capitalist property shall have been socialized, the holders of compensation deeds will not be able to purchase either fresh
means of production or producers. " Thus, gentlemen,"
he said, " to those who put forward the objection that
if, when expropriating capital, compensation is not given,
it is sheer robbery, and, if it is, capitalism will be reconstituted, I reply that between the title-deeds of socialized
society and those of capitalist society there is this fundamental difference : that the latter are means of domination and exploitation, which are constantly renewed
at the expense of human labor by the play of interest
and profit, whereas the others will only be means of
consumption and will exhaust themselves by degrees,
leaving labor unhampered and organized."

Jaurès then declared that whatever the judgment of

his opponents might be as to the wisdom of the socialist order, they must nevertheless admit that they were in the presence of doctrines that offered a precise and definite solution of the present antagonism between labor and capital. And he further declared that, having stated the socialist position, the socialist party had a right to demand of "the party of democracy and progress" what its doctrine was.

"What can you do?" Jaurès demanded. "What can you republicans and radicals do to liberate and organize labor?" He then showed that Clémenceau and all the radicals had for over twenty years criticised the existing order with the same severity as the socialists, and that even Clémenceau had once signed a manifesto declaring that "whoever is not a socialist is not a republican." This conscious stirring up of class strife, he said, was wicked and immoral unless those doing it had also at the same time some means for remedying the evil. "It is a great mistake to discredit in the eyes of the workers a system which you do not know how to abolish. While you were in opposition, it was perhaps natural that your attitude should be critical; but now," he continued, "you are not only in power, you are the power, not only in appearance, not only in part, but by the simultaneous arrival of a government whose members are radicals and of a radical-socialist majority. You have full power and therefore full responsibility. I ask you then: What are you going to do?" Taking up the radical program, he showed its inconsistencies and fundamental weakness. They had sent representatives to the Hague to support any proposition for the limitation of military expenditure, and they had begun their government by an increase in that expenditure. They had said nothing

on the question of railways, and in passing upon some
new mining laws, they had not attempted to insure to
the workers better conditions or a higher reward for
their labor.   He traced this weakness to the fear of the
government lest a policy which should be in the slightest
degree positive in these matters would frighten investors
and alarm the stock exchange.

Clémenceau, answering Jaurès, stated that he and the
cabinet were in entire agreement with the socialists in
nearly all of their practical program.   In his opinion
the socialists and the radicals could move together for
some time upon the lines of their immediate program,
and that ought to suffice.   But he condemned the larger
scheme of socialization, which he said would only produce a disastrous catastrophe if it were attempted to
put it into operation suddenly.   " Here is a list of M.
Jaurès' immediately realizable reforms," he said.   " An
eight-hours day, the right of state employees to com-
bine, national insurance against unemployment and
sickness, a progressive income tax and death duties, the
return to the nation of the monopolies, and proportional representation.   Why, that is a horribly bourgeois
program, and when M. Jaurès asked me, ' What is your
program ? ' I could scarcely refrain from answering at
once, ' My program ?   Why, it is in your pocket.   You
have picked it from mine.' "

But Clémenceau's old individualist views forced him
in opposition to Jaurès with regard to strikes.   " I hold
that every man who wants work," he said, " has the right
to ask society and the public powers to protect him in
the exercise of that right."   The government must use
its power to put down violence and to maintain order.

Jaurès, in his reply, showed the difference between

the position of the capitalists and that of the workers. "What you mean by the maintenance of order," he said, "is the repression of all excesses on the part of the workers, while admitting violence on the part of the employers. You forget the difference between the condition of laborers and employers. Yes; violence is gross, visible, when used by the workers. A threatening gesture, a brutal act; they are seen and noted. Their author can be promptly dragged before judges, and dealt with. But how about the employers ? They have no need to indulge in violent language, in gestures. Their violence can be carried out in orderly fashion. A few men meet in private, in full security, like an orderly board meeting, around a table. And, like diplomatists, without violence, without shouting, without gestures, they calmly decide that a reasonable wage shall be refused. They decide that those workers who keep up the fight shall be excluded; that by some secret sign in their work-book they shall be known to all employers, — that they shall be marked men. That is the silent method; it is the murderous engine which has caught the unfortunate victim and silently crushes him, without any grating noise in the machinery.

"When it is sought to fix personal responsibility in any trouble, the same difference is seen. The workman's share is easily fixed; any violent act is soon brought home and punished. But when it comes to the responsibilities of the masters, in such a case as the Courrières disaster (a terrible mining disaster which killed 1500 men), then difficulties arise. Their responsibilities are wrapped up in the complications of anonymous capital, of limited liability companies. There are subtle evasions which can defeat the ends of justice. An engineer can say that although men were sent down into the mine when it was known to be on fire, according to chemical and theoretical discoveries there was no reason to fear the danger which, as events proved, existed. And thus, while the workman's violence is ever apparent, palpable, and easily repressed, the deep and murderous responsibility of the great employers, of the great capitalists, ever disappears in obscurity."

Aside from the really fundamental differences between the two parliamentary groups, Jaurès agreed that there was something in common in their immediate programs, and he assured the radicals that the socialists would give them every assistance in carrying out their program of reforms. " If you are in earnest," he declared, "in your desire to nationalize railways and mines, and to carry out reforms, let it be clearly stated, and you will have our support. No reform will be wrecked by our opposition, but while our method is that of peaceful reform our goal will ever remain the revolution ; namely, the complete transformation of the present social system."

I once heard Jaurès speaking to an audience of perhaps 7000 people. In that immense hall he seemed a different man from the one I knew in the chamber. His voice had the power of a great organ, with endless changes of tone and expression, with modulations without limit and with a sustained emphasis and climax that seemed to me as extraordinary as anything I had ever heard. His finished oration had the roundness and perfection of a poem. On another occasion I heard him speaking to the men of the street. His power in this instance was again of quite a different character. He became a mob orator equal to John Burns in his best days. The influence he exercised over his audience was such that if he had desired to lead this crowd of men to storm the streets of Paris, I think not one would have failed to follow him.

In the chamber Jaurès is clever and adroit. For nearly twenty years he has been in the midst of every important parliamentary crisis. He knows the secret of parliamentary influence, and he uses his knowledge of parliamentary tactics and his skill as a debater in a manner that attracts and fascinates the whole of Paris. When it is known that Jaurès is to speak, the galleries are crowded, and hundreds and sometimes thousands beg for admittance. During the last few months his interpellations have covered a wide range of subjects, and in every case he has demonstrated to the public the desire of the socialists to support the radical ministry in all the reforms that it can be induced to carry through. At the same time with extraordinary skill he has put forward the difference between their programs.

It is hardly too much to say that Jaurès has done more during the last twenty years to form political thought than any other man in France. His battles against the royalists, the Bonapartists, the Liberals, and the nationalists, his extraordinary activity during the Dreyfus affair, and his exceptional power in harmonizing the new socialist views with all the republican traditions and freedom-loving aspirations of the French people, have given him a personal power and a following that are not equalled by those of any other man in the French chamber. As long as he had to battle with out and out reaction his position was comparatively easy, but at present he faces a more subtle form of opposition. As was said, the present government is the most radical that France has known in recent years, and when Clémenceau, late in 1906, took the place of Sarrien at the head of the ministry, the first utterances of the cabinet were so advanced that it seemed as if the radicals had taken over everything except the revolutionary proposals of modern socialism. The cabinet declared for the separation of the church and state, the suppression of martial law, the abolition of the dangers of the white lead industry, the nationalization of the Western railways, the strict enforcement of the law providing one day's rest each week, and finally for old-age pensions and a graduated income tax. Besides, Clémenceau invited three socialists to take positions in the cabinet. Millerand refused, but Briand and Viviani both accepted responsible posts. It would be difficult to convey an idea of the popular enthusiasm that prevailed in Paris over the announcement of the program and the composition of the new ministry. However, the situation seemed critical for the socialist party, for, if the program were carried out, and if the ministry were fearless and uncompromising in its support of the working-class, the socialist party might have been forced into a position where it would have been impossible for the people to distinguish between its work and that of the radicals.

It would be difficult, however, to imagine how any party could have met the situation better than the socialist party. Without expressing confidence in the ministry it definitely held that it would support all reforms of a truly fundamental character. In the chamber the socialists have pursued a most skilful course. They have forced the fighting. The ministry has been prodded and goaded. Its program, which now it almost wishes to forget, is placed before its eyes and those of the

country on every possible occasion. Unlike most opposition parties the socialists want to keep the radical
ministry in power, and on one or two occasions it would
have fallen if it had not been for their support and assistance. They take a long view, and see that nothing
is so important at the present moment as to prove to the
French people that the radicals will not carry out a program of fundamental reform. Thus it is necessary to
keep them for a considerable period in a position of responsibility so that they may be tested in the most thorough and conclusive manner.

So long as radicals are always in the opposition (as, for
instance, Hearst and Bryan are with us) they appear almost as revolutionary as the socialists themselves. But
now that the French socialists are fortunate enough to
have them in power, it only remains to demonstrate the
impossibility of their accomplishing any important reform. In other words, it seems as if the French people
are being conducted through the last stage of their illu-
sions. When it is once proved that the radicals will not
carry out their promises, it seems reasonable to think
that the people will turn to the socialists. Even now
the party is beginning to expose the barren record of
radicalism. *Le Socialiste* asks, " Where are we now?
The suppression of martial law? Mutilated. The
law about white lead? Stillborn. The nationalization
of the Western railways? In danger. The law about
Sunday closing? Nerveless and weak. Old-age pensions? Adjourned. Graduated income tax? Proposed.
But so absorbed are the radicals in fighting the working
men that they cannot spare the time or effort to trans-
form the proposition into an act."

If the radicals can be kept in power for a few months

more, and if they fail, as they have failed up to the present, to carry out a single one of their proposed economic reforms, it would seem probable that the socialist party alone can hope to win the adherence of an actual majority of the French people.   The situation in France, from the point of view of the parliamentary power of socialism, is, therefore, at the present moment the most dramatic in Europe.

In giving so much prominence to the parliamentary power of socialism in Germany, Italy, England, and France, I do not want to convey the impression that it is limited to, or of exceptional importance in, those countries.   Vandervelde is at work in Belgium, Victor Adler in Austria, and other men of ability are at work in nearly all the other parliaments of Europe.   Their strife against the established order is similar in character to that of the socialists in the countries I have mentioned.   They influence the thought of their countrymen to no less a degree, and in some cases they have accomplished more for the welfare of the masses than the socialists of France, Italy, or England.   And yet nearly everywhere the socialist parties have only a small minority in parliament, as the reader will see from the table on the opposite page.   In Austria and Finland at the moment the socialists have the largest representation, and in Russia, if the electoral law permitted, they would easily obtain a majority.   In the countries under review in this book, the tactics and the immediate ends of the party vary in many details from those in Russia and other countries.   What I have given of the parliamentary effort of the socialists in certain countries is, therefore, not necessarily typical of their work in the others.   The duties of a party are necessarily determined by the state of economic, political, intellectual, and moral development that exists in its particular field of action.

*Russia	132	socialists	out of total of	440	representatives
Austria	87	"	"	353	"
Finland	80	"	"	200	"
France	52	"	"	584	"
Germany	43	"	"	397	"
England	32	"	"	670	"
†Belgium	30	"	"	166	"
Italy	25	"	"	508	"
†Denmark	24	"	"	114	"
Sweden	15	"	"	230	"
Norway	10	"	"	117	"
Holland	7	"	"	100	"
Luxemburg	7	"	"	45	"
Switzerland	2	"	"	167	"
Servia	1	"	"	160	"
	547	"	"	4251	"

* This is the representation of the socialists in the second Duma, and not in the present one. The electoral law has been changed in such a wholesale manner that nearly all the workers and peasants have been disfranchised. If there had been universal manhood suffrage, a much larger number would have been elected. Nearly all the socialist members of the second Duma have recently been sent to Siberia.

† In Belgium the Labor Party has also seven representatives in the Senate, and in Denmark the socialists have four.

A new phase of international unity and solidarity begins to manifest itself that should not pass unmentioned. Of the numberless parties in the various countries the socialists alone seek to bring the national organizations into international accord. They have, therefore, decided to create an interparliamentary union for the purpose of conference, and in case of necessity, of joint action. The first congress of this body was held in London in July, 1906. Very little notice was taken of the meeting, although nearly every European parliament was represented by one or more delegates. Three days were spent in this interparliamentary conference, which it was decided should be secret because a representative of the Duma, Anakine, had come to place before the congress the desperate situation that faced the Russian socialists. I shall never forget the intensity of that memorable gathering while listening to the impassioned address of the Russian peasant. He was a gifted speaker, and although strong and fearless, he had the saddest face I have ever seen. In the course of his address, he said he had come to London despite his belief that upon his return to Russia he would be imprisoned or perhaps secretly murdered. On the day following the congress the representatives spent the afternoon on the estate of a sympathetic Englishman. Tchaykovsky, now in prison in Russia, was there with Anakine. As we drove along the lovely lanes, and looked upon the smiling hills of Surrey and Kent, and walked through Chaucer's Pilgrims' Way, the sadness and brooding melancholy of this Russian peasant's face cast a gloom over us all, and for weeks afterward it haunted me. His parliamentary duties called him back to Russia immediately, and a few days later we saw in the papers that he had hardly landed from the boat in Finland before he was set upon and beaten into insensibility by a band of thugs employed by the police.

I realize in terminating this chapter that some of my readers may conclude that the socialists have abandoned their revolutionary aims and have settled down to a peaceful policy of gradually reforming the present order; but if they do arrive at such a conclusion, it will show an utter misconception of socialist political tactics.

DIE ABGEORDNETEN DER ARBEITERPARTEI DER RUSSISCHEN REICHSDUMA.

Deputies of the Labor Party in the Duma.

Socialists have no desire to pursue the desperate method of inciting the workers to insurrection. They realize that violence is a sign of weakness. Increasing influence, and a growing assurance that socialism will eventually attain complete power, have encouraged them to work with confidence toward the end of converting a majority of the nation to their views. In parliament they never lose sight of that end, and Liebknecht well says, " All legislative measures which we shall support, if the opportunity is given us, ought to have for their object to prove the fitness of socialism to serve the common good." Following out that policy, the socialists are zealous promoters of every humane measure that can advance the welfare of the community. Whatever will increase the opportunities of working men for education, whatever will give them leisure to read and study, whatever will assure them health and pleasant surroundings at home and at work, the socialists exert their utmost to obtain. A humane interest in the welfare of all inspires these legislative efforts ; but the reader must not forget that in this work the socialists have also a special and revolutionary end in view. They are confident that when the workers free themselves from the conditions which now brutalize them, and when they gain sufficient leisure to read and think, there will come as an inevitable result a more consistent and intelligent revolt against the oppressive conditions of capitalism. At the same time anything which raises the standard of life, morality, and mentality of the workers makes them increasingly fit to assume complete control over industry.

This work of ameliorating conditions is supplemented by other efforts equally revolutionary in their aim. In every country the socialists are endeavoring to win for

the political organizations, the unions, and the coöperatives, greater powers of resistance.   Toward this end
they have already obtained in many countries additional
political rights, such as an extension of suffrage and the
right of free speech and assembly.   For the unions they
have endeavored everywhere to obtain, or to preserve
from reaction, the right of combination, of striking, and
of peaceful picketing.   They have rendered it increasingly perilous for the government to interfere in industrial disputes by the use of the army and the police.
For centuries the state has favored the interests of property as against the interests of the workers, but slowly
the new governing principle evolves ; namely, that in the
conflicts between labor and capital the state shall as
nearly as possible maintain an attitude of neutrality.
The result of all this socialist activity is the gradual
breaking down of political and economic oppression, and
the placing in the hands of the workers the means of
their own emancipation.

This forcing up of the standard of life, and this winning of economic and political power, when viewed from
the socialist standpoint, are essentially revolutionary
in their tendency.   They are determined efforts to
strengthen the workers in their struggle against capitalism.
A clergyman recently condemned socialism because, as
he said, it looks upon humanity as a god.   A prominent
socialist answered, " That is at least a higher ideal than
the one possessed by present society, which looks upon
property as a god."   There is truth in both assertions,
and they roughly explain the basis of the conflict now
being waged between capital and labor.   It is a war
à outrance between two ideals, and there is evidence to
show that property as a divinity is losing much of its

former prestige. Its influence over the masses is no longer what it once was, and when the opponents of socialism come before a propertyless populace, claiming to be the guardians of private property, and seek their suffrages on that ground, it creates as little enthusiasm as did the old plea of the divine right of kings at the time the rising democracy put an end to autocracy.

And yet that is the claim now being made by the radicals in France and the liberals in England. All private property is to them a sacred thing, an unalterable, unchangeable institution ; and to speak of its evolving from age to age, changing its form and scope to fit itself to the requirements of social evolution, is sacrilegious. Of course socialism attacks only one form of private property, as the abolitionists attacked only one ; that is, the private ownership of the instruments of production. But that, of course, makes socialism none the less subversive, and the capitalists, realizing the danger, try to defend private property categorically, even when it is most injurious to the public welfare. Rooted in the belief that private property must be maintained at all hazards, they cannot evolve from their own thought any method of ameliorating the social and industrial evils which result from the domination of the propertied interests. Nevertheless, they are terrified by the growing power of socialism, and finding compromise a necessity, they weakly borrow the immediate program of their opponents. Thus Campbell-Bannerman in England, Clémenceau in France, von Buelow in Germany, and other government leaders, find the only political course open to them is to adopt a socialistic legislative policy. It is unquestionable that by so doing they alleviate somewhat the misery, and for a time diminish the discontent; but their action is in deadly conflict with their political and economic faith. They thus leave themselves and their followers without principles, and their parliamentary policy degenerates into a petty struggle to save what they can in the face of an aggressive opposition.

CHAPTER IX

SOCIALISM IN ART AND LITERATURE

ALTHOUGH, as we have seen, modern socialism is of very recent growth, one can already clearly discern two distinct periods in what may be called the literature of socialism. The first period was a heroic one, corresponding nicely with the unorganized and not always intelligent revolt of the working-classes previous to the eighties. Nearly all the great minds in art and literature, consciously or unconsciously, translated into their work the spirit of unrest and blind revolt characteristic of the time. Wagner in music; Millet in painting; Turguéneff, Grigoróvitch, Nekrassoff, Tolstóy, Hugo, Zola, Herwegh, Freiligrath, Whitman, Carlyle, and Ruskin in literature, to mention only a few, were all expressing in varied form the widespread discontent with the existing social order. Matthew Arnold, similarly engaged in his keenly intellectual and passionless essays, summed up his complaint in the powerful sentence, "Our inequality materializes our upper class, vulgarizes our middle class, brutalizes our lower class." Ruskin came to the conclusion that "all social evils and religious errors arise out of the pillage of the laborers by the idlers." And in 1871 he began to write "Fors" — letters to the workmen of Great Britain — by declaring: "For my own part, I will put up with this state of things, passively, not an hour longer. I am not an unselfish person, nor an evangelical one; I have no particular pleasure in doing good; neither do I dislike doing it so much as to expect to be rewarded for it in another world. But I simply cannot paint, nor read, nor look at minerals, nor do anything else that I like, and the very light of the morning sky, when there is any — which is seldom, nowadays, near London — has become hateful to me, because of the misery that I know of, and see signs of, where I know it not, which no imagination can interpret too bitterly."

Carlyle could not think of modern society without bursting into rage. The disorganization of labor; the spectacle of society covering the fair face of England with filthy furnaces and boundless slums; the silly commonplaces of political economy, which he called "the dismal science"; the anarchy in industry and commerce, led him to write his bitter political satires that seethe with brimstone and fire. Hugo, in France, was writing his immense drama of modern society, picturing the life of that outcast saint whom the modern world could not understand, and perforce must crucify. Whitman, in America, was singing his great songs of Democracy. Tolstóy was writing two novels : one picturing the horrors of war, the other the foibles and vanities of Russian society. Turguéneff was watching the rising revolt among the masses, and becoming almost a guiding force in its progress by his pitiless analysis of the character of its leaders. It would be difficult to find in any other period of recent history men equal in power to these master minds, all of them struggling to voice the rising revolt, and yet incapable of discerning or of adequately expressing the new idealism coming to birth.

Amidst the storms then raging over Europe there was something magnificent in the Titanic labors of these men. Analyzing the warring elements, describing the discord, lamenting the carnage, they sought for some guiding principle, but in vain ; they could only voice the spirit of their restless, questioning, dissatisfied age. They were the prophets, rather than the teachers, of the new time of which they saw but the dawn. " I know not if I deserve," said Heine, " that a laurel-wreath should one day be laid on my coffin. Poetry, dearly as I have loved it, has always been to me but a divine plaything. I have never attached any great value to poetical fame ; and I trouble myself very little whether people praise my verses or blame them. But lay on my coffin a *sword;* for I was a brave soldier in the Liberation War of humanity." The same wish might have been expressed by all these men, for without exception they placed higher than their art their work in the service of humanity.

It is not a mere coincidence that during the same period another group of great minds was trying to form an International Working Men's Association. Marx, Engels, Bakounine, de Paepe, Mazzini, Professor Beesley, were all minds of a high order, and all were connected with the International at some time in its history. It represented in active life what the other group represented in art and literature. Both groups felt instinctively the modern revolt; both saw the evils of our economic system ; both recoiled from the anarchy in society, the bitter poverty of the many, the arrogant dominance of the few. But the Internationalists, like the artists and writers, could arrive at no common program ; and, after a few years of troubled existence, their organization broke into dissension and discord, which was also characteristic of the time. With the exception of Marx and Engels, much of the spirit of the International was destructive and nihilist rather than constructive and creative, with the result that it merely incited the masses to blind and futile revolt instead of organized and constructive action. The fact is, all these men were living in the eventide of a great historical epoch. It was Carlyle who voiced the vague, despondent spirit of these forerunners of modern socialism when he said, "There must be a new world if there is to be any at all."

The eighties mark a new period in the literature as well as in the politics of socialism. There began to appear at that time in all the countries of Europe a new force. There was the same revolt against the anarchy of society, against poverty and riches, but with it there came a master passion which differed fundamentally from the vague democratic yearnings of the older men. Carlyle, as well as the others, had noticed the growing proletariat, but he no more than they understood the historic rôle they were destined to play. Arnold said: "Our present social organization has been an appointed stage in our growth; it has been of good use, and has enabled us to do great things. But the use is at an end, and the stage is over." Nearly all the older men were of a similar view. They felt that society was on the eve of new developments, but of these their thought was vague and uncertain. In general their attitude was destructive and negative; more in accord with Bakounine than with Marx, who was coming to be the dominant spirit in the rising movement.

Socialism was beginning to manifest itself in definite

THE · WORKERS · MAY · POLE

[An offering for May-Day 1894 from Walter Crane]

form in Germany, in France, in Belgium, and even in England. It was no longer a mere revolt, and as an organized and disciplined movement it began to play an important rôle in the political life of Europe. It was hardly to be expected that the older men would fully understand the new movement, and it was but natural that in the main it was the younger men in literature and art who gave it expression. In any case nothing could be more remarkable than the rapid change following the seventies. After the vague democratic yearnings and the purely destructive criticism of the older generation, succeeded a gospel that dominated men of widely different talents; as, for instance: William Morris, Anatole France, Bernard Shaw, Maurice Maeterlinck, Alexander Kielland, Maxim Gorky, H. G. Wells, Giovanni Verga, Gerhart Hauptmann, Edmondo de Amicis; the scientists, Alfred Russel Wallace, Zanarelli, Lombroso, Grant Allen, Enrico Ferri; the poets, Giovanni Pascoli, Ada Negri, Edward Carpenter ; and the artists, Walter Crane, Steinlen, and van Biesbroeck. Like the older men they too are in revolt. And yet that which had begun to take place among the disinherited, and to assume definite and constructive form, found these and other men of talent ready to give it expression in painting, in sculpture, in music, and in literature.*

* It is a matter for regret that I can merely mention the socialist poets Edward Carpenter, of England; Graf, Guerrini, and Pascoli of Italy; and Mrs. Roland Holtz, of Holland, whose poems are frequently printed in socialist papers as the songs of the movement. Nor can I more than mention Maurice Maeterlinck, John Galsworthy, Granville Barker, and Richard Whiteing, and the artists who make possible such first-rate comical and satirical socialist journals as " L'Assiette au Beurre," " L'Asino," and " Der Wahre Jacob." Walter Crane, the English, and Steinlen, Grandjouan, Delannoy, and Naudin, the French artists, lavish their great talents upon socialist

Whether we take the work of the forerunners of modern socialism, or that of the present exponents, we find the same methods used to interpret the social spirit. Both depict the life of the peasant and the industrial worker, interpreting the soul of the people in its patient and quiet dignity. Both portray the evils of modern society by problem plays and novels. Both struggle to give expression to the quest for the ideal whether in the individual or in social organization. And nearly all the writers leave at times the field of art to issue revolutionary pamphlets upon economics and politics.

Perhaps the highest social use of literature is in awakening a sympathetic understanding between different races or different classes of the same race. In the days of slavery, when whites looked upon blacks almost as beasts devoid of human sentiment, the work of Harriet Beecher Stowe proved a revelation, and aroused in all civilized countries profound human sympathy. Whatever defects it may have as a work of art, "Uncle Tom's Cabin" made the thought of slavery intolerable. It has always been easy for men to believe that they differ from other men, and that color, race, or nationality,

propaganda. In the expository literature of socialism, the Fabian tracts and essays rank high. Bernard Shaw's work stands out from among the others, and perhaps no other modern writer is capable of treating economics in so interesting a manner. Anatole France's "Monsieur Bergeret à Paris," and H. G. Wells' "The Misery of Boots," are pure literature; and while the work of Robert Blatchford is largely of a propagandist nature, he is richly endowed with that greatest gift of the artist, the power of seeing things and of making others see them.

Many well-known American writers and artists also feel the socialist impulse. William Dean Howells, Edwin Markham, Finley Peter Dunne, Jack London, and Upton Sinclair are among the best known, although nearly all of the younger men are coming under the influence of socialist thought.

religion, blood, or riches, almost any distinctive thing, separates them from the rest of human kind, and creates a gulf between what they are pleased to call superior and inferior people. Between races such feelings are more easily explained; although when such books are read as Du Bois' "The Souls of Black Folk," unfortunately too little known, the feeling of superiority is apt to give place to a humiliating sense of shame. But among people of the same race such feeling is less readily understood; and yet it is almost as common. The slaves of our country were of a different race from their masters; but the serfs of Russia were of the same race and creed, the same language and tradition, as the upper class. And yet Kropotkin says: " Human feelings were not recognized, not even suspected in serfs, and when Turguéneff published his little story of ' Mumú,' and Grigoróvitch began to issue his thrilling novels, in which he made his readers weep over the misfortunes of serfs, it was to a great number of persons a startling revelation. ' They love just as we do; is it possible?' exclaimed the sentimental ladies."

A similar effort to that of the above-mentioned writers is made by those who endeavor to picture the suffering grandeur of the toiling masses of field or factory. To two Belgians, one a painter, the other a sculptor, we are indebted for some of the most affecting pictures of misery that art has given us. Charles Degroux belongs to the earlier period, but his pictures serve even to-day to mould socialist sentiment. His canvases are tragic. His figures are broken by the burdens of misery, and a spirit of brooding sorrow and inevitable misfortune pervades his work. The other Belgian, van Biesbroeck, is a young man, who after achieving an excellent reputation

throughout Europe came back to his native town of
Ghent at the request of the socialists. They have built
him and his father a studio, and assure to them what
they require; and these two work together to make
beautiful the various coöperative establishments owned
by the socialists. The older van Biesbroeck is a philosopher; the younger, an artist of exceptional talent. His
portraits of the workers of Ghent will become historic,
representing to future ages the barbarism of modern industrial society. His men, women, and children labor
and mourn. They are superb figures, forcibly drawn,
wonderfully chiselled, with the power to evoke precious
and inexpressible emotions of sympathy and comradeship. Resembling Degroux in some ways, van Biesbroeck understands better the heart, and knows how to
interpret in human terms the meaning of all the crushing
burdens borne by those who labor. You see sympathy
in all his work, — the sympathy almost of a mother for
her child; and yet how powerful the lines, how firm
and sturdy the figures.

Millet and Meunier have, of course, done an even
greater work in picturing the soul of the people. They
meet humanity at a higher level than Degroux or even
van Biesbroeck, and yet it is not often possible to find
in their work the same sympathy that pervades the
work of the latter. Millet sometimes painted a brutish
form without intelligence or spirituality, such as "The
Man with the Hoe"; but his greatest work was to interpret the peasant full of elemental, primordial force.
To see the superb action of "The Sower," the quiet
power and skill of "The Man spreading Manure," to
come across that lovely landscape with "The Glean-
ers" at work in the foreground, to grasp the infinite

"The Dock Laborer," by Meunier.

sweetness of those uncertain "First Steps," and the glorious spirit of paternity expressed in the affectionate outstretched arms of the father, or to incline the head with those two fine figures in "The Angelus," is to come at one mighty sweep into perfect sympathy with these patient bearers of life's burdens.

Meunier in sculpture did for the industrial workers what Millet in painting did for the peasant. Labor had a strange and overpowering fascination for Meunier, and he used to sit for hours in wonder and admiration, watching the turmoil of the docks in Antwerp. In the black country he would lose himself in a mass of miners rushing home from their work or watch at night superb figures before the flaring furnaces. In Meunier's sketches one is given some idea of how black and sinister he conceived modern industry to be, and at times his work is pervaded with a pathos that almost unnerves one; but the feeling is rarely dominant. He sometimes saw among the workers of Belgium a spent toiler, but none the less superb. I know of nothing in sculpture that seems to me more god-like than the head which he calls "Antwerp," symbolizing Labor; for that is what Antwerp meant to him. It is quiet, yet it breathes of action. There is not that refinement of the Greek which shows softness and weakness; there is no superfluous flesh. It is the face of a conqueror obeying a cosmic instinct; the symbol of the indomitable spirit of Labor which creates from the raw materials of hill and valley the necessary products of civilized life. Most of Meunier's work was devoted to portraits of peasants, miners, puddlers, glass workers, dockers, and laborers.*

* A striking tribute has recently been paid Meunier by the dockers of Genoa, who have purchased his "Le Débardeur" from their union funds.

It was the faithful effort to picture the lives of the men, women, and children of toil. The best examples of his art are in Brussels, and nowhere could they be more appropriately found or their teaching be more necessary. Belgium is the workshop of Europe, and it is well to have there these figures typifying Labor the Conqueror, a prophecy of what shall one day arrive.

Grigoróvitch and Turguéneff did much to acquaint the intellectuals of Russia with peasant life, and Gorky, during the last ten years, has done remarkable work in the same direction. Gorky is a rebel; not as many writers are, in the library only. He is an active, con-spiring revolutionist; in the open when possible, under-ground when necessary. When you have once seen Gorky, you understand the source of his power. His eyes — they make one think of high-power searchlights — have a force of vision which penetrates into the inner meaning of things. Life cannot deceive Gorky, and if one reads "Malva," "Tchelkache," the "Ex-men," or "Twenty-six and One," — those searching short stories in which Gorky is at his best, — and thinks them overdrawn, he does not know the life of the abyss. Gorky's tramps and outcasts are never completely lost or vanquished. They too are idealists and rebels, as are most Russians of the working-class. Although too broken in body to be effective, there is hardly one whose spirit is unworthy of our admiration. His pictures of lodging-house and slum, of factory and tenement, are no less wonderful than those appealing landscapes which so often form the background in his masterly pictures of Russian life. In his plays and novels even the most miserable of his characters have the instincts of man and the fire of rebellion. As with Meunier, one always feels when reading Gorky that however adverse the conditions, and however terrible the oppression, the spirit of man is unconquerable.

It is to Giovanni Verga that we must go to find pictures of Italian life comparable to those that Gorky has drawn of Russian life. In " The House by the Medlar Tree " we are shown the lowest misery, that of a Sicilian village. With powerful realism and infinite detail Verga portrays the peasants, the fisher folk, the toilers crushed under their burdens, and the vanquished wrecks; and above these unfortunates, the political, social, and religious parasites that prey upon ignorance and helplessness. In " Master Don Gesualdo " he pictures the middle-class provincial; in " The Duchess of Leyra," the silly vanities of the upper class; in a later book, the political corruption and petty intrigue so prevalent in Italian life; and at last he personifies in " The Man of Lusso " all the social and political vices that are crushing the Italian people. He is powerful, but his lines are often hard and his realism without grace. In some respects he is more like Zola than Gorky, for his sordid, ghastly pictures of misery are too often unaccompanied with that sympathy which one notes in the work of all Russians.

Matilde Serao and Ada Negri are two remarkable Italian women, — one a novelist, the other a poet, — both expressing the same revolt and picturing, each in her own effective way, the evils of modern society. Matilde Serao's " Il Ventre di Napoli," say the authors of " Italy To-day," is " a passionate appeal, straight from a woman's heart, to the rulers of Italy, pleading that no mere ' gutting ' of Naples by a few new streets can avail aught in healing the terrible social and economic miseries of her people. Few books move the reader more than this little volume of a hundred pages, telling of the moral and physical diseases that lie festering beneath the fair sky and picturesque beauty of this metropolis of the South — the gross, half-pagan superstition, the universal lust for gambling, the poverty, the squalor; yet withal a people of quick intelligence, patient of toil, naturally gentle, with an inbred love of music and color. Let those who attempt to indulge a facile indignation at the more obvious vices and darker features of Neapolitan life turn to the last chapter of this book, and learn somewhat of the exquisite refinement of its charity, the inexhaustible springs of human pity and neighborly love, that sweeten the lives of this much-maligned people, and make up a daily martyrdom of incalculable self-sacrifice."

Ada Negri is a product of the poor, and her bread was earned in one of the most miserable of Italian professions, that of schoolmistress. Her mother was a factory hand, and she never knew her father. In the early nineties there first appeared some of her extraordinary poems. To quote again, " It is difficult to give the reader who is unfamiliar with the originals an adequate conception of the concentrated passion, the nervous energy, that quiver in every fibre of this frail, solitary daughter of the people athirst for love and social justice and beauty. Wielding a lash that seems knotted with scorn, she scourges the dominant classes of society. . . . As she broods over her fate, the pale figure of Ill-fortune by her bedside claims her, yet bids her remember that the sun of glory illumines those who labor in blood and tears ; that sorrow gives wings to the ideal ; that victory is for those who have brave hearts and fight on. An

' enigma of hatred and love,' she weeps with pity for the ill-fed in her class of eighty children ; she cannot look upon a poor, ragged, shoeless street arab, and think of his probable fate, without yearning to clasp him to her breast in a supreme embrace of pity and sorrow.   She hears the infinite hordes of toilers advancing with a noise of thunder, in serried ranks, bareheaded, with fevered eyes ; from fireless hearths and sleepless beds, from alley and hovel, they press upon her ; she feels their hoarse breath on her cheeks.   She gives the pity they ask, but mingles it with fierce indignation.   In ' Tempeste' she tells of the sacrifice and tragedies of the poor — the workless, the ejected, the dead and wounded of the mine, the victims of machinery."

In contrast to the work of this fiery and bitter Italian is that exquisite little story of Anatole France — " Crainquebille."   It is one of the masterpieces of modern literature, this story of a Parisian pushcart pedler.   To come close to the emotions agitating this poor soul, to realize how little the busy turmoil of to-day takes account of its simple wonder, to see its hope and pride crushed by the brutal methods of police administration, is to awaken in a new and powerful way to the almost universal and ruthless disregard for the weak and defenceless.   As we go through this simple annal we feel a growing sense of comradeship with the old man, and we realize that all about us, in the poorest and meanest of these human souls that touch our elbows, there exists something that is infinitely sweet and precious.   By the side of " Crainquebille " belongs that prose poem of Leo Tolstóy," Where Love is, there God is also," the story of Martuin Avdyeitch, the sweet old shoemaker living in his cellar-dwelling — a story which takes us for a precious and peaceful half-hour among homely and simple lives that the world knows not.

Closely related to the portrayal of these types of the people is the work of the various writers who have interpreted the leaders of the revolt. The two novels, "Tragic Comedians" and "Vittoria," by George Meredith, centre about the lives of Ferdinand Lassalle and Mazzini. Both leaders of revolutionary movements, they become to Meredith material for two extraordinary psychological and social studies. And yet, interesting as they are, they hardly rank with the monumental work of Turguéneff, the Russian. Turguéneff was a revolutionist, who in his youth assisted Hérzen in editing a revolutionary paper, and who through his entire life was the standard-bearer of Liberal Russia. " He never preaches any doctrine whatever," says Stepniak, "but gives us, with an unimpeachable, artistic objectiveness, the living men and women in whom certain ideas, doctrines, and aspirations were embodied. And he never evolves these ideas and doctrines from his inner consciousness, but takes them from real life, catching with his unfailing artistic instinct an incipient movement just at the moment when it was to become a historic feature of the time. Thus his novels are a sort of artistic epitome of the intellectual history of modern Russia, and also a powerful instrument of her intellectual progress."

In six great novels Turguéneff traces in a series of types the intellectual currents running through Russian life from the forties through the seventies. Rudin, one of his most striking characters, is a man of the forties, under the ferocious despotism of Nicholas I. He is fascinating from the moment you meet him, and amazes all by his intellectual audacity.   His eloquence, range of knowledge, and popular sympathies arouse the enthusiasm of all who know him.   But that is the end. Brilliant and fertile in intellect, he is altogether barren in action.   He is an intellectual vagrant, turning from one thing to another, incapable of anything useful or practical.   At the end, hungry, homeless, and friendless, he dies on the barricades in Paris, during the revolution of 1848.   In a second volume, "The Nobleman's Retreat," we have Lavretsky, who has the idealism of Rudin with will-power added ; but his plans for practical activity are shattered by an unfriendly environment and a hapless marriage.   In his next volume, " On the Eve," published 1859, he develops in " Helen " a true type of the Russian young woman then beginning to join in all the movements for Russian freedom.   Kropotkin says, " She is the woman who conquered her right to knowledge, totally reformed the education of children, fought for the liberation of the toiling masses, endured unbroken in the snows and jails of Siberia, died if necessary on the scaffold, and at the present moment continues with unabating energy the same struggle."

In the next novel, "Fathers and Sons," published 1862, we have the nihilist type in Bazároff, perhaps the strongest character in Turguéneff's novels.   He is rough, fearless, absolutely sincere, denying all authority, and accepting nothing unproved.   He is rationalist and revolutionist.   The skilful artistic contrast which Turguéneff works into the book in the person of the smug, brainless Peter Petrovitch is dramatic.   The latter represents all that Bazároff detests ; the foolish vanities of life, silly superstition, personal elegance,

T

conformity to all conventions. A storm of protest greeted the appearance of this powerful novel. The youth whose type Turguéneff was seeking to portray in Bazároff were indignant, and thought they saw a desire to caricature their ideal. But despite the rudeness of Bazároff, Turguéneff loved him for his truth, sincerity, and courage, and the indignation of the advanced young liberals so affected Turguéneff that he contemplated for a time giving up literature altogether. In his next novel, " Smoke," written in 1867, he voices a spirit of despair, and pictures the hollow vanities of the handful of bureaucratic despots then ruling the destinies of the mighty Russian empire. In " Virgin Soil," the last of the series, he pictures that extraordinary movement of the seventies, " To the People." The Russian youth of intellect and conscience were at the time casting aside all thought of personal advancement, social position, and ease, to carry the revolutionary propaganda into the villages of Russia. The historic circle Tchaykovsky was then meeting in St. Petersburg, with Kropotkin, Stepniak, and a host of other brilliant and capable young men and women, all of whom are now dead or in exile. The series is one of the most remarkable in literature, picturing from decade to decade the variation in the revolutionary ferment, and serving in no inconsiderable degree to teach the new generation saner lines of action and nobler paths of sacrifice.

Much of the literature and art of socialism is devoted to the portrayal of the evils of society. The individual seems lost amid the play of social forces, while the crushing power of evil conditions is shown in all its magnitude. There are factory hells and slums, social vices and hideous industrial wrongs, which ruin and destroy what is good and precious in man. Among present-day writers perhaps no one has equalled Émile Zola in describing the devastating power of these relentless inevitable social forces. However much he may at times revolt us, we must admit that Zola attempted a laudable and gigantic task in the twenty volumes published under the general title, "Rougon Macquart." He could not tolerate the silly romanticism of the empire, and he determined to picture with pitiless realism the whole of contemporary society. In these volumes the life of all France passes before the reader. The descriptions of the vile degradations into which man falls are terribly realistic, and embrace a record of modern life so revolting as almost to choke and stifle one. In "L'Assommoir" Zola takes us into the depths, among intoxicated wrecks and hopeless outcasts. He leaves no vice unspoken, no horror undescribed. In "Germinal" we have a picture of the mines, and the movement of dark forms in the bowels of the earth as they struggle toward the light. Following this great series, Zola wrote three volumes, "Lourdes," "Rome," and "Paris," to show the decay of superstition and the rise of rationalism. In the latter he seemed to have lost confidence in any efforts for the regeneration of society, except the destructive attempts of the anarchists and the constructive work of science. Not content with picturing life as he saw it, he then wrote four gospels to convey to the world his idea of social salvation, the last volume remaining unfinished at his death. One of the four is "Le Travail," and in that he finds his inspiration. Labor, — the God of humanity; the glorious creator; the serene power that shapes the destiny of man, — he finds joyless, unknown, degraded, enslaved, crucified. It must be resurrected, and made free, and holy, and joyful, and beautiful. And he traces the outlines of a new social order arising through the associated efforts of the workers.

There is much that is similar to the work of Zola in the writings of nearly all of the younger men of our generation. The literature of social problems represents perhaps the main current in the literary effort of the last twenty years. Realism is in full swing throughout Europe. In the Balkan States there is a school of writers, several of whom have Zola's vivid descriptive power, combined with a reverential regard for the spiritual character of man that reminds one of Millet. Nearly all the younger men work with a conscious social purpose, and they see more clearly than Zola did through the bewildering chaos of contemporary life. Many of them owe their impulse directly to the socialist movement, and labor to accentuate in art the inspiration that comes from social democracy. Among the most noteworthy of the writers of the north is Alexander Kielland, the Norwegian. He closely approaches Zola in " The Laboring People," and in " Elsie " and in other short stories and novels he gives evidence of possessing a profound social philosophy.

Among Englishmen, the late George Gissing approached the realism of the Frenchman. He says in one of his novels : " Art nowadays must be the mouthpiece of misery, for misery is the keynote of modern life." In one powerful story, " New Grub Street," he traces the slow ruin by overwork, hunger, and care, of every sweet and ineffable gift of spiritual and artistic

Group by van Biesbroeck in Socialist Cemetery, Ghent.

power. " The Odd Woman " is a tragedy that describes the poverty of helpless, unnecessary odd women, — women the world has no place for, unnecessarily born, unnecessarily reared, without husbands, without duties, women whom the world passes by without a thought of their pitiless struggle for bread.   " The Nether World " is like one of Degroux's paintings : it is all black misery ; gaunt starvation ; ruin of spirit, mind, body ; slums, abysses. A terrible book, with no glint of light, no rift in the clouds ; which stares out of its pages at you like that grim and frightful " Melancholia " of Albrecht Dürer.

In connection with this type of literature one should not fail to mention two Russians who have accomplished a definite and important work. Tolstóy in " War and Peace " has done in literature what Vereschágin has done in art. Vereschágin is the Hervé of Russia, preaching to the whole nation the revolutionary views of the anti-militarist. He could not speak or write his views, or form a political party to carry them out, so he gave them to the world in paint. The effect exercised by these two anti-militarists upon Russia "was already apparent," Kropotkin says, "during the great Turkish war of 1877–1878, when it was absolutely impossible to find in Russia a correspondent who would have described how ' we have peppered the enemy with grapeshot,' or how ' we shot them down like ninepins.' If a man could have been found to use in his letters such survivals of savagery, no paper would have dared to print them."

In portraying the evils of modern society, perhaps no writers have done a more effective work than the dramatists. Hermann Sudermann's " Die Ehre," " Sodoms

Ende," and " Heimat," the latter well known in America as " Magda," are all militant dramatic protests and
strong social satires.   Young Sudermann and his contemporary, Gerhart Hauptmann, were the leaders of a
new movement in German literature which voiced the
democratic revolt and socialist idealism of the German
youth during the eighties and nineties.   " The Weavers "
of Hauptmann is perhaps the most powerful socialist
drama that has been written.   It is a sombre picture of
a people crushed by toil and driven to revolt by misery
and hunger, ending in a bloody struggle between the
soldiery and the starving workmen.

Ibsen, the Norwegian dramatist, is a psychologist
rather than a sociologist, battling against sophistry,
hypocrisy, and mistaken ideals.   Even in his so-called
social dramas, " The League of Youth," " The Pillars of
Society," etc., he is far more interested in individual
than in social pathology.   Again and again he pictures
the individual restive under the restrictions of modern
society, and in revolt against the slavery of some modern
conventionality.   With considerable feeling he once
expressed the gist of his philosophy in the following
words : " Liberty, equality, and fraternity are no longer
the same things that they were in the days of the
blessed guillotine ; but it is just this that the politicians
will not understand, and that is why I hate them.
These people only desire partial revolutions, — revolutions in externals, in politics.   But these are mere trifles.
There is only one thing that avails — to revolutionize
people's minds."   In carrying out this program Ibsen
waged a veritable warfare upon philistinism.   He conceived his most necessary work to be of a destructive
character with the bias of an anarchist, which he once

confessed himself to be in a letter to George Brandes, the Danish critic. He is the avowed representative of the Bazároffs that Turguéneff presents so powerfully in " Fathers and Sons."

It is unnecessary to say that Bernard Shaw, the British dramatist, is a socialist, who purposely uses his art for propaganda purposes. He employs the drama for social and political ends as the church once did for moral and religious ends. For destroying what seems to him false and evil in present society his method is sometimes that of the anarchist, and John Tanner in " Man and Superman " personifies this attitude toward life. Realizing the necessity for some destruction, some clearing away of old ideas and institutions before new ideas and institutions can take their place, Shaw is often purely destructive, and to the casual reader this may seem his entire aim. But a careful reading of his novels and dramas, lectures, criticisms of art and literature, will give proof of his constructive purpose. He can resist the tendency so little that he prefaces all his dramas to make his point clear, and — to slip between the covers a socialist tract.

Many of Shaw's admirers fail to grasp the fundamental purpose underneath his work, mainly, I think, for the reason that wit is so rarely found among social reformers and idealists. He is too often considered merely a man of literary fancy and conceit, fond of trifling with the world's great movements, and jeering at cherished ideals and ancient beliefs. But in all his novels, which were written in the early eighties when most of his time was spent in propaganda for the socialist movement, and in his plays, which have been written during the last ten years, a definite social philosophy manifests itself. "John Bull's Other Island" is a political tract on the Irish question, and "Widowers' Houses" shows, as Shaw himself says, "middle-class respectability and younger son gentility, fattening on the poverty of the slum." "Mrs. Warren's Profession" deals with the problem of wage-earning women under modern economic conditions, and attempts to prove, to use Shaw's own words again, that "any society which desires to found itself on a high standard of integrity of character in its units should organize itself in such a fashion as to make it possible too for all men and all women to maintain themselves in reasonable comfort by their industry without selling their affections and their convictions. At present we condemn women as a sex to attach themselves to 'bread-winners,' licitly or illicitly, on pain of heavy privation and disadvantage." "Man and Superman," "Major Barbara," and "The Doctor's Dilemma" have a broader social outlook. They embrace Shaw's acute criticisms of modern life and the elements of his constructive social philosophy. As Holbrook Jackson says, what Shaw "has aimed at doing for the English stage is what Ibsen, Tolstóy, Strindberg, Brieux, and others have done for the European stage; that is, to inaugurate a problem drama of modern ideas, to exhibit dramatically the vital part of human beings struggling against things and conditions."

"The Perfect Wagnerite," one of Shaw's most brilliant critical essays, performs a double service, in enabling him to show the revolutionary sympathies of the great musician, and at the same time to portray in a masterly manner the vices of capitalism. "The Ring," Shaw explains, was begun immediately after Wagner escaped to Switzerland, following the German revolution of 1849. His sympathy for the poor led him to participate in their battle against the rich and the wrong, along with his friend Auguste Roeckel, and Michael Bakounine, the famous apostle of revolutionary anarchism. Wagner's "Art and Revolution," which was also written in Switzerland, shows how thoroughly the socialist side of the German uprising had his sympathy; and for three years he spent much of his time pamphleteering on social questions.

According to Shaw, "The Ring," with all its gods, giants, and dwarfs, its water maidens and valkyries, its wishing cap, magic ring, and miraculous treasure, is a dream of to-day, symbolizing the struggle for gold and power. Wotan represents monarchy, and Loki (the lie) assists him, with all the logic and imagination of an ordinary corporation attorney, in trying to maintain his power. His wife Frika represents law, constitutions, and other inflexible things, while Siegfried signifies the coming of man. As Shaw says, it is pretended that there are as yet no men on the earth. There are giants, dwarfs, and gods, and he warns us against the danger of imagining that the gods are of a higher order than the human. This he says is not at all true. Man must come to redeem the world from the lame and cramped government of the gods.

In the first opera, "The Rhine Gold," we find Alberic, a dwarf, endeavoring to rob the Rhine-maidens of their treasure. He is the typical capitalist, and after he once obtains the power which gold gives, "hordes of his fellow-creatures are thenceforth," says Shaw, "condemned to slave miserably, overground and underground, lashed to their work by the invisible whip of starvation. They never see him any more than the victims of our 'dangerous trades' ever see the shareholders whose power is nevertheless everywhere, driving them to destruction. The very wealth they create with their labor becomes an additional force to impoverish them; for as fast as they make it it slips from their hands into the hands of their master and makes him mightier than ever." But when Alberic becomes the possessor of all this wealth, others more important than he by tradition endeavor to rob him of it; and all the rest of the opera, and the two that follow, are taken up with an undignified and bitter struggle for the gold. Finally Siegfried, representing in Shaw's mind not socialism but anarchism, comes to make an end of the gods.

He calls Siegfried a young Bakounine, and says that while anarchism as a panacea is just as hopeless as any other panacea, and will be so even if we breed a race of perfectly benevolent men, nevertheless in the sphere of thought anarchism is a necessary preliminary to progress. Anarchism represents the revolt against authority no matter what force and tradition it may have behind it. It is, therefore, to Shaw's mind, a critical faculty essential to intellectual progress. But he says Anarchism "will not be replaced by Anarchism. As to the industrial or political machinery of society, Anarchism there must always reduce itself speedily to absurdity. Even the modified form of Anarchy on which modern civilization is based, that is, the abandonment of industry, in the name of individual liberty, to the upshot of competition for personal gain between private capitalists, is a disastrous failure, and is, by the mere necessities of the case, giving way to ordered Socialism. For the economic rationale of this," Shaw dryly adds, " I must refer disciples of Siegfried to a tract from my hand published by the Fabian Society and entitled ' The Impossibilities of Anarchism.' "

Whether or not Wagner ever reached in his own mind a further stage than that represented by anarchism, Shaw does not indicate, but he does tell us that Wagner, like Shelley in " Prometheus Unbound," ends his great drama with rapturous loving strains that have no particular social significance. As a matter of fact, Wagner began "The Ring " when intensely sympathetic to the revolutionary cause, and ended it at a period when the passion of the dramatist, artist, and musician was uppermost. The cycle, therefore, represents infinitely more of the spirit of revolt at the beginning than at the end, which is, of course, true also of Wagner's life. " The Perfect Wagnerite " is interesting not only in itself, but also because it is typical of Shaw. Whether he works as a novelist, dramatist, musical or literary critic, he never forgets the passion of his life, which is socialism.

William Morris deserves a first place in the Literature of Socialism. It must have been a surprise to his friends when in 1883 he became a militant member of the party. The superficial observer of this poet and craftsman during the seventies could hardly have imagined the change that was to come. Few men have led a life more completely given over to culture. As he himself said, he was " the idle singer of an empty day." The titles of his books indicate how remote was Morris's thought from all that is modern. After " The Earthly Paradise," he wrote the story of the Golden Fleece, called " The Life and

Death of Jason," which gave him a foremost position among English poets. He saturated himself with the mythologies of Greece, Persia, and the North, and his translations of the Icelandic Sagas, Virgil's "Æneid," and the Epic of Sigurd were the poetic harvests of these early years.

When not engaged in literature, Morris carried on a stupendous work, endeavoring to reinstate domestic decoration as one of the fine arts. With a group of poets and artists, including Burne-Jones, Dante Gabriel Rossetti, and Philip Webb, he lavished labor and love in erecting a really beautiful house in the suburbs of London. In the course of his labors, he recreated the mediæval arts and handicrafts, including painted windows, mural decoration, furniture, metal and glassware, paper and cloth wall hangings, painted tiles, jewellery, printed cottons, woven and knitted carpets, silk damasks, and tapestries. From the household arts he went to bookmaking, and reëstablished as an art printing, illustration, and illumination. There were several indications, it is said, that when he "plunged into politics he was on the brink of a new departure in the field of romance. One may even conjecture the path it would have taken, as the heroic cycle of Iran had long held in his mind a place next to those of Greece and Scandinavia."

But the socialist movement came to claim him, and during the early eighties Morris had no thought for the passions of his former years. He was in the street, leading the unemployed, speaking in Hyde Park, lecturing in little out-of-the-way holes in London, distributing hand-bills in front of lecture halls, and selling socialist tracts to the audiences. During this period he produced little of artistic or literary value, although he wrote chants for the movement, and assisted in editing two socialist journals. When his passion for an immediate revolution gave way to a saner outlook upon life, he began the "Dream of John Ball," one of the finest romances in our language.

In this book Morris goes back to the England of the fourteenth century, which he knew so well and loved so fervently, to grasp the hand of John Ball, the leader of the peasants' revolt. The peasants are rising all over the country, and are on the way to London to demand a declaration of freedom from the king. Morris represents himself as the voice of the future, and after watching a hard battle between the masters and the men, he and John Ball spend an entire night in conversation in the choir-stalls of an exquisite little Gothic church. Ball is the type of the impassioned idealist who thinks he is attacking a root evil, and that when the serfs are freed, misery will have been banished from the earth. He tries to learn from Morris whether or not his project will succeed, and what will befall the people in the time to come.

There is something of anguish in the answers of Morris as he outlines to John Ball the increase of misery and wretchedness which shall come during the next five hundred years, until the climax is reached in the middle of the nineteenth century. He tells of the days when the landlords will force the peasants from the fields, enclose the commons, and confiscate the lands. He pictures the abject misery of the workers who must sell themselves day by day for leave to labor. He pictures the coming of the machines when one man shall do the work of a hundred men, yea of a thousand or more; and he says: "I tell thee many men shall be as poor and wretched always, year by year, as they are with thee when there is famine in the land; nor shall any have plenty and surety of livelihood save those that shall sit by and look on while others labor."

"Now am I sorrier than thou hast yet made me," said John Ball; "for when once this is established, how then can it be changed? . . . Woe's me, brother, for thy sad and weary foretelling! And yet saidst thou that the men of those days would seek a remedy. Canst thou yet tell me, brother, what that remedy shall be, lest the sun rise upon me made hopeless by thy tale of what is to be? And, lo you, soon shall she rise upon the earth."

"In truth the dawn was widening now, and the colors coming into the pictures on wall and in window; and as well as I could see through the varied glazing of these last (and one window before me had as yet nothing but white glass in it), the ruddy glow, which had but so little a while quite died out in the west, was now beginning to gather in the east; — the new day was beginning. I looked at the poppy that I still carried in my hand, and it seemed to me to have withered and dwindled. I felt anxious to speak to my companion and tell him much, and withal I felt that I must hasten, or for some reason or other I should be too late; so I spoke at last loud and hurriedly: —

"'John Ball, be of good cheer; for once more thou knowest, as I know, that the Fellowship of Men shall endure, however many tribulations it may have to wear through. Look you, a while ago was the light bright about us; but it was because of the moon, and the night was deep notwithstanding, and when the moon-

"The Glass-worker," by Meunier.

light waned and died and there was but a little glimmer in place of the bright light, yet was the world glad because all things knew that the glimmer was of day and not of night. Lo you, an image of the times to betide the hope of the Fellowship of Men. Yet, forsooth, it may well be that this bright day of summer which is now dawning upon us is no image of the beginning of the day that shall be; but rather shall that day-dawn be cold and gray and surly; and yet by its light shall men see things as they verily are, and no longer enchanted by the gleam of the moon and the glamour of the dreamtide. By such gray light shall wise men and valiant souls see the remedy, and deal with it, a real thing that may be touched and handled, and no glory of the heavens to be worshipped from afar off. And what shall it be, as I told thee before, save that men shall be determined to be free; yea, free as thou wouldst have them, when thine hope rises the highest, and thou art thinking not of the king's uncles, and poll-groat bailiffs, and the villeinage of Essex, but of the end of all, when men shall have the fruits of the earth and the fruits of their toil thereon, without money and without price.'"

There are too many beautiful and precious things in literature for one to say lightly that this or that is most lovely; and yet I cannot go far astray when I put in my Golden Treasury that handgrasp of sympathy and fellowship which reaches out through a long night of dreary centuries and unites in comradeship these two great souls.

Morris realized, and meant to show in "John Ball," that the development of society was an evolutionary process, and that no man could mould it to his ideal. In writing, therefore, his "News from Nowhere" he had no intention of picturing a definite social order that might be brought into being by the conscious effort of the socialist movement. As a matter of fact, Morris wrote "News from Nowhere" as a retort to the machine-like utopia of Edward Bellamy. Loving labor, he did not want to be freed from it, and he could not tolerate the thought of a civilization founded upon bell-buttons and automatic machines. It was his ideal that all work should be worth doing, and be in itself pleasurable. He says, "It is right and necessary that all men should have work to do which shall be worth doing, and be of itself pleasant to do ; and which should be done under such conditions as would make it neither over-wearisome nor over-anxious." This claim is the basis of all his socialism. "To feel," as he says, "that we were doing work useful to others and pleasant to ourselves, and that such work and its due reward *could* not fail us ! What serious harm could happen to us then ? " "News from Nowhere" is the dream of a society based upon that claim.

H. G. Wells has also ventured into the realm of socialist anticipation, but in "A Modern Utopia" he does not attempt to plan a future society. His book is really a series of utopian speculations based upon the scientific achievement of to-day, and a vision of the enormous possibilities for human development in a society in which thought and labor shall be dominated by the passion for human welfare. Anatole France, in "Sur la Pierre Blanche," pictures a society arising out of the socialist movement now growing in strength and acquiring power in all the countries of Europe. In this story an international group of parliamentary socialists begin to exercise toward the end of the twentieth century an enormous influence upon the various governments, with the result that, after a period of terrible warfare over the colonizing policy of the capitalist régime, war is finally through the power of the socialists rendered impossible. Capitalism, having developed gigantic trusts, finds itself incapable of managing the great forces of production, and, incited by greed, its economic warfare leads to a series of convulsions and disasters. This accentuates the class struggle, and a period of chaos ensues, until at last socialism emerges triumphant. Socialist republics are established in all the European countries, and their delegates, assembled at Brussels, proclaim the United States of Europe.

This Utopia is compressed into about sixty pages. There is no effort to plan in detail a new society, and on the whole it resembles the work of H. G. Wells, except that the utopian speculation upon the progress of science is more definite. Flying machines and wireless telegraphy have abolished the frontiers; agriculture is a department of chemistry; architecture is the highest developed art, as it is the most useful; in education there is no more necessity for studying theology and law; and wireless telegraphy has done away with the need for police. Music retains its old power, and in the theatre the lyrical replaces comedy and tragedy. Invasion from American and Asiatic countries hostile to socialism is rendered impossible by a belt of powerful electrical instruments that a boy can set in motion. " Sur la Pierre Blanche" is a delightful piece of imaginative writing, and incidentally presents in their most attractive form the fundamental principles of the modern socialist movement.

U

Another effort of writers and artists, akin to the search for an ideal society, is the quest for the ideal adjustment between the individual and society. Tolstóy's "Resurrection" should be placed under this general heading. Although the whole range of modern society is presented in Tolstóy's novel more powerfully than in the work of any other Russian, "Resurrection" is really the testing of a soul, the story of the evolution of the moral and spiritual life in its search for individual and social righteousness. It is a story of the birth, the growth, the death, and the resurrection of the spirit in a world of torment and anguish.

A similar work has been done by Fogazzaro in the trilogy recently translated into English. The Italian has, in a quite remarkable way, shown the evolution of the individual soul in its relation to that social environment of its time which moulds it from the outside. In "The Patriot" we have the beginning of the revolt, the young Italian filled with the revolutionary spirit of the seventies. "The Sinner" is the story of the testing of the individual not yet awakened to definite ideals. In "The Saint" the hero, "Piero Maironi," wavers between the individualism of Tolstóy, the monastic perfection of St. Francis, and the passion for social righteousness expressed in the socialist movement. The series is a notable contribution to the literature of socialism, taken either as a quest for the ideal individual or the ideal social principles. Without, perhaps, a definite intention to be symbolical, Fogazzaro has pictured in the first two volumes the spirit of Italian life during the seventies, eighties, and early nineties, — the spirit which I have tried to describe in the chapter on Italy. The people, after losing the individualistic ideals of the Mazzinian period, were sunk in the vices of political corruption, petty intrigue, and materialism.   In "The Saint" there is an equally symbolical picture of the rebirth of the Christian idealism, which has been so potent a factor in all the reform periods of Italian life, and the rise of socialism.   It may be that Fogazzaro meant to keep strictly to the method of the psychologist and moralist; nevertheless, one finds in his work an immense social teaching.   He tells the story of the evolution of the soul of the Italian people. He pictures Italy passing from the heights of the political passion of the earlier period, through the valleys of despair and corruption, and then on to the heights of the new socialist idealism.

It is rare to find in modern literature a book so exquisite, mingling a romanticism so delicate with a realism so powerful, as "De Kleine Johannes," or "The Quest," by Frederik van Eeden.   I know of nothing in literature more sweetly fantastical.   Hovering about the infancy of Johannes are fascinating little fairies who lead him hither and thither through the world of fancy.   There is "Windekind," whom he wants to take him to the setting sun streaming out of the golden cloud-gates.   There are the little angels of fancy that introduce him into the entrancing world of four-footed creatures and of the winged beasts of the air. "Wistick" and many other little fairy gods try to show him the beauty of all other creatures but man, and the exquisite harmony of all other societies except the human.   And then there is "Pluizer," who takes Johannes into the dirty narrow streets of the city, where the little strip of blue sky looks only a finger's breadth, where children creep over cold floors, and little girls

hum melodies to their thin, pale nurslings. Following "Pluizer" comes "Marcus," a gaunt, wandering
scissors-grinder, who goes about among circus folk
and factory hands preaching a kind of Christian socialism. He takes with him little Johannes, who looks
upon the wandering missionary as a kind of deity,
despite his long hair, silly old cap, and frayed-out
trousers. As they lie one night upon a hard mattress
in a wayside garret, Johannes falls to weeping over
the toil, the poverty, and squalor they see and suffer.
"When I see your shabby clothes and blackened
hands," sobs Johannes, "when I hear you addressed
as comrade by these poor and filthy people, when I
see you sharing their hard and unlovely life, then I
cannot keep from crying." "It is dreadful," Marcus
answers, "not on my account, but because of the necessity for it." "But how can there be any need of
your being so plain and sad? Is there anything good
in plainness and sadness?" "No, Johannes; plainness
and sadness are evils. The beautiful and the joyful
only are good, and it is they we must seek."

I do not know what "The Quest" means. It is
vague and uncertain, as I suppose a quest must be, but
as a picture of the unrealities we love and of the real-
ities we hate there is not its like. And yet what a painful journey; with its vague, pervasive longing for some
certainty, for peace, beauty, and goodness, for kindli-
ness, for human sympathies, for respect for each other's
soul and each other's individuality. It is all quest, —
lonesome, uncertain quest for that hidden ideal, always
seeming to be in the near future, yet ever evading our
grasp when we seem to reach it. It is a sorrowful
tale; and our hearts ache with the little Johannes as

he goes through the big world on this serious business. But it helps us to understand the inevitable impulse of the ever active brain and the ever yearning heart to struggle forward toward the light; a struggle not only of the individual, but of masses of individuals. It is the sole worthy and important portent of the modern socialist movement, of all quests the greatest.

CHAPTER X

THERE is a lapse of nearly two thousand years between the birth of the first International and the second. There are many points of resemblance between the two, as without doubt there are profound differences. The first, like the second, began among the poor, capturing organizations of working men, carrying on its agitation wherever there was distress and misery, and raising its banner wherever the working men were in revolt. It preached a gospel, which in its essence meant liberty, equality, and fraternity. The slaves were among the first to accept the new gospel, and wherever they were organized in unions the Christians found a welcome. One historian says it was at Pergamus, the seat of the great uprising of working men under Aristonicus, that the Christians built one of their most celebrated churches. The people were in the throes of one of the bloodiest class conflicts of history. Their powerful trade union had enabled them to keep themselves free from slavery ; and the new gospel, preaching the equality of workman and master, of slave and slave-owner, came to them as a powerful spiritual support in the struggle against their oppressors.

Back of nearly all the uprisings of slaves and workmen were the Christian agitators. In this way, partly, Christianity spread from Jerusalem to Rome, and from Rome throughout the empire. Its propagandists went forth to convert and conquer the world, forming on their way new organizations of working men, establishing benefit societies, mutualities, and coöperatives. They built wherever they went " Houses of the People," and preached an economic doctrine akin to modern socialism. Lecky says that "Christianity was not merely a moral influence. It was also an institution definitely, elaborately, and skilfully organized, possessing a weight and a stability which isolated or undisciplined teachers could never rival, and evoking, to a degree before unexampled in the world, an enthusiastic devotion to its corporate welfare, analogous to that of the patriot to his country." This is the main reason why the governments persecuted the Christians. Then, as to-day, there was, according to Lecky, " no principle in the imperial policy more stubbornly upheld than the suppression of all corporations that might be made the nuclei of revolt." One other thing there is in common between the old International and that of to-day : Wherever the early Christians formed a section of their movement they raised, so Osborne Ward says in " The Ancient Lowly," the same red flag which has passed from revolutionist to revolutionist through all periods of history down to the working men of our own time.

The members of this early International were subjected to criticisms familiar to our ears. They were called " enemies " or " haters of the human race." At a time when the general moral standard was very low they were charged with deeds so atrocious, Lecky says, as to scandalize the most corrupt. They were represented as habitually celebrating the most licentious orgies, indulging in the worst of evil practices; and it was even steadfastly rumored that they fed on human flesh.   Christianity was to the mind of the upper classes the same revolt of unchained appetites as that of modern socialism; it preached the same dangerous and sub-versive doctrines and was led by the same sort of irresponsible revolutionists.

Christmas was once the fête day of labor.   It drew men, women, and children together to celebrate the advent of peace on earth and good-will to men.   The first of May is the fête day of the modern movement. In every city, town, and hamlet where socialists are to be found, this May Day is a festival.   In Germany, France, Italy, Austria, Belgium, Russia, America, and even in the Antipodes, millions of workmen assemble.   There are parades, public meetings, orations, concerts, mani-festations, and banquets.   As the people meet they greet each other as comrades, and before them as they march they bear a flag which represents to them a higher ideal than that of family, country, or nation — the ideal of universal brotherhood and peace on earth. Their poets compose songs for the day, and their artists paint pictures to celebrate the approaching victory of Labor.

Like the ancient one, this modern movement is not a mere spasm of solidarity.   Wherever there is a mine, a mill, or a factory, there are unions, brotherhoods, and other manifestations of this now almost universal or-ganization of the workers.   Its unions, coöperatives, friendly societies, and mutualities are bound together in district organizations, in national organizations, and finally in international organizations.   The membership of the unions alone numbers between eight and ten million men and women ; a million in France, two mill-ion in England, over two million in America, and about the same number in Germany. The members of the coöperative associations and friendly societies can also be numbered by the million; and the political organizations of every city, town, and hamlet are organized by district and nation into a great international, numbering again about ten million members. If one counts women and children, also, the total would approximate thirty-five or forty million. Wherever capitalism takes root, — in Russia, Japan, and China, as well as with us, — this movement follows it; and no matter what method of organization may be chosen at the beginning, whether it is trade union as in England, coöperative as in Belgium, political as in Germany, the complete organization of the working-class ends by welding all forms of its revolt into one movement, which harmonizes its varying methods of conflict.

This amazing organization of working men is of comparatively recent growth, being mainly the work of the last half century. Accustomed to change, the modern world seems incapable of surprise; and even this miracle of miracles becomes a commonplace. Yet only a few decades ago it was a dream, a wild, fanciful dream of two lonely men. One of these was a Jew, who had been driven from country to country, until finally he found shelter and protection amidst a foreign population in the Rome of the modern world. He was in desperate poverty and sometimes without food. Once a political exile, almost as poor as himself, gave him money to buy a poor pine coffin for his dead child. He was a dreamer who saw, as no one else of his time saw, that economic and social evolution, and the march of events, would make his dream come true.

Yet what could have seemed more impossible in

1848 than the international organization of working men ? It was a year of revolutions. In nearly every country of Europe, liberalism, then the political name for capitalism, was striking its final blow for victory. Fighting under a banner that promised liberty to all, it obtained it for itself alone. Liebknecht has said, " The German capitalists who now applaud the thought of empire, and see in this day the essence of the most brilliant diplomatic wisdom in Bismarck's blood and iron policy, were fifty years ago, from first to last, liberal and democratic, hating militarism, ridiculing police rule; in short opposing everything they venerate, or at least deem necessary, to-day." So it was, and is, throughout Europe. Nevertheless, in the forties, amidst these political upheavals, the working-class bore aloft the banner of the Liberals.

The socialists, as well as all other advanced thinkers, looked to liberalism for the salvation of the people. The Fourierists, the Cabetists, and St. Simonists were forming societies, mostly among the middle class, to carry out their ideals. Weitling was at the head of a similar movement in Germany. Robert Owen was working among the manufacturers of England, endeavoring to persuade them to become the real organizers of labor, and to reconstruct industrial society upon lines offering equal opportunities to all. The political socialists of France were endeavoring to convert capitalists to the necessity of organizing labor through state socialism. Proudhon condemned all state action, and urged the working-classes to emancipate themselves by the coöperative method. With the exception of the latter, no one looked upon the workers as capable of emancipating themselves.

The working-class was divided, ignorant, and sunk in the depths of misery. The chaos of industry, the economic crises, the rapid introduction of new machines, had without warning thrown multitudes out of work into a state of forced starvation. In revenge they burned factories, destroyed the new machines, and generally throughout Europe they were striking, rioting, devastating, without intelligence or organization. Speaking of an English insurrection, Carlyle says: " A million of hungry operative men rose all up, came all out into the streets, and — stood there. What other could they do? Their wrongs and griefs were bitter, insupportable. . . . A million hungry operative men started up, in utmost paroxysm of desperate protest against their lot; and certain hundreds of drilled soldiers sufficed to suppress this million-headed hydra, and tread it down, without the smallest appeasement, or hope of such, into its subterranean settlements again, there to reconsider itself." There were many socialists in Europe, great-hearted idealists, who saw this misery, and wept; but even to them labor appeared like Millet's " Man with the Hoe": plundered, profaned, and disinherited, promising his whirlwinds of rebellion; but "stolid and stunned, a brother to the ox." He was too gross and stupid and crushed, they thought, to raise himself, or to realize the cause of his misery; and it was, they imagined, only instinctive that occasionally there ran through him a paroxysm of blind and brutal revolt. " Look around you," Carlyle said to the masters. " Your world hosts are all in mutiny, in confusion, in destitution; on the eve of fiery wreck and madness."

What reasonable man could have looked in the

direction of the people with any confidence ? The great minds, then working to find a solution for the intolerable misery of the masses, looked upon them with compassion and not with hope. There were, however, two young Germans, Karl Marx and Frederick Engels, working among some fugitives and political exiles in Belgium and Paris. The Communist Alliance, mainly a conspiratory organization, had been founded in 1836 by some revolutionists. It had gradually spread to all the German working men's clubs of England, Belgium, France, and Switzerland, and in order to make it international it was decided to admit members from other nationalities also. When Marx entered the alliance, it became an open organization for propaganda instead of secret and conspiratory. Rejecting its ridiculous ideas of insurrection, it began seriously the work of education, and became a school for socialism. Although it never exercised any considerable influence upon other nationalities, it continued to grow as long as the flood of German political exiles continued.

Two congresses were held in 1847, the second of which decided to publish a manifesto, which Marx and Engels were delegated to write. In the following year, shortly before the February revolution, the now famous Communist Manifesto was issued. Its significance was immense; for besides giving a rapid survey of industrial evolution it proclaimed for the first time the idea of a Labor Party, independent of all other political organizations. Amidst the chaos of the time Marx alone saw the forces gathering, out of which were slowly evolving a definite political and economic organization of the workers. He recognized that the working-class was not then sufficiently developed to constitute itself into a distinct party, and consequently that the struggle of the workers could not immediately assume a political character; but he prophesied that that would be the outcome of industrial evolution. In the manifesto he traced briefly the character of the revolts then taking place against capitalist institutions, and pointed out that the working-class was being driven more and more to organize for protection and mutual assistance. He admits that the organization of the proletarians into a class, and consequently into a political party, is continually being upset by the competition between the workers themselves; but nevertheless it ever rises again stronger, firmer, and mightier. The communist associations, through which he had hoped to carry on an international propaganda, failed to bring definite results. They were, to begin with, exotic, and consisting almost entirely of German exiles it was impossible for them to influence their fellow-workmen of other nationalities. As soon, therefore, as the number of political refugees decreased the clubs became weaker, and within a few years extinct.

Meanwhile the workers throughout Europe were actively engaged organizing trade unions, coöperatives, and mutual societies to aid in their struggle with capitalism. It was a period of great activity, and while Marx and Engels devoted most of their time during the next fifteen years to scientific and literary work, they were not without hope that the organization of the working-class would develop international strength. Toward the sixties they believed that the time was arriving for the launching of an organization comprising the labor movements of the various countries, and when a meeting took place in London in 1863 for the purpose of expressing sympathy with the Polish people, who had just been crushed again by Russia, the idea was broached and sympathetically considered. A short time later a second meeting of sympathy for Poland was held in London, in which some French workers took part, and after a debate on the social question, it was finally resolved to form the International. On the 28th of September in the following year, at a memorable meeting in St. James's Hall, London, the International Working Men's Association was founded. Marx edited the inaugural address, the program, and the constitution. It was not to be a fighting organization, but rather, so far as possible under the conditions prevailing at that time, a centre for all endeavors toward the emancipation of the working-class. In a measure it was a practical fulfilment of the appeal addressed to the workers sixteen years before in the Communist Manifesto, — " Proletarians of all countries, unite ! "

The new movement was an attempt to bring together all the organizations, and to harmonize all the diverse tendencies represented in the revolutionary movements of Europe. It included working-class leaders, from the extreme anarchist to the moderate republican of the Mazzini type. In England the members were mostly trade unionists ; in Germany, socialists ; in France and the Latin countries, anarchists. A few working men's organizations in America allied themselves, and in other countries there were many affiliated groups. Nearly all the leaders, however, were of the middle class, and many able thinkers sympathized with and supported the movement. It started with every promise of success ;

but it was loosely organized, and it mirrored the chaotic condition of the working-class itself. More brilliant than substantial, it was not long before bitter feuds broke out among the leaders, which added to the general confusion, and divided the workers even more grievously than before.

The various tendencies represented not only a difference in view as to economic theory, but as to tactics as well; and Marx and Engels soon saw that no harmony could exist between their method of political action and that of the anarchists, who believed that the new society must be founded upon the entire destruction of the old. In addition to these two diametrically opposed views there were countless minor tendencies, almost as impossible to harmonize. The Blanquists were conspirators, hoping to capture by stealth the French government. The Proudhonians were opposed to all parliamentary action, and the republicans and liberals were unable to see the necessity for a working-class party independent of the old political organizations. Instead, therefore, of uniting the workers, the International became the storm centre of divisions, of warring personalities, of jealous and ambitious intellectuals, until finally Marx became a dictator.

Marx was a trained polemicist. At the age of twenty-four he and some friends founded a German paper. His attacks upon the government were ferocious, but his literary ingenuity was such that the censors could find nothing to condemn. The authorities again and again changed the censor, and then his articles were submitted to a double censorship; but even that was ineffectual, and in despair the government was forced eventually to suppress the paper. As editor of this and other

German papers, and as a literary free-lance, Marx conducted for about twenty years a relentless campaign against the governments, the Liberals, and the hypocritical politicians. He was an unsparing critic. The Chinese say that if you have an enemy, treat him as an elephant, even though he be a mouse. Some of Marx's opponents were of little consequence, but he always treated them as leviathans.

One of Marx's greatest polemics is " The Eighteenth Brumaire of Louis Bonaparte." Liebknecht says of it : "The words are darts and spears, and the style one that stigmatizes and destroys. If hate, if scorn, if burning love of freedom ever found expression in flaming, annihilating, and elevating words, then it was surely in the Eighteenth Brumaire." In answer to the criticisms sometimes made against Marx's writings, that they are obscure and unintelligible, Liebknecht, speaking of this book, asks: "Is the dart incomprehensible that flies straight to its target? Is the spear unintelligible that, hurled by a steady hand, penetrates the heart of the enemy?" Another polemic is " Mr. Vogt," where Marx gives play to his extraordinary gifts as humorist and satirist. At twenty-eight years he engaged in an intellectual duel that is now famous in the history of socialism, with one of the greatest French economists. Proudhon and Marx knew each other intimately, and often spent entire nights together discussing socialism. But they could not agree, and when Proudhon published his " Philosophy of Misery," he wrote to Marx, saying, "I wait your criticism." A few months afterward Marx published his scathing " Misery of Philosophy." It was terrific, and ended their friendship forever.

This critical power of Marx was his most terrible

Karl Marx.

weapon, and he used it without the slightest mercy against all whom he considered to be mistaken either in their economic views or socialist tactics. A school of great thinkers, the early French socialists, rest to-day under the stigma of his powerful critique — they were Utopians. He condemned the state socialists and even the theories of Lassalle in Germany, who always considered himself a disciple of Marx. Finally he turned upon Bakounine and the anarchists, who formed one of the most powerful sections of the International. Bakounine was a great intellect, and his influence in Russia, France, Italy, Spain, and Switzerland was immense. It was a battle royal, which finally in 1872 forced Marx, in order to rid the movement of the dangerous tactics of the anarchists, to destroy the International itself.

At this stage of Marx's career he could hardly have appeared to the superficial observer as an attractive personality. His influence in the movement seemed purely destructive. He appeared monstrously quarrelsome, and his enemies spread throughout Europe the impression that he was a dishonest and ambitious politician, consumed with egotism. To them he was a mere charlatan who had forced himself into a position of dictatorship in the International, and they expected the most disastrous consequences. Perhaps the kindliest criticism that one finds of Marx amongst his enemies of that period is that of Bakounine. "I have known Marx for a long time," he says, "and although I deplore certain defects truly detestable of his character, such as a tempestuous and jealous personality, susceptible, and too much given to admiration of himself, an implacable hatred, which manifests itself in the most odious calumny, and a ferocious

x

persecution against all those who, while sharing the same tendencies as his, have the misfortune not to be able to accept either his particular system or his supreme and personal direction ; . . . nevertheless I have always highly appreciated and rendered complete justice to the truly superior science and intelligence of Marx, and to his unalterable, enterprising, and energetic devotion to the great cause of the emancipation of the proletariat. I recognize the immense services he has rendered the International, of which he has been one of the principal founders, and which constitutes to my eyes his greatest title to glory."

Opposed to the criticisms of his enemies we have the eulogies of his friends ; few men have possessed more devoted ones. Liebknecht, in his charming memoir of Marx, shows how great he was in heart and mind. "This generous heart," he says, "that throbbed so warmly for everything human and for everything bearing human features. . . . He was not only the most loving of fathers ; he could be a child among children for hours. He was also attracted as by magnetism toward strange children, particularly helpless children that chanced to cross his way. Time and again he would suddenly tear himself away from us, on wandering through districts of poverty, in order to stroke the hair of some child in rags or to slip a penny into its little hand." What a contrast this, to the pitiless, iconoclastic Marx one thinks of in the International. His charity, his faithfulness, his courage despite the oppressive poverty to which he was nearly always subjected, and his disinterested devotion to the workers, cannot be questioned if one reads the few sketches of his personality that are left to us by his friends.

Far from being vain and egotistical, "Marx was," Liebknecht says, "one of the few among the great, little, and average men I have known who was not vain." He "was too much like a child to simulate." He was a poor diplomatist, as "he was truth personified, free from guile and hypocrisy." He worked tremendously hard, and being often hindered during the daytime took refuge in the night. When he went home from some meeting or session, he would sit down regularly for a few hours, and these hours were more and more extended until finally he was accustomed to work all night. Liebknecht sums up his estimate of Marx in these words: "Happily I became acquainted with great men so early in life and so intimately that my belief in idols and human gods was destroyed at a very early period, and even Marx was never an idol to me, although of all human beings I have met in my life he was the only one who has made an imposing impression upon me." Liebknecht's memoir is simple and unaffected, showing every sign of complete sincerity. Frederick Engels, the lifelong, devoted friend and inseparable companion of Marx, was something of a hero-worshipper, and time has yet to justify what he wrote just after Marx's death: "The greatest mind of the second half of our century has ceased to think."

The time has not arrived to make a complete estimate of Marx, but at least it can be seen that the fears of his opponents in the International were without foundation. If he presumed to be a dictator, it was not because he was personally ambitious or desired to conduct a personal warfare; it was because he had a constructive policy which he profoundly believed contained the essential principles upon which the working-class movement should be conducted. His warfare was against policies and not men. Like other great intellects he often pursued his ends with relentless vigor and almost brutal power. However much of sentiment there was in his personal relations, it did not affect the conduct of his policies. That individuals were injured did not count, and sentiments of mercy found no place in his great campaign for synthesizing the doctrines and defining the tactics of working-class organization. A man in whom sentiment was predominant could not, after having, for the sake of working-class unity, created a great movement like the International, for the same reason destroy it, after a brief existence of nine years.

But there was much left to Marx after the fall of the International. It had at least rendered him one great service. He had selected from amongst its members men who proved to be some of the ablest leaders in the European movement. It is most amusing to read of the methods Marx used in selecting his disciples. He was not a zealous devotee of phrenology, but he believed in it to some extent, and when young men of prepossessing ability came along, Marx put them through an examination which was terrifying, and often submitted their skulls to a minute examination. He then put them through a course of study, and those who came to him in London were sent to the reading room of the British Museum to pass a certain time each day. Every morning he would shout to his pupils, as he sent them off to the Museum, this imperative, " Learn, learn !" Liebknecht says that " while the rest of the fugitives were laying plans for the overthrow of the world, and intoxicating themselves day by day, evening by evening, with the hasheesh drink of, ' To-morrow the revolution will start'; we the 'sulphur gang,' 'the bandits,' were sitting in the British Museum, trying to educate ourselves and to prepare arms and ammunition for the battles of the future."

In this way Marx schooled many of his disciples who were to give form during the next few years to the political movement of the working-class in nearly every country in Europe. Wherever they went, they conducted the same battle that Marx had previously led in the International. In Italy they opposed the purely republican policy of the followers of Mazzini and Garibaldi, although at a congress in 1881, at which the latter presided, socialists and republicans sat side by side. For over twenty years the Marxists used their utmost efforts to win the working-class from the anarchists and from other leaders of the violent type, and it was not until the nineties that a definitely political movement came into being. In France, amidst a wild confusion of doctrines, they were forced to battle with the anti-parliamentary views of Proudhon, the secret and conspiratory methods of the Blanquists, the ruinous patronage of the republicans, and the blind and violent policy of the anarchists; but as early as 1878 Jules Guesde, Paul Lafargue, and Gabriel Deville brought a section of the French workers into the political movement.

In Germany there was a similar struggle going on between the Marxists, the Lassallians, the anarchists, and the sentimental socialists. That incomparable agitator, Lassalle, had for several years been engaged in organizing the Universal Workmen's Association. Liebknecht, when he returned from London, began to promote the International; and soon converted August Bebel

to the Marxian view.   The movement, however, was divided until 1875, when finally through the oppression
of Bismarck the two rival sections were forced together,
and a compromise program was adopted.   De Paepe,
in Belgium, long found it impossible to unite the warring factions, and the conflict between the followers of
Proudhon and Marx continued uninterruptedly until
1885, when the Labor Party was inaugurated.   In Holland the movement was also taking form, although in
1890 differences of a serious character arose between
the followers of the famous anarchist, Domela Nieuwenhuis, and the Marxists.   In Denmark a socialist
labor party was the work of the International, but it
soon degenerated into a simple trade union, although it
retained its political program.   Eventually, however,
the Danish socialists in 1878 came to an agreement
with the unions, left the middle-class parties, and
formed a social democratic organization.   A similar
thing happened in Sweden, but in Switzerland the
foundation of a party was delayed until 1888.   In
Spain a strong anarchist tendency among the workers
prevented the growth of socialism until Pablo Inglesias founded a paper in 1888; and shortly afterward a
socialist party was formed.   In Austria a political
movement was organized about the same time as the
German party, but because of unequal suffrage it
remained weak in parliamentary representation until
1907.   In Russia there have been endless ruptures,
which are not yet healed.   All sections of the Russian
movement have used terrorist methods.   The anarchists have been the most influential among the peasants,
while the Social Democratic Party, with a Marxian program, has made great headway in the industrial centres.

In England the working men have only recently as a body adopted the independent political attitude. Besides these national organizations of the old world there are now branches of the international movement in America, in Brazil, in Argentina, in Australia, in South Africa, and in Japan.

From this rapid survey of the spread of socialism throughout the world some idea is gained of the organizing ability and untiring labor of the socialists after the death of the International. It gives at the same time convincing proof of the practical foresight of Marx, and of the unifying and potent character of his program. The Marxian position has been adopted as the basis of action by practically all socialist political organizations. The doctrines and literature are everywhere the same, and it is common for a speech of Bebel, Jaurès, or Guesde to be translated into ten or more different languages, to become a part of the propaganda in every working-class district in the world. This work of internationalizing socialist thought, and of uniting the workers of all the world upon a common program, is certainly one of the greatest achievements of modern times, and the credit of it belongs to Marx. After his death in 1883, Engels wrote to Liebknecht, "Whatever we all are, we are through him; and whatever the movement of to-day is, it is through his theoretical and practical work; *without him we should still be stuck in the mire of confusion.*" It is a just tribute, as not even the most bitter opponent of Marx could deny. It was his labor that brought the workers out of an indescribable chaos of discordant and contradictory doctrines, and it was his disciples that won the workers from the disastrous methods of conspiracy, insurrection, and riot advocated by the anarchists. What seemed in the day of the old International to be wild destruction and petty personal warfare on the part of Marx has proved to have been the necessary demolition of obstructing and demoralizing policies to make way for the stupendous constructive work of working-class organization.

The influence of Marx has been so dominant in the development of modern socialism that its critics outside of Germany have repeatedly said that socialism is wholly a German product, and that like other exotics it would not take firm root in the unfriendly environment of other lands. Events have proved the falsity of this prophecy; but that socialism is German in origin often goes unquestioned. Without wishing to minimize in the least the immense contributions made by the Germans, it is nevertheless indisputable that socialism is no more German than capitalism is English or the trusts American. They are all essentially international, and owe their development to steam power and the machine. Every nation has made its contribution to the upbuilding of both capitalism and socialism. It is unquestionable that Marx played a stupendous rôle in the evolution of socialism, both as a philosophy and as a political movement, and the German organization was the first concrete working out of his political views; but the second fact is largely accidental, and the first is not proof of German origin.

Marx was no more a German than Heine. He was born in Germany of Jewish parents. But his father taught him Voltaire and Rousseau, and his father-in-law, Baron von Westphalen, recited to him by heart Homer and Shakespeare. To Germany he owes his

exceptional early education, and to Germany's persecution he owes a life of exile in Holland, Belgium, France,
and England, which brought him into intimate contact
with all the great revolutionists of his time, and gave to
his thought its international character. Marx knew
nearly all modern languages, and he wrote in English,
articles for the " New York Tribune," and in French,
articles for various continental papers. His book on
the Eastern question shows the world-wide scope of his
outlook in diplomacy and international politics. His
economics came largely from England, where capitalism
was furthest developed, his socialist sympathies from
the French writers, and his scientific method from the
Germans. He was far removed from the national or
provincial mind, and while he drew his materials from
the science, philosophy, politics, and economics of all
lands, no one nation can claim to have had an exclusive
or decisive influence upon his thought. Marx's critical
capacity and logical method enabled him to accept the
best in the thought of the early French socialists without becoming their disciple, of benefiting by the re-
search of the early English economists without accepting
their conclusions, of making the most of the thought of
others without necessarily agreeing with their convictions. He was synthetic, assembling the views of others
into a homogeneous whole, discarding inconsistencies
and confusion, and working out into a logical and
methodical system material much of which others had
gathered.

There was hardly an economist, and certainly no great
socialist thinker of any country, who did not contribute
something through Marx to modern socialism. The
philosophy of socialism owes most to the intellectual

initiative of the French, in whose literature we find in the germ nearly all of its basic doctrines. It is customary to-day for socialists to look upon the early French thinkers as hardly worthy of consideration, and many seem to feel that the Marxian philosophy has displaced and rendered valueless the work of this immortal school. In great degree this is due to the fact that Marx classed them as Utopians; but Marx, in using this word, was referring to their methods and tactics and not to that infinite wealth of material in economics, philosophy, and history, which they left as a heritage to all mankind. Marx himself drew innumerable riches from these vast reservoirs. St. Simon was an incomparable historian with a truly philosophic mind; Fourier knew commercialism to its roots, and so early and so thoroughly grasped the nature of modern capitalism that one must look back upon his analyses and prophecies as evidences of the almost miraculous critical power of the French mind. Besides these two great socialists there was Considerant, whose power of portraying the evils of capitalism has never been excelled. These are but three of the Frenchmen to whom Marx was indebted, and one need only mention others such as Babœuf, Pierre Leroux, Louis Blanc, François Vidal, Pecqueur, and Cabet, to convey some idea of the greatness of this early school of French socialism. Marx's quarrel with the French socialists was largely due to the fact that they wanted to create an artificial society, thus substituting sentimentalism for the natural evolutionary processes which were of themselves working out a radical social reconstruction. Above all they had no confidence in the working-class, and it never occurred to them to think of the workers as the sole revolutionary and regenerative force. They wanted socialism to be established by a class that did not desire it, for a class sorely in need of it, but incapable of achieving it for themselves. The scientific views of Marx would not harmonize with this sentimentalism of the French socialists, and although he drew plentifully from their store of social criticism and historic analysis, he departed radically from their conclusion as to the method to be pursued in the up-building of the socialist movement.

The English contribution to socialism is entirely in the field of practice. To begin with, it was the classic land of capitalism, and Liebknecht has said that Marx's "Capital" could not have been written except in London. Side by side with capitalist evolution was the growing antagonism of the workers, which was in the middle of the last century more clearly defined in England than any-where else in Europe. From the very beginning the English movement has been a perfect example of the class struggle, and a striking and almost fatalistic working out of the Marxian view. Even when it was limited to trade unionism, it was still the best demonstration in Europe of an organized instinctive association of the disinherited produced largely by the force of economic conditions. The lack of idealism in the English move-ment disconcerted Marx and Engels less than it does the socialists of the present day; and as late as 1892 Engels wrote that the working-class in England "moves, like all things in England, with a slow and measured step, with hesitation there; with more or less unfruitful, tenta-tive attempts here; it moves now and then with an over-cautious mistrust of the name of socialism, *while it gradually absorbs the substance;* * and the movement

* The italics are mine.

spreads and seizes one layer of the workers after another. It has now shaken out of their torpor the unskilled laborers of the East End of London, and we all know what a splendid impulse these fresh forces have given it in return. And if the pace of the movement is not up to the impatience of some people, let them not forget that it is the working-class which keeps alive the finest qualities of the English character, and that, if a step in advance is once gained in England, it is, as a rule, never lost afterward.   If the sons of the old Chartists were not quite up to the mark, the grandsons bid fair to be worthy of their forefathers."

That Engels should grant that the English movement gradually absorbs the substance of socialism while distrusting the name proves how thoroughly he understood the English character.   In no other country have revolutions been more profound and more democratically beneficial, although, as Mathew Arnold says, in all this struggle the English have proceeded by the rule of thumb.   What was intolerably inconvenient to them they have suppressed, not because it was irrational, but because it was practically inconvenient.   They have seldom in suppressing the evils of the past appealed to pure reason, as the French invariably do, but always if possible to some precedent or form or letter, which serves as a convenient instrument for their purpose, and which saves them from the necessity of recurring to general principles.   " They have thus become," as Arnold goes on to say, " in a certain sense, of all people the most inaccessible to ideas, and the most impatient of them ; inaccessible to them, because of their want of familiarity with them, and impatient of them because they have got on so well without them."   " There is a world of ideas, and there is a world of practice," he continues. "The French are fond of suppressing the one, and the English the other."

If the French have contributed to socialism a wealth of ideas, and the English an impressive instance of the inevitable antagonism of the workers to capitalism, the Germans have contributed something equally important. They have combined the idea and the practice. Without the instinctive idealism of the French, or the instinctive practice of the English, they are both doctrinaire and practical. The Germans were the first to build up a political movement of the workers founded upon the doctrines and philosophy of socialism. They put into the concrete the socialist views of Marx, and made out of a doctrine a powerful living reality. Combining the practical and the abstract, the methodical and scientific Germans have given an example to the world of working-class unity and solidarity. Without French thought Marx could not have produced the fundamental doctrines of modern socialism; without a knowledge of English labor organization it is doubtful if he would have perceived so clearly the capacity of the working-class for organized and consistent action; and without the gift of the Germans for combining the idea and the practice, modern socialism could not have reached its present position of having a conscious aim, a simple and precise doctrine, and an organized practical movement.

Marx died in 1883, and, therefore, did not live to see the new International, as it was not until 1889 that the various national movements decided to hold a joint congress. In that year nearly 400 delegates from twenty different countries met in Paris to express their mutual accord and to work out some plan for international organization. Two years later another congress was held in Brussels, with delegates from every country of Europe, America, and Australia, and in 1893 an imposing gathering assembled at Zurich. At the London congress in 1896 an important question engaged the attention of the delegates. The anarchists had begun again to insinuate themselves into the movement, with the hope of turning it away from peaceful and parliamentary methods. After a heated discussion as to whether or not they should be admitted, it was finally decided by an almost unanimous vote to exclude them altogether; and to exclude them is now the avowed policy in all countries. The congress held four years later was not important, and I have reviewed briefly in another chapter the chief debate which took place at Amsterdam in 1904. That congress marks an epoch in the history of modern socialism. Its greatest accomplishment was the unifying of the socialists in France. To achieve this result, it was forced, though almost against its will, to adopt a policy of international socialist tactics, which, it is reasonable to think, prevented a serious crisis, and perhaps a rupture in the European movement.

A notable event occurred on the opening day of the Amsterdam congress. After Troelstra had spoken in the name of the socialists of the city, Van Kol followed with a word of welcome. With that fine emotion so characteristic of this old warrior, he turned to the delegates from Russia and Japan, then at war, and warmly complimented the socialists of both countries upon their courage in pronouncing themselves against the war when it was at its greatest heat. Katayama, the Japanese delegate, and Plechanoff, the Russian, grasped hands amidst thunders of applause from the delegates, who had all arisen to their feet. When Van Kol had finished, Katayama, mounting to the tribune, was given a tremendous ovation. His words describing the unhappy condition of the workers in Asia were listened to in religious silence, many of the delegates standing while he spoke. He deplored the war, and rejoiced especially to have been seated at the side of a delegate who represented the workers of Russia. He expressed the hope that the time would soon come when not only the war of the extreme Orient would be at an end, but when the state of war which capitalism implies would be at an end also. Following him, Plechanoff saluted the delegates of the International, and especially his Japanese brother. He said it was not the Russian people who had made war upon the Japanese. It was the worst enemy of the Russian people, the imperial government. After reviewing shortly the conditions in his stricken country, he sat down amidst an enthusiastic demonstration. The editor of the proceedings of the congress says: " An untranslatable impression of grandeur and of force pervaded the inaugural session. The three presidential addresses at once elevated the minds and hearts of the delegates to the lofty and serene conception of an international which will assure by solidarity and by science the peace of the world and the happiness of all."

From the first congress of the new International in 1889, to that of 1904, the socialist movement realized an immense progress. Van Kol, in his address, recalled the fact that the old International had gathered for the last time at the Hague in 1872. A little café was sufficient for all their purposes. At Amsterdam twenty-three nations were represented by about 450 delegates,

and the success, the harmony, and the increasing power
exercised by socialism, encouraged the delegates to believe that the movement was strong enough to storm the
citadel of reaction; it was, therefore, decided to hold the
following congress in 1907 in some city of the German
empire.

Nothing could be more significant of the growing
international power of the movement than the fact that
despite the intense hatred with which the emperor and
the bureaucracy view the German party, they were,
nevertheless, powerless to prevent it from holding a
great international meeting upon German soil. Little
more than a decade before, every German social democrat was an outlaw, and although the legal status had
since changed, the attitude of the upper classes had not.
Again and again it was rumored that the International gathering would not be permitted. There was a
certain thrill of excitement, therefore, and a degree of
uncertainty, when nearly a thousand delegates, representing thirty nationalities, arrived at Stuttgart.

On Sunday, the day before the official opening of the
congress, workmen with their wives and children began
to arrive from the neighboring towns. Bands and
singing societies paraded, carrying before them their
treasured red flags. Thousands upon thousands came,
and before the noon hour the streets leading out to a
great open space near the city were lined with men,
women, and children. When I arrived at about two
o'clock in the afternoon, between forty and fifty thousand people had assembled to hear the socialist orators
from all the world. Ten or twelve platforms had been
erected, and upon each was a little group of the most
distinguished militants in the movement. Over this

mighty throng, in many languages, came the voices of the great agitators, bearing a common message ; and although we could not always understand the words, we knew their meaning and were glad.

On the following day the delegates assembled in the largest meeting-place in Stuttgart. The Germans had organized the congress in their characteristically efficient manner, and tables were arranged about the halls with banners indicating the seats of the various delegations. It was an impressive sight, when they had all gathered, to look about the great hall and to see assembled, from every industrial district of the world, the extraordinary men who, in the face of incredible obstacles, and despite the opposition of every government, had forced socialism into its present position of power and influence. Nearly all the older men had been in prison or had undergone years of exile, and some of them, like Hermann Greulich, — that sterling old Swiss socialist with the fine white head that resembles Tolstóy's, — had even been stoned by the workers themselves. There were 300 representatives from Germany, about a hundred from France, and 150 from England. North and South America, Australia, and all the smaller nations of Europe were represented, and there were two delegates from Japan and two from India. Nearly every one was a person of consequence in the working-class movement. About a hundred were members of European parliaments, many of them represented important unions, and there were few that did not speak for thousands of organized men. One delegate alone represented a million workers. The following table gives the number of votes obtained by the various national parties at the last elections. I am unable to find the vote for Russia, although the socialists elected 132 members to the second Duma. In Hungary the socialists have a great following, but little electoral strength, as the suffrage is restricted : —

	Votes
Germany, 1907	3,258,968
Austria, 1907	1,041,948
France, 1906	900,000
Belgium, 1904	469,094
United States, 1904	409,230
Great Britain, 1906	350,000
Finland, 1907	330,000
Italy, 1904	320,000
Denmark, 1906	77,000
Switzerland, 1905	70,000
Holland, 1905	65,743
Norway, 1906	45,000
Sweden, 1905	35,000
Spain, 1904	29,000
Chili, 1906	18,000
Bulgaria, 1903	9,000
Argentine, 1906	3,500
Servia, 1906	3,133
Total	7,434,616

The discussion was carried on in three languages, and despite the brilliant qualities of many of the speakers the sessions became rather tedious. Five important matters were discussed: women's suffrage, emigration, the colonial question, the relation between the trade unions and the party, and militarism. They were all practical questions, which was significant of the enormous change in the socialist movement during the last few years. No difference of opinion manifested itself concerning the doctrines of the party, and the time of the congress was entirely occupied in earnest effort to come to some agreement upon these questions of immediate importance.

Infinitely the most vital from the European standpoint was militarism, and for five days the ablest debaters at the congress were engaged in the difficult problem of drafting a resolution which would satisfy the various sections. The newspapers at the time printed reports which exaggerated the differences. As a matter of fact the views of the mass of party members do not differ in any fundamental principle. They are all anti-militarist, and they are all agreed to use their utmost influence against war, and to do all possible, inside and outside of parliament, to prevent the increase of armies and navies. But the French evolve theories out of every situation in which they become engaged, and certainly anti-militarism does not mean to the Germans what it means to Hervé; namely, anti-patriotism. Both Jaurès and Bebel emphasized the priceless value to a people of its national character. The main difference between them lies in the fact that the French are likely to be more extreme in their expression and more violent and impractical in their methods than the Germans. Victor Adler, the able leader of the Austrian socialists, summed up the matter in these effective words: "We Germans are not fond of empty threats. We are prepared to go further than our promises. We cannot and will not say what we should do, but you may rely upon it that we should act with as much energy as any one else."

The importance of the International Congress did not lie in its debates and resolutions, and it is unnecessary to go into details concerning them. Certainly nothing was accomplished at Stuttgart that can compare with the resolution on tactics passed by the delegates at Amsterdam. But the gathering was significant, profoundly significant. That a thousand delegates, representing the working men of thirty nations and close on to ten million voters, should confer for one week together is perhaps the most impressive event of modern times. It suggests the beginning of great things, and presages development of stupendous moment. Think of German, French, Italian, and English working men, living under governments that, armed with every conceivable form of murderous and destructive apparatus, glare at each other across their frontiers and spread hatred and suspicion among the masses, that spend millions upon millions for fortresses, military manœuvres, and navies, — think of them coming together to grasp each other by the hand, to march behind one flag, and to call each other comrade. Their forebears were for centuries at each other's throats, massacring, pillaging, and conquering. A word from their kings and emperors sufficed to create rivers of blood — here they were at Stuttgart, in the face of their opposing governments, inspired by a common idea, and planning to fight for instead of against each other. Kings, emperors, and ministers, as well as the entire press of the world, were discussing the Hague Peace Conference, and chose to think it significant. Many of the continental rulers would have done anything to prevent these working men assembling to declare themselves comrades, and to discuss seriously as comrades universal peace. The discussion of war and peace at Stuttgart was not in itself of especial importance; but the week's fellowship, expressive as it was of universal brotherhood, — that was significant.

A flood of interesting thoughts surged in upon one attending that memorable gathering of men from all lands. The want of a common language was agonizing at times, and one often grasped the hand of a comrade without being able to speak a word of greeting. Despite every evidence of unity of purpose and cordial fellowship, the national characteristics were strong. The national groups were differentiated one from another, so that they seemed almost well-defined individuals, thus affording a rare opportunity to observe traits of national psychology. There were the French with their fine idealism, worshipping the abstract as something human, concrete, and tangible. Nervous and passionate, they permeated the entire gathering with their electric mentality. What a contrast were the scientific, doctrinaire, erudite Germans, whose methodical efficiency was everywhere in evidence. The gifted Belgians seemed at times to be Frenchmen, at other times stolid and practical Germans. The slow-moving, sluggish man of the north had little to say and much to show for his quiet and effective labor. Fair and big and phlegmatic, he was the counterpart of the dark, hot-blooded, emotional Italian whose nimble mind and imaginative flights carried him to all sorts of excesses. And then there was the sad, brooding, spiritual Russian, whose sacrifices know no bounds while the ideal is unattained.

These differences in national psychology convey some impression of how varied an edifice socialism will be when finally it comes into being. One cannot doubt the socialism of Italy will be very different from that of England. I can even imagine that the socialism acceptable to the men of the north will be intolerable to the men of the south. There must be a common foundation, if socialism is to weld the peoples together, and such a foundation exists in the doctrines and fundamental principles of socialism. But this basis resembles the earth itself, in that upon it must be built edifices that will vary in use and beauty according to the gifts of the associated builders. Socialism will vary as our democracy and political institutions, our literature and cathedrals, in short as the peoples themselves vary. For the present the international movement signifies a common battle against capitalism. It means to destroy wage-slavery, and to raise what are now the subject classes into a position of dominant influence. In that, there is no variation in doctrine or belief. It involves war to the end against the destructive forms of competition which create our modern chaos, our contrasting wealth and poverty, and which make of the masses of men mere pawns in the great international game of industrialism, commercialism, and war.

THE MOVEMENT IN OTHER COUNTRIES

(SUPPLEMENTARY CHAPTER)

Russia. — It is difficult to give any concise statement of the position of socialism in Russia, because of the tremendous upheavals of recent years. Suffice to say that the brief and eventful career of the Duma has clearly demonstrated that under normal conditions, and with universal suffrage, the socialists would be in possession of governmental power. Never was there a time when the autocracy had to fight so strenuously to preserve its privileges, and even its existence. Panic-stricken, the authorities have gone to the extreme in their efforts to suppress the various nationalities they have conquered; to propagate race and religious antagonism, in order to obscure from the toiling masses the real cause of their misery; and to stamp out by the most horrible methods the spirit of revolution.

The first traces of the socialist movement were apparent in the forties, but for thirty years it was confined to small groups of university men and students, with a few remarkable working men. About the time Bakounine was agitating in Western Europe, and the International was effecting working-class organization, young men and women of the more prosperous classes left their families and fortunes in order to propagate socialism among the people. The Russians, especially the peasant class, have always had communist aspirations, and the emancipation of the serfs was to them the realization of a long-cherished ideal. Nevertheless the spread of socialistic ideas was at first very slow. The various socialist circles were broken up again and again by the government, and their members banished or imprisoned.   This persecution led to the adoption of terrorist tactics on the part of the socialists for about four years, culminating in the death of Alexander II in March, 1881.   The coming of industrialism in its most intense form marked an epoch in socialist propaganda.   What with the opening of the coal and iron fields in the South, and the textile trades in St. Petersburg, Moscow, Nijni Novgorod, and Lodz, something like two million people were drawn off the land and concentrated in factories.   Consequently it needed but few years of capitalist exploitation for them to realize class-consciousness.   Beginning with the great fight of the weavers in St. Petersburg in 1896, strike after strike took place all over the country, skilfully engineered by the socialists, up to the memorable general strike of 1903 ; which, commencing in the South, spread until a quarter of a million workers had ceased production.   The industrial crisis which had set in, however, rendered strikes to a considerable extent ineffective, and the starving populace had nothing left to do but demonstrate in the streets, with the consequence that massacres by the soldiery were frequent.   Amid the general ferment the revolutionary movement, in which the socialists were the directing force, spread with marvellous rapidity.

There are three principal socialist organizations in Russia : the Socialist Revolutionary Party, who accept terrorism as a transitory necessity ; the Social Democratic Party, pure Marxists, advocating the class movement as against individual action ; and the Bund, composed exclusively of working Jews. Roughly it might be said that the two former are divided principally on the matter of terrorist tactics and concerning the land question.   With regard to the latter problem, the Social Democrats, consisting for the most part of the industrial workers of the towns, favor only the expropriation of large landowners.   In this respect they might be considered opportunist in their tactics, as they do not want to alienate the sympathies of the small holders. On the other hand the Socialist Revolutionary Party stands for the out and out expropriation of the land, and events have demonstrated that the peasants are fully in accord with their advanced agrarian program. Says Mr. English Walling: "Whether or not this program succeeds depends largely on the action of the Social Democrats. The government and the bourgeois parties are already doing everything in their power to break up the village commune and increase the number of small proprietors. If this process is not stopped, the number of small proprietors will be doubled within a few years, complete nationalization will have become impossible, and Russia will have to wait decades or generations for the social revolution." The Socialist Revolutionists say that the signal for the expropriation of the land will be the signal for the general insurrection of the people. But while preparing for this, they will not cease the daily struggle. They claim that history has justified their terrorism, both individual and collective. And, moreover, "We shall not cease to use terrorist tactics in the political struggle until the day when shall be realized the institutions making the will of the people the source of power and legislation."

In view of the tragedy of October, 1905, the socialists deemed it wiser to do all in their power to retard any further open struggle until the masses, and especially the agricultural population, should have been properly organized. Unfortunately the march of events did not obey their will, and the insurrection of Moscow broke out. However, this served to prove the possibility of an armed uprising, because during the eight days of barricade fighting, the government trembled for its existence. And when the revolutionists abandoned their positions, having served their purpose, the government, imagining that the revolution had played itself out, burst into a frenzy of reaction and persecution. " But only the blind could think that the colossal social and political crisis which affects our immense country could be closed within the limits of two or three months."

Considering it fruitless, the Socialist Revolutionary Party decided not to take part in the elections to the first Duma, but to apply themselves energetically to opening the eyes of the people to the mock constitution that had been set up; and while the government was engaged in managing the elections, the socialists had exceptional liberty in their propaganda. Books, pamphlets, and newspapers were published by the million; the committees which had been smashed up were reconstituted; and all together the socialists had a great day. However, notwithstanding their statements that they would have nothing to do with the Duma, revolutionists were elected by the people, and a strong labor group was formed. This it was decided to make use of in the furtherance of the socialist cause. But the first Duma, in which so many hopes had been placed by the people, only lasted ninety days; and the interval between the first and second parliaments proved to be one of the blackest periods of unbridled government terrorism, pogroms, courtmartials, and executions. The authorities were absolutely ferocious because the Duma had not been amenable to their power, and as usual their ferocity was greatest against the socialists, who were obliged to retort with acts of terrorism. The flower of the socialist forces perished in the prisons, in Siberia, and on the scaffold. The average existence of a committee was two months; of a journal, two numbers. But the influence of the socialists grew enormously, thousands of meetings were held, and a huge amount of literature was distributed in secret.

At a meeting of the council of the party in November, 1906, it was resolved to take part in the election for the second Duma; considering it now compatible with their tactics, as the presence of members of the party in parliament could be utilized for propaganda purposes. The war and famine had favored the exploits of bands of thieves, and their depreda-

Russian Socialist Deputies listening to the Report of a Peasant who has come on Foot from a Country Town to lay before them the Desires and Grievances of their Constituents.

tions were baptized with the name of " expropriations." As this was likely seriously to compromise the socialist movement, the council considered it necessary to take some action in the matter. Members were, therefore, invited to abstain from the expropriation of private goods, or goods belonging to private societies. However, confiscation of all goods detained by the Czarist government was admissible, but this must be under the immediate control of the regional committees, who would restitute all funds to the central committee for use for the common good. The regional committees were moreover invited to organize the masses by military methods.

Perhaps the greatest achievement of the party in the second Duma was in the matter of their agrarian measure, put forward for the second time. In the first parliament this project, which claims the socialization of the land, only received 33 votes; in the second it received 105, which included the peasant deputies. So that the agrarian program of the party has been indorsed by the whole progressive peasant population.

Among the soldiers and sailors the socialist propaganda has made great progress, as is shown by the perpetual unrest and frequent mutinies in those two services. Even the Cossacks have commenced to reflect and comprehend the horror of the rôle they are made to play. Very encouraging also is the progress among the boatmen and other employees along the Volga, and the great railroad union.

The confidence that the autocracy had put in the peasants in the first and second Dumas was altogether misplaced. Instead of supporting reaction, the peasants sent their own representatives to parliament. The government, therefore, changed completely the " constitution," so that the effect of the third election to the Duma is that an absolute majority is given into the hands of 135,000 of landed proprietors and rich bourgeois. Thus the parliament is composed of the privileged classes and their creatures. The new electoral law has given nearly three-fourths of the seats to the nobles, one-fourth to

the rich bourgeois, leaving only a twentieth to the other classes.
The erstwhile socialist members have been sent to Siberia or
to prison.   And the struggle goes on.

Austria. — Because of the multiplicity of languages within
the empire the Austrian Social Democratic Party is composed
of several national groups — Germans, Czechs, Poles, Italians,
Slavs, and Ruthenians — autonomous to a large extent, but
forming what has been called a " Little International."   Definite organization was achieved at the close of the eighties.
The strong trade unions were driven by autocratic oppression
into political action, and they became affiliated with the socialist party.   The trade unions now make a great point of
their social democratic character, and vigorously repudiate the
" neutrality " idea.   But the general situation in Austria was
until recently most unpromising.   The unsettled relations
between Austria and Hungary, the animosity fostered by the
various nationalist parties, the frequent massacres of striking
laborers, had a depressing effect upon industrial conditions,
and starvation was prevalent.   In Galicia especially, thousands
died of starvation every year, while the blind revolts of the
proletariat were ruthlessly crushed by the soldiery.   Because
of the restricted suffrage, and the amount of electoral thimble-
rigging that was possible, there was little hope for the people
in the ballot-box.   Besides, open intimidation at the polls by
the police was general.   Nevertheless, in 1901 the socialists
assembled 780,000 votes, and elected ten members to the
Reichsrath.   The group, maintaining a strict independence in
parliament, and the party outside, concentrated their efforts on
the campaign for universal suffrage.   The propaganda, mainly
oral because of the illiteracy of the people, was superbly organized, and the workers generally gave them enthusiastic support.
As an illustration of the intense feeling at Vienna, so disgusted
were the printers at having to set up articles abusing the
socialists and universal suffrage, that they struck work and tied
up six of the big capitalist newspapers.

The fight for and the winning of universal manhood suffrage in Austria is one of the brightest pages in the history of socialism. The granting of a "constitution" in Russia, and the suffrage fight going on in Hungary, had a stimulating effect, and at the annual congress of the party in 1905, all sections were eager for battle. It was while the congress was in the midst of a discussion of the question that the Czar's constitutional manifesto was published in Vienna; and the delegates jumped to their feet, sang songs of battle, and made a solemn declaration that they would fight to the end whatever the issue, even if it meant a general strike. The same evening more than 30,000 working men and women united in a great demonstration before parliament and the Hofburg. Enthusiastic meetings followed in all the towns and provinces, and collisions with the soldiers and police were frequent. The minister Gautsch, who had previously ridiculed the idea of universal suffrage, was panic-stricken, and made promise of electoral reform before the next general election. On the 28th of November, 1905, parliament reassembled, and the working class generally declared a holiday throughout the empire. Everywhere they had meetings and processions, and at Vienna a quarter of a million working men and women bearing red flags paraded before parliament. It was a day never to be forgotten, and created a profound impression of the enormous influence of socialism. A deputation of workmen waited upon the presidents of the council and the two chambers, and made a request for immediate electoral reform. In reply, Baron Gautsch announced the deposit of a process based upon universal suffrage.

But it was not until February, 1906, that the government took any steps to fulfil its pledge; and then it was immediately obvious that they were not going to satisfy the demands of the socialists. They refused to women the right to vote. Even the limited measure provoked the resistance of the privileged classes, and showed that more vigorous tactics were necessary if the socialists were not to be again betrayed. To display any weakness on the part of the proletariat at this moment would be to lose all that they had been fighting for. The campaign was, therefore, continued with greater energy, and the excitement of the populace was such that the government was stirred to action. The bourgeois fought strenuously against the proposed reform, and then the socialists had seriously to consider whether they should not have recourse to the general strike. They decided to commence with a strike of three days in Vienna as an experiment. All the preparations were perfectly made, down to the last detail, and at a given signal all work would have ceased. The government was quite *au courant* with the situation, and had taken precautionary measures. The order to mobilize for the occupation of the stations and factories was given; while in the city a large military force was massed. But the threat of the strike was sufficient. A special commission of the Reichsrath was set seriously to work, and on the 21st of July there was a repartition of the representation by nationality. The greatest difficulty had been overcome. But in the autumn the enemies of universal suffrage tried again to thwart the people by introducing a system of plural voting which would have been completely subversive. However, the danger was again averted by the prompt action of the socialists in arousing the public feeling, and the first of December, 1906, saw the new measure, giving all men over twenty-four the right to vote, adopted in the chamber of representatives, and in the following month by the upper house.

The work to which the socialists had consecrated long years of effort was crowned with success at the elections in May, which will live in the memories of all. Instead of only eleven seats in parliament, the socialists captured no less than 87; such old militants as Victor Adler, David, and Ellenbogen receiving enormous majorities. The socialist vote amounted to 1,041,948, nearly a third of the total vote cast. The Christian Socialists, who are bitterly opposed to the Social Democratic Party, and have little in common with socialism except the name, obtained 96 members with only 722,314 votes, and the Czechs obtained 83 members with only 600,909 votes. But although in some parts the socialists had failed to touch the agricultural population, the various nationalist parties were almost crushed out; which in itself is a great step in advance. A coalition was immediately formed against the socialists, but the significance of the elections was made apparent in the emperor's address, which promised a wonderful list of social reforms. The Women's Social Democratic Party, controlling the women's trade unions, was of great aid during the fight, and the effective work done among the men is shown by the fact that in two years the number of trade unionists was increased from 180,000 to over half a million.

Hungary. — As the constitution of political organizations is illegal, it is impossible to indicate the strength of the socialists in Hungary; but through the troublous times of recent years they have increased enormously. As early as 1867 two working-class organizations were started : the one to follow Schultze-Delitsch, who afterward founded the movement for agricultural banks, and the other to follow the ideas of Lassalle. The former was but short-lived, but in 1869 a democratic union was formed and a "Laborers' Journal" founded. The movement was subjected to brutal treatment on the part of the government. Hundreds were exiled, shot, or imprisoned, and the leaders were photographed and placed in the rogues' gallery of criminals. As a result of this persecution it was not until 1890 that the organization became fairly well established ; and electoral disabilities caused it to assume more of a trade union and economic character. Little could be done in parliamentary work, and although the socialists did extremely well in the municipal elections, it was not of much avail, because the local authorities have little autonomous power. In the development of trade unions splendid progress has been made, as from 1905 to 1906 the number of organized workmen increased from 71,173 to

129,332, or over thirty per cent of the total workers. But it is among the rural workers that the propaganda has been most effective. The country population is in an incredibly poverty-stricken condition, and the sympathetic character of the socialist movement has appealed strongly to these starving people. They have already been organized into over 600 groups, with a membership of 50,000.

During the last few years especially has the development of the socialist party been of a very agitated character, and it is now transformed into a group of conspirators, submitted to espionage and domiciliary visits by the criminal police, and proscribed by society. The bourgeois parties sought to sidetrack the movement by agitating for a separation from the Austrian empire, and the whole country was in a ferment over the language question. The Austrian government, driven to action, threatened to accede to the demand for the recognition of the Hungarian language, but that they would couple with it the granting of universal suffrage. This not only chagrined the Hungarian bourgeois, and caused them hastily to abandon the nationalist movement, but it also proved unfortunate for the imperial authorities; for the socialists, who had hitherto kept out of the nationalist embroglio, entered with all their force into a campaign for universal suffrage. And such was the effect of their propaganda, that parliament promised to give the matter attention. However, parliament was prorogued indefinitely, and the socialists had to keep up their agitation. Eventually the constitutional difficulty was cleared up somewhat, and parliament was reopened with a promise from the throne that universal suffrage would be put in the first place. Again nothing was done, but when the elections of 1906 took place, not a single candidate could be found who would declare himself against electoral reform. However, it was soon apparent that the people had again been betrayed; and when the socialists renewed their campaign, a veritable reign of terror was instituted against the workmen's unions. They even discussed in parliament a measure sanctioning to the landed proprietors the right of bastinado in the treatment of their agricultural laborers.

On the 10th of October last year the people ceased work, and a hundred thousand men traversed the main streets of Buda Pesth, accompanied by bands playing the " Marseillaise," to the house of parliament, where a deputation waited upon the president of the chamber. With simple dignity they declared : " We have interrupted the industrial activity of the country in order to give expression to the claims of the downtrodden and suffering people. We demand universal and secret suffrage." They went on to give statistics showing the miserable condition in which the workers lived, what a great number were emigrating, and how those remaining were being mown down by tuberculosis. The state had created no new schools, and the workmen remained in their ignorance, 38 per cent being illiterate. The government had dissolved 354 trade unions. The universal vote had been promised, but parliament had allowed nineteen months to elapse without dreaming of presenting any measure. On the contrary they had presented laws which had put the proletariat more and more at the caprice of the possessing class.

All the deputation received in reply was a contemptuous speech from the president, while a socialist deputy was refused the right of interpellation. This reactionary attitude, added to the governmental terrorism in attempting to suppress the trade unions, has created profound resentment among the workers ; and so intense is the feeling, that the situation of the Hungarian cabinet cannot be tenable for long, especially in view of the winning of the suffrage in Austria.

Finland. — The trade unions were the foundation of the Finnish Labor Party, inaugurated in 1890 with a program based upon that of Erfurt. This has since been elaborated, in 1903, when the movement took the name of the Finnish Social Democratic Party. As soon as the program was published it was confiscated by the police, and the name of the

z

party was not allowed to appear in any newspaper, nor even extracts from such writers as Marx, Engels, and Lassalle. The population being very scattered, and the winters long and severe, the difficulties of propaganda are great; but nevertheless the Finns made splendid progress. They have fixed certain periods of the year for special agitation, and these have become permanent institutions in the life of the people, in addition to the general celebration of the First of May. Up to 1905 the paying members of the party amounted to nearly 50,000, including 10,000 women.

The chief accomplishment of the socialists, of course, has been their dramatic conquest of universal and equal suffrage for men and women. Notwithstanding the fact that every meeting was held under the supervision of the police, who interfered on the slightest provocation, the socialists attacked with vigor the constitution of the Diet. This assembly was made up of four distinct classes: the nobles, the clerics, the landed proprietors, and the rich bourgeois. Workpeople, soldiers, and sailors had no votes; two per cent of the inhabitants of a town controlled the electoral power. The agitation led to an immense popular demonstration at Helsingfors on April 14, 1905, when the huge crowd waited for six hours while their demand for the vote was being discussed in the Diet. The result was barren, and when it was communicated to the people, their emotion and excitement were terrible; and this feeling spread throughout the whole proletarian class in Finland, so that the 14th of April was called " the day of shame."

The socialists had already threatened to have recourse to more vigorous tactics. They declared that by means of universal suffrage the people would elect their own representatives, form a national assembly, and elaborate a new charter. This revolutionary idea was received with enthusiasm by the populace, and in October, 1905, during the trouble in Russia, the general political strike was declared. The socialists established practically a new government, with all the state departments, and order was perfect everywhere. The committee proclaimed the inviolability of the person, the right of free speech and of the press, and suppressed the ordinary police and the functionaries of the Senate. The bourgeois were in a panic, and disputed among themselves as to the methods to pursue. One section advocated the convocation of the Diet in order, as they said, to hand over the powers to the national assembly, while another section proposed that the Diet itself should undertake legislation for new representation, or in other words to legislate the old Diet out of existence. But the socialists would on no account allow the bourgeois to meddle. However, the imperial proclamation arrived on the 6th of November, conceding all that the workers demanded; and the strike terminated. The socialists had little confidence in this, and went on making preparations for another strike ; and soon mistrust of the government was general. An ex-secretary of the party, Kari, accepted a position in the government, and the party declared that by so doing he had himself severed his connection with socialism. As the socialists were now perfecting their elaborations for another political strike the authorities were again thrown into consternation and panic, and eventually a measure was rushed though the Diet, and the suffrage was sanctioned in St. Petersburg in July, 1906. Still several small groups of non-possessors were not franchised, but practically all men and women received the right to vote.

In April, 1907, the general election took place, and although the capitalist parties exploited to their utmost the racial and lingual differences between the Swedes and the Finns, the success of the socialists was an event never to be forgotten. For the first time a socialist sits in the parliament, and for the first time in any parliament women have also been elected. Indeed, perhaps the greatest praise is due to the women in the winning of the suffrage. On one occasion they held a meeting at which there were no less than 25,000 women. The socialist representation in the Diet numbers 80 out of a total of 200 members.   Nineteen women were elected, of whom nine were socialists.   One of them was a housemaid !

Sweden. — The proletarian movement dates from the seventies, up to which time the bulk of the people had been engaged in agriculture.   Pioneering was done by a Danish tailor named Auguste Palm, who started a newspaper entitled " The People's Will."   This was suppressed, and later a socialist organization was founded, which eventually branched off into trade unions. These unions came together in 1889 and formed the Social Democratic Labor Party, based on a program after the German pattern.   The party had thus the excellent foundation of a workers' economic movement.   It early had its internal tribulation, but after a set debate at a congress in 1891 the Marxian socialists triumphed over the anarchists.   The suffrage being very restricted, the socialists made electoral reform the main object of their propaganda, while at the same time they carried on an incessant agitation for improved conditions in industry.   Strike after strike was organized, and so admirably managed that working conditions have been vastly improved.   So advanced was the movement that in 1902, the government having played with the people so long on the matter of the suffrage, a general strike was declared.   In Stockholm there were no trams, cabs, gas, electricity ; and all production had ceased, 42,000 people having struck work in that city alone.   The government was in a dilemma, and a meeting of the two chambers hastily passed a resolution inviting the government to bring in a measure based upon universal suffrage.   However, this was but an insincere action in order to quiet the people, and the socialists had to continue their agitation.   In fact, it may be said that the socialists of Sweden achieved what success they have because of their suffrage agitation and their admirable organization of strikes. In the last seven years the number of trade unionists has increased from 46,000 to 144,395.

In 1904 the chamber rejected a measure brought forward

by the conservative government for so-called universal suffrage, as it left intact the predominance of the senate. To be a senator it is not necessary to pass examinations or submit to popular elections. A considerable income or a big fortune is the only necessary qualification. The senate deals with the budget, so that there is little chance for any legislation which meets with the disapproval of this house. During 1905 the government proposed a measure menacing the right to strike of the trade unions in the railway, gas, electricity and similar industries, obviously an attempt to frustrate any political general strike. There was great excitement over this, and without doubt there would have been a spontaneous general strike had the measure passed. But mainly owing to the strenuous efforts of the socialists, it was defeated by 112 votes to 110. During this same year took place the memorable strike of the metal workers, which ended in a decided victory for the workmen.

With regard to the separation of Sweden and Norway, the socialists in congress in 1905, when the Norwegian delegates were also present, proclaimed the absolute right of the Norwegian people freely to decide their own affairs. During the crisis the Swedish bourgeois were very excited and bellicose, and demanded the mobilization of the army; while for once the socialists and the royal family were in accord in the support of a peaceful arrangement.

At the general election of 1905 the party returned thirteen (since augmented by two) members instead of four as previously. A liberal-radical government came in, and they proposed a limited suffrage reform, to which, as it would increase the electorate from 400,000 to about a million, the socialists gave their support. The senate threw it out, and a conservative government then took office. The new parliament contrived an ingenious measure for universal suffrage, with proportional representation for both chambers. The opening of the senate to the people was more apparent than real, and the socialists, perceiving that it was an attempt to put the senate beyond destruction, opposed the whole measure by a vigorous campaign, and demanded a complete constitutional revision. "Down with the senate" was their cry, and so great appeared to be their influence that the bourgeois parties became alarmed. Liberals, and even senators who did not like the tampering with the upper house, gave the government measure support, and it was passed. It comes into operation in three years' time, and as it more than doubles the number of voters, the socialists are sanguine of electing quite fifty members to the chamber, and perhaps two dozen to the Senate.

Norway. — As it was one of the latest countries to be invaded by industrialism and capitalism, and as it was already one of the most democratic in nature, with an advanced system of education and social legislation, socialism did not make a beginning in Norway until late in the eighties, when the Labor Party was established; although as early as the fifties Markus Thrane, a young agitator, endeavored to organize the workers, for which he was many times imprisoned. Socialists, both men and women, soon made their way into the municipal councils; and it is, perhaps, in its municipal work that Norwegian socialism has been most successful, especially in Christiania and Trondhjem. It was not until 1903 that they were represented in the Storthing, when the four socialists elected included Dr. Ericksen and Professor Berge, the former a Lutheran clergyman, and the latter the only Roman Catholic in parliament. The press is well developed, and includes the "Social Demokraten," an influential daily. The membership of the party is now over 20,000, in 396 groups.

Naturally the attention of the Labor Party has been engrossed during the last few years by the crisis culminating in the separation of the states of Norway and Sweden. Since 1892 the socialists had declared for a severance from the dominance of Sweden, in order to put an end to the ruinous military expenditure, the perpetual fear of the Swedish nobles, and in order that Norway might devote herself to social reform. The separation was effected, but the Liberals, as soon as they had got what they wanted, — the establishment of Norwegian consulates, — showed themselves to be reactionary, finally dissolving and handing over the power of government to a conservative bloc, who gave to the Norwegians, up to that time governed after the manner of a republic, a Danish king. The socialists fought energetically for a republic, and although the time for propaganda was very short, it was thought that they would carry the day. The plebiscite, however, showed only 69,264 for a republic as against 259,563 for a kingdom. The subsequent action of the socialists in voting to welcome King Haakon to Norway was severely criticised throughout the world movement, and to their explanation that it would have been unconstitutional to have voted otherwise after the referendum, the German "Vorwärts" retorted, "Since when have socialists been bound by constitutions?" Eventually it was given as an excuse by the leading socialist review that the party was very young, and that it must be remembered it had not been built upon an economic foundation as in other countries.

The elections of 1906 proved a great time for the socialists, as they assembled no less than 45,000 votes as against 30,000 in 1903, and increased their representation to ten. Trade unionism has also rapidly developed, the number having in two years increased from 9089 to 25,308, and affiliated with the Labor Party. Propaganda is making progress among the farmers and the fishermen. The women throw themselves into the work with enthusiasm, and the young people's societies are of great help.

As both the conservatives and the radicals had long ago inscribed on their programs the granting of the suffrage to women, the Storthing could no longer refrain from granting this popular demand, and in August it became law. All men in Norway over 25 years have the right to vote without qualification, and the vote is now extended to women over 25, but with a revenue qualification. However, as, in the case of married women, they are entitled to vote if the specified amount of taxes is paid by the husbands, it is calculated that something like 300,000 women have been enfranchised, which includes a considerable majority of the married women.

Denmark. — It has been said that the progress of socialism in Denmark is more encouraging than in any other country. It was in the spring of 1871 that a young post-office official named Louis Pio, fired by the socialist ideals of the Paris Commune, issued a socialist leaflet which caused somewhat of a sensation. This was followed by the establishment of a newspaper, which lives to this day in "The Social Democrat." In the fall of 1871 a section of the International was established, and in twelve months' time it counted 8000 members. Attention was devoted to the organization of trade unions especially, and strikes were inaugurated and fought with tangible success to the workers; but after a period of ruthless persecution the movement was suppressed in 1873, and the leaders imprisoned. Nevertheless, the work went on in the economic field, and in 1878 the various unions and associations came together and founded the present Social Democratic Union of Denmark, based upon a program of the German type. The union embraces two organizations, the one political and the other economic, made up of the various trade societies. The political side elects two members on the general council of the unions, and *vice versa*. The political organization counts 35,000 members, and the trade unions 99,000; but as some are members of both, the round total would be somewhere about the encouraging figure of 120,000.

The fight between the landlords and the great farmers on the one hand, and the peasant farmers and agricultural laborers on the other, has now become very keen indeed; in participating in which the socialist cause has had an astonishing success, the real workers of the land turning to the socialists as their only saviours from the rapacity of the land monopolizers. There have been repeated attempts to split up the admirable organization of the party, by the institution of "Christian Socialist" parties, and by the anti-parliamentary tactics of a few anarchists; but all these attempts have been miserably abortive; and the Danish party stands out as one of the sturdiest and best-united sections of the international movement.

The socialists were very successful in the elections of 1906, as they increased their representation from 16 to 24 in the People's Chamber, out of a total of 114 seats, and from one to four representatives in the Senate, out of 66 seats. The total number of votes polled was 77,000. In the communal elections the party has also made great progress, as in 50 towns they have either in the council or in municipal posts 450 representatives, and 400 in the rural communes. In parliament the group has had a decided influence upon social reform. In 1891 a tax was put upon lager beer, a part of the proceeds of which was devoted to the establishment of an old-age pension system, without any previous payment on the part of the recipients. All over 60 years of age are entitled to a pension, half of which is paid by the state and half by the local authority. The socialists are now agitating for a liberal extension of the system. In the matter of factory legislation the group have also done excellent work, and they are now fighting strenuously for universal and equal suffrage in municipal elections, unemployed legislation, the eight-hour day, and for a radical reduction in military expenditure. Propaganda is principally by the 25 daily newspapers, of which "The Social Democrat" boasts a daily circulation of 55,000. Coöperative enterprises are spreading, and at Copenhagen the socialists have a bakery, a butchery, and a brewery.

Holland. — Up to 1870 there was no movement of importance in the Netherlands, but when Domela Nieuwenhuis gave up his pastorate in the Lutheran Church at the Hague in order to preach socialism, the new gospel was received with enthusiasm. The group of pioneers met with as bitter persecution as perhaps the socialists have experienced anywhere except in

Russia. In 1888 Nieuwenhuis, on his release from imprisonment for lèse majesté, was elected a member of parliament, and
so great was the indignation of the bourgeois that one school-
master made an earnest appeal to the government to strike the
" red district" represented by the socialist from the map!
The solitary socialist had a rough time in the assembly, and
the fact that he could make no headway there made him despair of parliamentary tactics. He then went to the extreme
of revolutionary propaganda, and this eventually led to a seces-
sion from the movement. In 1894 the present Social Democratic Party was formed by twelve men, known now as the
twelve apostles, including the present leader Troelstra. In
1901 the party ran candidates in 51 out of the hundred electoral districts, and with a vote of 40,000 they returned seven
members to parliament, an increase of four on 1897. " Het
Volk," the chief party organ, has had a considerable influence
in propaganda. With the gradual decline of agriculture, as
compared with the oncoming of the capitalist régime, the trade
unions have developed rapidly, side by side with a young and
sturdy coöperative movement on the lines of that of Belgium.
One of the strongest trade unions, which has played a prominent part in labor battles during recent years, is that of the
diamond workers, which has Polak for a leader. There have
been many successful agitations and strikes in the various
trades, notably in the jute industry, and even among the agricultural laborers. Workmen's coöperatives, quite distinct from
the bourgeois, are devoting part of their profits to the political
and economic fight. Special effort is being made on the question of the eight-hour day, and on universal suffrage.

The elections of 1905 saw the fall of the much-hated Dr.
Kuyper, who was the personification of reaction, and the arch-
enemy of the proletarian movement. So far as the workers
were concerned it might almost be said that their only desire
was to defeat this man, at whose hand they had suffered so
much; and his fall was celebrated with great rejoicing through-

out the land.   During his ministry he had waged unceasing warfare against the workmen's organizations, and by a stroke of the pen had taken away the right to strike from the workers on the railroads and in the public services.   As, however, the elections were still under the influence of the Liberals and the Clericals, the socialists were unable to get a straight fight upon their principles, and they were unable to increase their representation, although their vote was 65,743 as against 38,279 in 1901. The Clericals held 48 seats and the Liberals 45, and thus the socialists are to a certain degree in possession of the balance of power, which they use to effect in stimulating social reform.

Internally the party has been troubled by the syndicalist element.   Indeed, from its earliest days the Dutch movement has been agitated by those of an anarchist tendency; and because of their hostile attitude there was recently great danger of a disruption of the party.   "Het Volk" was charged with becoming lax in Marxian principles and with favoring revisionism.   However, after a long dispute and much personal bitterness, the overwhelming majority of the members have supported the central committee in a resolution demanding that the criticism of the syndicalist section should be kept within reasonable limits; and at the congress of 1907 the malcontents submitted, a fact that has considerably brightened the outlook for socialism in the Netherlands.

Switzerland.—During the past few years the Social Democratic Party has been passing through tribulation, but the members derive much satisfaction from the fact that while the political movement has made little headway, there has been a wonderful development of trade unions, coöperatives, and local reform societies.   Known as the most democratic country in the world, Switzerland had very early its radical associations and socialist societies.   One of the oldest and most powerful was the Grutliverein, which dominated the working-class movement until recent years; but as most of its leaders were Liberals, the result has been similar to that in England: the development of a distinctly socialist party has been comparatively slow. Until the quite recent advent of industrialism, there were few proletarians ; and possessed of his right to the referendum, the individual was not enamoured of political parties. One effect of the referendum is that, every important question having to be submitted to the populace, it follows that a great amount of political education on the subject is necessary, with the result that the peasant class especially is inclined to be conservative and impatient of politics, and the politician tends to become opportunist.

The Social Democratic Party was founded in 1888, and as the Grutliverein had become permeated with socialism, a union was effected in 1901, and also with the trade unions. Although this amalgamation, bringing in as it did the extensive organization and funds of the Grutli, had a strengthening effect upon the proletarian movement, its socialism was somewhat diluted. There have been many reports as to the sad way into which the Swiss socialist party has gotten, but to a large extent it is due to the fact that many of the Grutli were merely radicals and could not accept the socialist principles in full. It is the weeding out of this element that explains very largely the apparent weakening of the cause of socialism in Switzerland.

The socialists have done most excellent work in the municipal councils, and there are signs on every hand that they are gaining the sympathies of the workers. The electoral system is open to much fraud, which is unscrupulously practised by the capitalist parties to keep the workers from representation in the National Council. At the last election the socialists assembled 70,000 votes, by which they claim to have won 25 seats, but they were only allowed six. Recent inquiries have been made into the extent of exploitation of child-labor, with the appalling revelation that 53 per cent of the children attending school are also employed in laborious daily work. The school teachers complain that the mentality is now very low, and that 40 per cent of the children are stunted. Capitalism has become intense, and with it an almost savage system of oppression has been instituted by the government. The fact that there are three different languages in the country hinders very much the propaganda of the socialists, while the anarchist tendency is still strong in the trade unions.

Switzerland has become notorious for the frequency with which the soldiery is used against striking workmen, and in 1906 the socialists held an extraordinary congress to discuss the whole military question. Although the military system of this country is much belauded in other parts of the world, the Swiss socialists passed a resolution declaring themselves in accord with all the other socialist parties in the demand for the suppression of all acts and means of war, admitting for the present the need for a militia exclusively for defensive purposes. They demanded a guarantee against the gross abuse of the employment of soldiers against strikers; and failing any such assurance, they counselled all soldiers to disobey commands to attack workmen, guaranteeing to indemnify such soldiers for any financial charges they might incur, and to support their families. To this end a special fund was established. Recently the socialists have been subjected to much persecution. The editor of the Zurich daily has been banished, and the writer of a leaflet has been sent to prison for eight months.

Spain.— Many attempts were made between 1878 and 1882 to found a socialist party, but they failed, until Pablo Inglesias, who had propagated socialist ideas for many years, founded a paper, " El Socialista," in 1888. Then a Socialist Labor Party was formed at Barcelona, its program being taken from the French and German parties. But ever since the International the anarchist spirit had been prevalent, for which no doubt the corrupt state of the government, and the apparent hopelessness of parliamentary action, were largely responsible. The socialists had this spirit to combat as well as the ordinary difficulties of propaganda, but nevertheless they made steady progress, and in 1904 they counted 10,000 members, and mustered 29,000 votes at the parliamentary elections.

But the terrible industrial crisis which followed the Philippine and Cuban wars has had a discouraging effect upon the socialist organizations as well as upon the trade unions. Trade is practically at a standstill, and whole villages have been deserted. Another reason for the backwardness of the proletarian movement is the illiteracy of the people. Out of 9,087,821 men 5,086,056 can either not read or write, and of 9,530,265 women no less than 6,806,834 are illiterates. In the year 1902 alone, all together 51,593 people emigrated, about half of these to America. Nevertheless, despite the enormous power exercised by the clergy over the ignorant, there has been an encouraging growth of a republican spirit. The socialist party now only counts 6000 members, but it is working in very cordial relations with the general union of workmen, whose membership totals 34,537 as against 56,905 before the industrial crisis. There is a section of anarchists, but the unions are directed and the tactic is determined by the socialists.

Government, both central and local, is in a parlous condition. The universal suffrage, the self-government, the fundamental liberties, exist on paper only; and the bureaucracy is dominant. Terrorism has existed for some time at Barcelona, and it has been proved that the authors of bomb outrages were the police themselves. At the parliamentary election in 1907, the bureaucracy received an unexpected blow. What was known as the solidarity movement, originating in the department of Catalonia, resulted in a large number of members being returned pledged to fight for autonomy in local government. But during the year the government have put forward measures revising the system of local government, which are only underhand blows at universal suffrage. The bureaucracy has for a time strengthened its hold in the communities, and it is calculated that it is well-nigh impossible for workmen to elect their own representatives in a majority of these local bodies.

Bulgaria. — The Socialist Party was founded in 1894, and in 1902 obtained seven seats in parliament, with 20,307 votes, but in the following year lost them all. This was partly due to the terrorism exercised over the electors by the government, but principally to a very serious split in the ranks of the socialists. Up to quite recently the membership consisted for the most part of the educated classes and petty bourgeois, while the proletarian workers were in a small minority. It was declared that because of this character of the movement the party was nothing more than a seat-hunting body for the bourgeois, who had abandoned the principles of the class struggle. Some of the opportunists, as they were called, advocated the collaboration of classes, while the other section demanded that the movement should be kept on strictly Marxian lines. The opportunists repudiated the charges of their opponents, but nevertheless a split took place in 1903, and up to the present there are at work two distinct socialist parties. As a consequence the cause makes but slow progress in Bulgaria, so far as representation on public bodies is concerned.

Servia. — The Erfurt program was adopted as the basis of the Social Democratic Labor Party, founded in 1903. There had been an active trade union movement since late in the eighties, but because of the unrest and disturbances leading up to the *coup d'état* in 1903, there had been little work of a political character, the authorities doing their utmost to stamp out any organization. The socialists had hardly got started when the annual parliamentary election was upon them. However, they put forward candidates, and despite the very limited suffrage, they elected one member. In 1905 they won two seats, but in 1906 they could again only secure one, although their votes had increased. In the communal elections they have done much better. The membership of the party at the end of 1906 was 1400, and they work in perfect harmony with the trade unions.

They are now concentrating on the fight for universal suffrage.

Poland. — Of twenty million Poles, ten million are upon Russian territory, four in Austria, and three and a half in Prussia, while the rest are scattered all over the world. Hence the Polish Socialist Party is divided into three sections. In Russia such are the oppression and secret methods of the government that extreme precaution has to be exercised in admitting people to membership. Under such circumstances the formation of trade unions is difficult, but nevertheless the socialists were the guiding spirits in a whole series of strikes from 1899 to 1903, with more or less tangible results to the strikers. And then the industrial crisis almost brought about the suspension of the movement. During the recent years, however, the propaganda has been very effective, extending to the rural workers, where the socialists have the opposition of the nationalists and the clergy, who do not hesitate to assist the police against them. Much is made of the First of May in Warsaw, and the custom has extended of utilizing the funerals of socialists for demonstrations. It is not infrequent that scores of the mourners are afterward lodged in jail. The Austrian section is largely in Galicia, a country still under a regular feudal system, and where the people die of starvation by the thousand. The socialists were, of course, much agitated over the revolutionary happenings in Russia, and at a great demonstration in Krakow the portrait of the Czar was burnt. In the subsequent police riot many people were wounded. Incidentally the chief of the police had his ears soundly boxed! Even in Prussia the Poles are subjected to severe persecution, and in the endeavor of the authorities to crush out all national characteristics, the children are imprisoned if they are discovered studying their own language or literature. The consequence is that the intellectual development of the Poles in Prussia is being arrested. A Pole arriving from Warsaw or Krakow is a suspect, merely because he is a Pole. Nevertheless, the socialists carry on an active propaganda, and the party coöperates enthusiastically with the German socialists. There is a branch of the party in America.

Japan. — In 1897 a socialist agitation was commenced by Sen Katayama, who was present at the Amsterdam Congress in 1904, but at almost every meeting he was stopped by the police, who kept pace with his movements everywhere. However, he engineered several successful strikes. In 1901, a Social Democratic Party was started in Tokio, and was immediately suppressed. Another effort, a month later, was also suppressed ; but a third attempt, when a program was adopted on the lines of the Communist Manifesto, was more successful, and the movement took root. The spread of socialist ideas has been accelerated by the feverish growth of capitalism and the industrial crisis following the war. Several socialist newspapers were started, of which " Hikari " has played a prominent part. Kotoku and Nishikawa, the editors of one of the journals, were sentenced to imprisonment, and the journal suppressed. In 1906 Tokio was for several days in a state of civil war consequent upon a socialist agitation against the shameless exploitation of the people by the tramway monopolists. Latterly the government has redoubled its persecution, the recently started daily newspaper has been suppressed, and for the time being the socialists have decided to carry on their propaganda in a secret manner. Socialism is undoubtedly spreading fast, especially among the more intelligent of the populace and the students.

Chili. — As early as 1850 Francisco Bilbao propagated ideas of equality, and founded a Society of Equality ; and for his pains he was condemned as a blasphemer and exiled. The year 1887 saw the establishment of the Democratic Party, which is socialist in character, and has recently expressed a desire to become affiliated with the International. The men who started the movement were subjected to much persecution, which is continued up to the present, as quite recently the editor of the official journal was condemned to eighteen

2 A

months' imprisonment, which he avoided by leaving the country. Because of the revolution of 1891 there was a check in the work of the party, but afterward it resumed with greater vigor, and in 1894 scored its first political success by electing a deputy at Valparaiso. In 1906 there were six members elected, and the socialist vote totalled 18,000. Eighty representatives were elected in the municipalities, and in five towns the socialists were in a majority. A significant feature of the present situation in Chili is that the government cannot get sufficient men to join the police, and not 20 per cent of the conscripts present themselves for service in the army.

Argentina.— Notwithstanding the heterogeneous character of the population, and the illiteracy of the poorer classes, socialism is making considerable progress in the Argentine Republic. The Socialist Party was established at Buenos Ayres in 1896, when a program was adopted similar to those in Europe, but modified to local necessities. At the beginning of 1907 there were more than 3000 members. The weekly paper " Vanguardia " has a circulation of 6000. The electoral system is corrupted and abused by the landowners, but nevertheless the socialist vote has increased from 1254 in 1904 to 3500 in 1906. One socialist deputy was elected in 1904 for four years. There are two or three federations of trade unions, one of which is distinctly anarchistic.

Australasia. — Geographical isolation, and the tolerably comfortable condition of the workers, account in a great measure for the tardy appearance of socialism in Australia. Up to 1890, the year of the great maritime strike, there was no political movement among working men, but in their defeat on that occasion they learned a severe lesson. In the following year they signalized their entrance into independent politics by electing a large number of labor members to the various state parliaments. At this time the Australian Socialist League, founded in 1887, did excellent propaganda. In 1892 there was a congress at Sydney for the purpose of uniting the various socialist bodies that had sprung up in different states, but by 1896 this had disappeared. The labor movement fought shy of socialism, while the question of protection versus free trade has hindered progress generally. However, during the past few years quiet work has been done by the Socialist League in South Wales, the Social Democratic Party in Victoria, the Social Democratic Vanguard in Queensland, the Social Democratic Federation in Western Australia, and the Clarion Fellowship in Adelaide. Tom Mann, formerly of England, has been the guiding spirit at Melbourne, giving up work with the Political Labor Council about two years ago to go for out-and-out socialism. As an incident in the socialists' fight for free speech Mann was sentenced to five weeks in jail. In New South Wales especially, as the result of Mann's work, there is now an excellent and virile organization, with a socialist Sunday school in Melbourne that is doing good work.

The trade union movement is very strong, and signs are multiplying that it is becoming permeated with the spirit of the class struggle. To a certain extent the Labor Party have been forced to come out into the open because of being labelled socialists by their opponents; and at the Interstate Labor Convention in 1905, the following was decided upon as an objective : " The securing of the full results of their industry to all producers by collective ownership of monopolies, and the extension of the industrial and economic functions of the state." The Labor Party have over a third of the representatives in the various parliaments, a large proportion of whom are avowed socialists, and in the Federal Parliament, where for five months in 1904 they were in power, two-thirds of the labor men are socialists.

So far as socialistic legislation is concerned, New Zealand is far ahead of any other country. They have universal suffrage for men and women, graduated land and income taxes, drastic factory laws, conciliation laws, old-age pensions, etc., but it is nevertheless a fact that at present there is much discontent among the industrial workers, and the country is being troubled by the problem of unemployment. Attempts are being made to get the labor organizations to adopt a socialist platform.

Canada. — During the eighties much excellent propaganda was done by numerous socialist parties and leagues in this vast and sparsely populated country, especially in British Columbia ; but it was not until the end of 1904 that the Canadian Socialist Party was founded. Notwithstanding the fact that Canada is but a new country, a large proportion of the inhabitants are industrial proletarians, and socialism has therefore found fertile soil. In February, 1907, the party succeeded in electing three socialist members to the parliament of British Columbia, and in other cases they were only just beaten by a few votes. In Toronto the party is also very active, especially in the municipal elections. The trade union movement is strong, but although socialistically inclined, is not yet disposed to declare straight out for socialism. So that at the twenty-second annual Trades and Labor Congress, held in Victoria, it was decided to form an independent Labor Party, and to work after the manner of the Labor Party in England.

America. — Because of its cheap land and political liberty America was for the first half of last century the experimental ground for all manner of communist and political schemes. The number of communities and brotherhoods established, each with its own particular panacea, amounted to several hundreds. The Owenite, Icarian, and Fourieristic movements attained large proportions, and in particular the latter attracted the sympathy and active support of many prominent writers and public men. But all these experiments had little or no effect upon the modern socialist movement, and after the Civil War there was hardly anything left of their various organizations. For some time the whole country was absorbed in repairing the effects of the war, industry flourished in an unprecedented manner, and the people generally were too busy for politics. In 1870 there was a great scarcity of labor, but it only needed a few years of the feverish industrialism which prevailed to bring about crises which resulted in a permanent standing army of a million unemployed workmen.

There are many things which would account for what might be called the backwardness of the socialist movement in America. It might be said that the transition from a comparatively prosperous state of affairs to one of industrial anarchy, with its concomitant of surplus labor, has been too swift to allow of the people acquiring that spirit of class-consciousness out of which have grown the socialist movements of Europe. And, with its "democratic" institutions, there has been no such common cause as the fight for the suffrage, which has been so much of a unifying and educational force among the proletariat of other countries. Again, the vastness of the country has been a great drawback. There has certainly not been union among the socialists themselves, but it is very easy to overstate the retarding effect of such want of unity. Undoubtedly the principal obstacle has been that, while numerous exotic socialist societies have sprung up during the last fifty years as a consequence of the presence in America of a population of widely different nationalities, the very difference of language and characteristics of the immigrants has militated against a union of the workers. Even when they had been brought together in trade unions, they displayed, up to quite recently, a positively hostile attitude toward political action. So that, fully considered, it must be said that in face of such formidable difficulties, in what they have accomplished up to the present, the socialists of America have done remarkably good work.

In the early seventies a number of sections of the International Working Men's Association were started, mainly by immigrants and political refugees from Europe; and when the seat of the Central Council of the International was removed to America a short time before its decease, there was an active period of socialist propaganda, which was accelerated by the spreading industrial depression. In 1876 the various organizations were brought together, and the Working Men's Party of the United States was founded, changing its name a year later to the Socialist Labor Party of North America. For twenty years this was the chief organization in the socialist movement. As not more than ten per cent of the membership were native Americans, the young party was confronted by the gigantic task of "naturalizing" the heterogeneous elements, and progress was inevitably slow. An attempt was made to convert the rapidly growing trade union movement, but the socialists received anything but encouragement from the union leaders. Failing to make any impression, therefore, a section of the socialists declared that it was not worth while troubling about the trade unions. Following strictly independent tactics the socialist party participated in elections, but it was only during temporary periods of unsettled trade conditions that they polled any considerable vote. It seemed as if the workers would only give attention to politics when they were on "short time" or out of work altogether. By 1878 the membership of the Socialist Labor Party had grown to 10,000, but during the subsequent trade depression it dwindled to about 2000. Eight papers in English which had been started did not survive above a year, but the "New Yorker Volkzeitung" has continued until it is to-day the leading German socialist newspaper in America.

For several years the energies of the party were taken up in fighting the vigorous anarchist movement which was developing. Various revolutionary clubs had come together and formed the Revolutionary Socialist Party in 1881, finding a popular leader in John Most, who had been excluded from the German Social Democratic Party, and had served terms of imprisonment in Germany, Austria, and England because of his revolutionary writings. The movement was transformed into the International

Working People's Association, on a basis of "social revolutionism," and with its main strength in Chicago. The depletion of the membership of the Socialist Labor Party, which in 1883 hardly counted 1500, was due in a great measure to the new organization, in which the workers thought they had found a more effective instrument for the achievement of better conditions of life. Vain attempts were made to unite the two bodies, and a bitter fight ensued. Manifestoes and counter-manifestoes were issued, and the socialists declared, "We do not share the folly of the men who consider dynamite bombs as the best means of agitation." Meanwhile both parties had an accession of members, the "International" in 1885 having a membership of 7000.

In that year the American Federation of Labor, the principal organization of trade unions, revived the agitation for an eight-hour day. In this the revolutionary party took a prominent lead in Chicago. There were many collisions with the police and riots, culminating in the memorable Haymarket affair. A squad of police suddenly presented themselves at the finish of a meeting, and just outside the hall a bomb was thrown among them, killing one and wounding others. Indiscriminate shooting ensued, and besides numerous wounded, seven policemen and four civilians were killed. The leaders of the "International" were tried for murder, and although not the remotest connection could be established between the defendants and the bomb-throwing, August Spies, Samuel Fielden, Michael Schwab, Albert R. Parsons, Adolph Fischer, George Engel, and Louis Lingg were sentenced to death. In the case of Schwab and Fielden the sentence was commuted, Lingg committed suicide in prison, and the other four were hanged. The Haymarket affair was the end of the International Working People's Association.

In 1886, extensive lecture tours by Wilhelm Liebknecht and Eleanor Marx Aveling, the daughter of Karl Marx, did much to aid the growth of the Socialist Labor Party. Politically, the socialists had a very chequered career. At first they had declared for the abolition of the position of President of the United States, but in 1880 they allied themselves with the Greenbackers, a party originally founded upon a program of currency reform, on their adopting a socialistic platform; but after the presidential election the alliance was dissolved. In 1886 the lively campaign of Henry George in New York was supported by the socialists, although they did not accept his views. It was a painful lesson for them, and they resumed their independent attitude. In 1892 they made their first presidential nomination, and their vote gradually increased until in 1898 they polled 82,204.

Meanwhile the economic organizations of the workers were making rapid strides. The Knights of Labor, established for the uniting of the trade unions, in order " to secure for the workers the full enjoyment of the wealth they create," developed until in 1886 it had over half a million members, an accession due in great measure to the "strike fever." Its disintegration, however, began shortly afterward, until now there are but a few thousand adherents. Another organization of unions which had started in 1881, was five years later transformed into the American Federation of Labor, with Samuel Gompers as first president. In a year's time it counted a membership of 618,000, and at the present day, something over 2,000,000 members are affiliated. The Federation would have nothing to do with politics, and the leaders especially resisted strongly the attempts made from time to time by socialists to obtain a declaration of socialist principles.

The Socialist Labor Party now assumed an attitude of bitter hostility toward the trade union movement, and in a resolution passed in 1896 declared that the trade union organizations were " hopelessly corrupt." With the idea of drawing from the Federation the large number of unionists who were socialistically inclined, a Socialist Trade and Labor Alliance was founded; but it only accentuated the difficulties, and far from attaining its object, it was the means of splitting up the Socialist Labor Party itself.

In 1897 a new movement had been started under the title of the Social Democracy of America, primarily to further colonizing schemes. It grew in numbers, but two years later split upon the question of colonization versus political action. The politicians, headed by Victor L. Berger, were in a minority, and seceded in order to establish the Social Democratic Party of America. The new party included Eugene V. Debs, who had come into prominence as the organizer of the great railroad strike, as an incident of which he had served six months in jail. Terms of unity with the pro-union section of the Socialist Labor Party were discussed, and amalgamation had been almost completed when there was division in the ranks of the Social Democrats. Thus both the social parties were split. It had been agreed, however, that Eugene V. Debs, of the Social Democrats, should be nominated for President of the United States, with Job Harriman, of the Socialist Labor Party, as Vice-President, and during the campaign much of the bitterness between the various sections was wiped out; and under the name of "The Socialist Party," they were united at a convention held in Indianapolis, in July, 1901, when it was reckoned that about 10,000 members were affiliated.

From that day the Socialist Party has steadily grown, while the influence of the senior party has rapidly declined. The Socialist Party has now about 35,000 members who pay dues of three dollars a year each. At the presidential election of 1904, when Debs was again nominated, the socialist poll was 409,230, as against 223,494 in 1902. The socialist press has increased enormously, and now numbers over fifty journals. Half of these are in English, eight are in German, of which two are dailies, four in Yiddish, as well as papers for Finns, Italians, Hungarians, Czechs, Poles, Letts, Lithuanians, Slavs, and Swedes. The Socialist Labor Party has published "The People" daily for four years, and the Socialist Party is now represented among dailies by "The Chicago Daily Socialist." Of the weeklies, "The Appeal to Reason" has a circulation of about 300,000.

Undoubtedly, of recent years, the cause of socialism has made considerable progress, and the most encouraging sign is the fairly rapid permeation that is going on in the trade unions. Many large organizations have definitely endorsed the socialist program. These unions have a total membership of 350,000, but in addition there are many big unions having a large proportion of socialists who have not passed resolutions. Reports are multiplying of the strong tendency toward socialism that is manifesting itself throughout the whole economic movement, and at least twenty of the trade union journals are consistent advocates for the cause. A large number of brilliant journalists and university men are sympathetic, and there is an Intercollegiate Socialist Society, which exercises a considerable influence in a quiet way in the universities. In 1905, Mrs. Carrie Rand left a large sum of money for the establishment of an institution for the teaching of socialism and the social sciences, and the Rand School of Social Sciences in New York is now occupying an important place in the advance of socialism.

Special mention must be made of the achievements of the socialists in the state of Wisconsin, and especially in Milwaukee. In the State Legislature the six socialist members have introduced no less than 72 measures of industrial and political reform, about a fourth of which have been put on the statute book. They have got established an eight-hour day for telegraphers, and important modifications in child labor laws. In the Milwaukee City Council the party has twelve socialist aldermen, and among other things, they have got established a public electric lighting system, secured a three-cent fare on a part of the street-car system, and an increased tax on street railway property.

The story of the attempt to put to death Haywood, Moyer, and Pettibone, officials of the Western Miners' Federation, is too fresh in the public mind to need more than mentioning. Not only did the affair attract world-wide attention, but it had a wonderful effect upon the whole working-class movement of America. Taken in conjunction with the recent setting aside by the law courts of much protective labor legislation, and the aggressive action of employers' associations and citizen alliances, it has done much to teach the workers the necessity for united political action. The unprecedented industrial depression, with the appalling number of unemployed, is having its inevitable effect,—the trade union organizations are turning to independent, class-conscious politics. And signs are multiplying of a decidedly unifying force throughout the whole socialist and labor movement.

A FEW AUTHORITIES

THERE is an extensive literature upon the program of socialism. "Modern Socialism," edited by R. C. K. Ensor (Harper Brothers, 1904), is a collection of the speeches and writings of the foremost socialists, and includes programs and documents of fundamental importance. "Socialism and Social Reform," by Richard T. Ely (Crowell and Co., 1894), covers somewhat the same field. It is less authoritative, but reviews the main doctrines of socialism, and includes in an appendix some important programs, manifestoes, and other official papers. "The Fabian Tracts" deal with a wide range of subjects and give the attitude of the English socialists upon nearly all questions of municipal and industrial reform. "Le Socialisme Français," by A. Millerand (Paris, 1903), and a biographical sketch, "L'Œuvre de Millerand," by A. Lavy, express pretty fully the attitude of the French reformists. "Essais Socialistes" by Émile Vandervelde (Paris, 1906), gives the socialist position in regard to alcoholism, religion, and other matters. Perhaps the most important volumes treating critically the program of socialism are "Socialisme Théorique et Socialdémocratie Pratique," by Ed. Bernstein (Paris, 1903), and "Le Marxisme," by Karl Kautsky (Paris, 1900). No one who is interested in socialism should fail to read with care the Communist Manifesto by Marx and Engels (Kerr and Co., Chicago), and an interesting critique by Marx upon the socialist program, "A Propos d'Unité, — lettre sur le programme de Gotha" (Paris, 1901).

The attitude of socialists upon agrarian questions is not well defined. There are, however, several books by prominent socialists which can be consulted ; notably "La Question Agraire," by Karl Kautsky (Paris, 1900), and "La Politique Agraire" (Paris, 1900), by the same author ; "Le Socialisme et l'Agriculture," by G. Gatti (Paris, 1902) ; "The American Farmer," by A. M. Simons (Kerr and Co.) ; and "La Question Agraire en Belgique," by Émile Vandervelde. With regard to militarism, two interesting books are

"Leur Patrie," by Gustave Hervé, and "Militarismus und Anti-militarismus," by Dr. Karl Liebknecht (Leipzig, 1907).

By far the most important contributions upon the details of the socialist program are the thousands of pamphlets and tracts issued for propaganda purposes by the various national parties. These can be obtained of socialist publishers, or at the national offices of the parties. For France they can be got at 16, rue de la Corderie, Paris; Germany, Buchhandlung Vorwärts, Berlin, SW, 68, Lindenstrasse; Belgium, " Maison du Peuple," rue Joseph Stevens, Brussels; America, Charles Kerr and Co., 264 East Kinzie Street, Chicago; and in England, of the Labor Party, 28, Victoria Street, London, S.W.; the Social Democratic Party, 37 a, Clerkenwell Green, London, E.C.; and the Independent Labor Party, 23, Bride Lane, Fleet Street, London, E.C.

Upon the doctrines of socialism, three important books for general readers are written by non-socialists — " Socialism," by Werner Sombart (Putnams, 1898); "The Quintessence of Socialism," by Dr. A. Schaeffle (Scribner's Sons); and "An Inquiry into Socialism," by Thomas Kirkup (Longmans, Green and Co., 1887).

The partisan view is expressed with extreme simplicity in "From Serfdom to Socialism," by J. Keir Hardie (George Allen, London), as well as in "Merrie England" and "Britain for the British," by Robert Blatchford (Kerr and Co.); while "The Coöperative Commonwealth," by Laurence Gronlund (Boston, 1900); "Socialism," by John Spargo (Macmillan, 1906); "The Social Revolution," by Karl Kautsky, and "Collectivism," by Émile Vandervelde (Kerr and Co.), are all important contributions. "Studies in Socialism," by Jean Jaurès (Putnams, 1906), "Principes Socialistes," by Gabriel Deville (Paris, 1898), and the Fabian Essays (London, 1904), will also be found helpful to the general reader.

"The Economic Interpretation of History," which is a basic doctrine in the socialist philosophy, is fully elaborated by Professor E. R. A. Seligman, a non-socialist (Macmillan, 1903). "Essays on the Materialistic Conception of History," by Antonio Labriola (Kerr and Co., 1904), and "Economic Foundations of Society," by Achille Loria (Scribner's Sons, 1899), are books in the same field. The historic basis of socialism is treated in a powerful sketch by Frederick Engels, "Socialism, Utopian and Scientific" (Scribner's, 1892); and in "Historic Basis of Socialism in England," by H. M.

Hyndman (London, 1883), and "Commercial Crises of the Nineteenth Century" (Scribner's, 1892), by the same author.

Socialist economics is extensively treated in nearly all of the above volumes; but the special student should consult "Capital," by Karl Marx. The first two volumes are translated into English (Kerr and Co.). A rapid review of the doctrines of the first volume is made by Edward Aveling in "The Student's Marx" (Scribner's, 1902). Other books are "Economics of Socialism," by H. M. Hyndman (London, 1896), and "Landmarks of Scientific Socialism," by Frederick Engels (Kerr and Co., 1907).

Necessarily the chapter on "Socialism and Social Reform" is based very largely upon current events, and much of the material comes from the various socialist newspapers, journals, magazines, and official publications. These are altogether too numerous to be mentioned, but the most important are "The Labour Leader," "The Clarion," and "Justice," in England; "Le Peuple" and "Le Mouvement Communale," in Belgium; "L'Humanité," "Le Socialiste," and "Le Mouvement Socialiste," in France; "Vorwärts" and "Die Neue Zeit," in Germany; "Avanti," in Italy; and "The International Socialist Review," Chicago. The attitude of the socialists toward social reform, as expressed in the decisions of the International congresses, is very clearly worked out in "La Tactique Socialiste," by Edgar Milhaud (Paris, 1905). The respective opinions of the revisionists and the Marxists on this matter are expressed by Bernstein and Kautsky in the books mentioned above. The renaissance in the Latin countries of the Proudhonian view is best expressed by the various organs of the new syndicalism, and by a valuable collection of documents upon "La Grève Générale et le Socialisme," edited by Hubert Lagardelle (Paris). The opposite view is given in a brochure by Karl Kautsky, "Politique et Syndicats" (Paris, 1903), and the current combat against this tendency can be followed in the new journal edited by Jules Guesde, "Le Socialisme." The Fabian position is clearly stated in the Fabian Tract No. 70, and also in an extremely interesting pamphlet, "The Fabian Society; its early history," by G. Bernard Shaw.

There is no book describing the organization and standing of the socialist parties throughout Europe. Professor Edgar Milhaud, of Geneva, has written an extremely interesting study of the German movement, "La Démocracie Socialiste Allemande" (Paris, 1903).

J. Destrée and Émile Vandervelde have issued a complete review of the progress of the Belgian movement, " Le Socialisme en Belgique," while Louis Bertrand has given in two volumes each, " Histoire de la Co-opération en Belgique " and " Histoire de la Démocratie et du Socialisme." Paul Louis has prepared three studies, " Histoire du Socialisme Français," " Les Étapes du Socialisme," and " L'Avenir du Socialisme." An interesting volume by a non-socialist is " Essais sur le Mouvement Ouvrier en France " by Daniel Halévy (Paris, 1901). Sidney Webb's " History of Trades Unionism in England " barely touches the movement of the last twenty years.

By far the most important sources of information are, of course, the reports of the proceedings of the various congresses, national and international. Some of them are very difficult to obtain, but there may be mentioned the reports of the German Social Democratic Party from 1880 to 1906; of the general congresses of French socialist organizations from 1899 to 1902; of the Parti Socialiste (Section Française de l'Internationale Ouvrière) from 1905 to 1907; of the congresses of the Belgian Labor Party from 1886; of the British Labor Party from 1900; and of the International Congresses at Paris, Brussels, Zurich, London, Paris, Amsterdam, and Stuttgart. A most useful little book is the collection of the agendas and resolutions of the International Congresses up to that at Amsterdam. " L'Internationale ; documents et souvenirs," by James Guillaume (Paris, 1905), is anti-Marxist, but contains a résumé of nearly all the official documents issued by the first International. Enormous and very difficult to consult is a multitude of biographical studies of the leaders and militants of the movement. Mention might be made, however, of " Karl Marx," by Wilhelm Liebknecht (Kerr and Co.) ; " Wilhelm Liebknecht," by Kurt Eisner (Berlin, 1906); " L'Enfermé," by Gustave Geffroy, a thrilling study of Blanqui; " German Socialism and Lassalle " and " Bismarck and State Socialism," by William H. Dawson (Scribner's) ; " Ferdinand Lassalle and Social Reform," by Edward Bernstein (Scribner's) ; " Mémoire d'un Communard," by Jean Allemane (Paris) ; " Life of William Morris," by J. W. Mackail (Longmans, 1901), and " Bernard Shaw," by Holbrook Jackson (Jacobs and Co., Philadelphia, 1907).

INDEX

BY THE SAME AUTHOR

POVERTY

AN ATTEMPT TO DEFINE IT AND TO ES-
TIMATE ITS EXTENT IN THIS COUNTRY

By ROBERT HUNTER

Cloth, 12mo, $1.50 net; by mail, $1.62

" Despite the abundance of sociological literature in this field, really good books dealing with poverty are conspicuously rare. To this exceptional class belongs, however, a volume on ' Poverty,' by Mr. Robert Hunter, formerly head of the New York University Settlement. . . . Mr. Hunter's book is at once sympathetic and scientific. He brought to this task a store of practical experience in settlement and relief work gathered in many parts of the country. His analysis of the problem is marked by keen insight and sound judgment. There is no sentimental foolishness, no hysterical extravagance in this book ; nor, on the other hand, is it the smug treatise of a cold-blooded statistician. It is the work of a man who has observed the evils of poverty at first hand, who feels strongly the injustice of what he has seen, and yet who thinks straight — a man with a heart and a brain. . . . Whether we agree or disagree with the particular measures of prevention proposed by Mr. Hunter, one can hardly dispute, on general principles, the correctness of his diagnosis and the wisdom of his advice."
— *The Social Settler* in *The Boston Transcript.*

THE MACMILLAN COMPANY
PUBLISHERS, 64-66 FIFTH AVENUE, NEW YORK
I

Mr. H. G. WELLS'S *New Book*

New Worlds for Old

AN ACCOUNT OF SOCIALISM

Cloth, 12mo, $1.50 net; by mail, $1.61

———————

In this book Mr. Wells's pleasant and always interesting style and the clearness of his logic lay solid foundations for the spread of a broadly human, enlightened type of socialism. Very simply, yet with undeniably strong arguments and a fascinating lucidity, he sets forth the two great ideas upon which he builds his faith. You cannot agree with him wholly, perhaps; certainly you cannot quarrel with his frank discussion; and it is equally sure that you will read on, captivated by his evident open-mindedness, his recognition of the difficulties in the way of bettering social condition, and the force of his enthusiasm without impatience.

Socialism is much in the air, but there is no book which states so clearly and so interestingly what it really amounts to.

The book should be read by every one who is interested in having an intelligent standard, at once sympathetic and unprejudiced, by which to measure current discussion.

———————

THE MACMILLAN COMPANY
PUBLISHERS, 64-66 FIFTH AVENUE, NEW YORK

By JOHN SPARGO

Socialism

A Summary and Interpretation of Socialist Principles

12mo, cloth, $1.25 net

"The 'man in the street' will find this little volume an up-to-date exposition of the Socialism that is alive in the world to-day."
— *Review of Reviews.*

"Anything of Mr. Spargo's is well worth reading, for it is written with conviction and with a sense of concrete life far removed from mere doctrinairism. . . . Anybody who wants to know exactly what the American Marxian of the saner sort is aiming at will find it here. In view of the present situation it is a book that every thoughtful person will want to read and read carefully." — *World To-day.*

By JACK LONDON

War of the Classes

By the Author of "The People of the Abyss," etc.

Cloth, $1.50 net; paper, 25 cts. net

"A series of correlated essays, direct and trenchant in style, fresh and vigorous in thought, and . . . exceedingly entertaining in manner."
— *New York Sun.*

The Iron Heel *A Novel* Cloth, *12mo, $1.50*

The power and sweep of the story, the grip of the drama that it unfolds, are bound to make their appeal ; the unquestionable sincerity of the author will move even the most casual reader to thoughtfulness ; and the undercurrent of reference to present facts makes the picture irresistibly convincing. No one can resist the feeling that Mr. London is intensely in earnest, and this earnestness, coupled with his great literary and dramatic gift, makes "The Iron Heel" one of the most remarkably interesting novels of the day. "A stupendous work of the imagination," the critics call it, "so charged with dynamic influence that in Russia it would be immediately powdered out of existence."

THE MACMILLAN COMPANY

PUBLISHERS, 64-66 FIFTH AVENUE, NEW YORK

3

" Socialism grew to be a very important question during the nineteenth century; in all probability it will be the supreme question of the twentieth."

—T. K.

———————

A History of Socialism

By THOMAS KIRKUP

Third Edition, revised and enlarged

Cloth, 8vo, 400 pages and index, $2.25 net

"The aim of the present book is twofold : to set forth the leading phases of historic socialism ; and to attempt a criticism and interpretation of the movement as a whole." — *T. K.*

———————

COMMENTS OF THE PRESS

"Unquestionably the best study of Socialism in the English language . . . of the utmost value." — *Manchester Guardian.*

"A book which should be on the shelves of every public library and every workingman's club." — *Pall Mall Gazette*, London.

"The chapter on the growth of Socialism has been completely re-written in order to bring it up to date. . . . He is singularly free from the exaggerated statement and declamatory style which characterize the writing of so many socialists, and the concluding pages of the present volume show him at his best. . . . None have surpassed Mr. Kirkup in philosophical grasp of the essentials of Socialism or have presented the doctrine in more intelligible form." — *The Nation.*

———————

PUBLISHED BY

THE MACMILLAN COMPANY

64-66 FIFTH AVENUE, NEW YORK

4